MAGNIFICENT SEVEN

Yorkshire's Championship Years
The Men, the Magic, the Memories

The Players' Own Story
with Andrew Collomosse

GREAT NORTHERN

Great Northern Books
PO Box 213, Ilkley, LS29 9WS
www.greatnorthernbooks.co.uk

ISBN: 978-1905080-74-8

Design and layout: David Burrill

Printed in the UK by CPI William Clowes Beccles NR34 7TL

CIP Data
A catalogue for thi[s]   [libr]ary

CONTENTS

INTRODUCTION

This is the story of the men who won a magnificent seven County Championships for Yorkshire and gave White Rose cricket its finest hour.

Between 1959 and 1969, under the captaincy of Ronnie Burnet, Vic Wilson and Brian Close, Yorkshire won more trophies than at any other time in the club's illustrious history: seven Championships and two Gillette Cups.

Four of England's most famous players, Fred Trueman, Raymond Illingworth, Close and Geoffrey Boycott, were pivotal members of that side and their careers have been well-documented.

Alongside them was a group of players whose names and deeds have been woven into the rich tapestry of Yorkshire cricket history but whose stories have not, for the most part, been told before.

Men like Philip Sharpe, slip fielder supreme who held over 600 catches in an 18-year first-class career with Yorkshire, Derbyshire and England, wicketkeeper Jimmy Binks, who made 412 successive Championship appearances, Mel Ryan, Bob Platt and Mike Cowan, Trueman's new ball partners in the early years, and all-rounder Richard Hutton, son of Sir Leonard, who followed his father into the England side.

Men like Bryan Stott, Ken Taylor, Doug Padgett, Brian Bolus and John Hampshire, selfless run-makers in the Yorkshire cause, Don Wilson, left-arm spinner and unquenchable enthusiast, Geoff Cope, the off-spinner who, more than most, would later learn all about cricket's triumphs and tribulations.

Some of those who made Yorkshire great have passed away: Burnet, Vic Wilson, Trueman, Tony Nicholson, who shared the new ball with Trueman from the mid-Sixties, and Chris Balderstone, equally at home in professional cricket or football. They are remembered here.

Only one of the 16 players invited to contribute to Magnificent Seven declined to do so. For the record, Geoffrey Boycott was born in Fitzwilliam, West Yorkshire, on October 21, 1940. An opening batsman, he was capped in 1963. He played in 414 first-class matches for the county between 1962 and 1986 and scored 32,570 runs, including 103 centuries, at an average of 57.85. He also appeared in 260 limited overs matches. Boycott captained the side from 1971 to 1978. He made 108 appearances for England, scoring 8,114 runs at an average of 47.72, and also appeared in 36 One-Day Internationals. Boycott served on the Yorkshire committee and is a member of the YCCC Board.

At the start of the 1959 season, Yorkshire had not won the Championship outright for 13 years, their worst sequence since securing the title for the first time in 1893. By the end of the 1969 season, they had set the record straight in the most emphatic manner.

Only Surrey, with seven successive titles in the 1950s, and the Yorkshire side of the 1930s, who won seven Championships in nine years, boast a comparable record of sustained success in 20th Century cricket.

But of course, neither of those Titans had the opportunity to win the Gillette Cup, which was not introduced until 1963. So we can only speculate on how successful or otherwise they may have been in knock-out competition.

What is beyond dispute is that in 1959, Yorkshire emerged from the dark days into the most productive phase of their long history. These are the men who restored White Rose pride.

Foreword

By Ray Illingworth

It was a beautiful summer. Good wickets and outfields like lightning. The start of my best period as a player, the dawn of a new Golden Age for Yorkshire cricket. Until 1959, my career had been a mixture: some years, I was better with the bat, others with the ball. But in '59 everything came together, for me and for Yorkshire. A memorable year.

We clinched Yorkshire's first outright County Championship since 1946 in sensational style in our final game against Sussex at Hove. Chasing 215 in 105 minutes, we got home by five wickets with seven minutes to spare. None of the Yorkshiremen who played under Ronnie Burnet on September 1, 1959, will ever forget that day.

I played a big part in the victory, scoring a hundred when we badly needed runs in our first innings and taking seven wickets in the match. I was at the non-striker's end when Brian Bolus hit the winning runs.

And the Championship was the climax of a marvellous year for me on a personal level, too. I played two Tests against India and in all first-class cricket, I scored 1,726 runs at 46.64 and took 110 wickets at 21.46; it was the second of my six doubles as a Yorkshire player.

Yet at the start of that season, Brian Sellers, the county's new chairman and the man whose refusal to offer me a long-term contract in 1968 forced me to leave the county, had poured cold water on our prospects of taking Yorkshire back to the top.

He predicted that it would be three years before a side that had been re-built after finishing a turbulent 1958 in eleventh place, would become a force. Sellers was wrong; we did it in one.

Was I surprised Yorkshire had come so far so quickly? A little bit, I suppose. I knew we had the potential to become a good side but I'd played through so many disappointments over the previous eight years that I wasn't sure we could do it with a relatively inexperienced side.

But once we had that first title under our belt, I was very confident indeed that we would go on and win it again. And we did. Six times in the next nine years. And Yorkshire also won the Gillette Cup in 1965 and again in 1969, the year after I joined Leicestershire.

It was a marvellous time for Yorkshire cricket, a golden era that no county has come close to matching in over half a century. Yet it had all been very different for me during the seven years after I made my first team debut against Hampshire at Headingley in August, 1951.

I was just 19 and I found myself in a dressing room where virtually everyone was an England international. Len Hutton, Johnny Wardle, Willie Watson, Bob Appleyard, Frank Lowson, Don Brennan and Norman Yardley, the captain, played in 168 Tests between them.

A year earlier, Brian Close had become the youngest player to turn out for England, aged 18, and Fred Trueman was ten months away from the start of a record-breaking Test career.

It should have been the perfect arena for a young player to develop and forge a successful career of his own. Instead, the atmosphere was acrimonious and the team spirit poor.

We finished second behind Warwickshire in my first season and then Surrey won the title seven times in a row from 1952. Yorkshire finished second three times and third once, not bad going for any other county. But not good enough for Yorkshire, who had won the title seven times in the thirties.

Now Surrey were a great side and they had matchwinners in all departments. But so did we and I'm sure that if the team spirit had been right and we'd really been pulling together, we would have beaten them on at least a couple of occasions during those seven years. Instead we had to wait until 1959.

Norman Yardley was my first captain. A lovely fella, he'd led England in 14 of his 20 Tests and off the field. You wouldn't find a nicer man. But he wasn't strong enough with some of the senior professionals. There were times when I'd be preparing to bowl and a senior player would come up and say, "What are you doing?"

"The captain's told me to bowl."

"On yer bike! I'm bowling here." And I'd have to wait another few overs before I got on.

I first started to make a real impact in 1953, the year England regained the Ashes under Hutton. Because of Test calls, Appleyard's health problems and injury that ruled out Close for virtually the whole season, I played in all 28 matches, scoring 717 runs and taking 69 wickets. In '54, with Closey and Appleyard fit again, I played in 18 games and I seem to remember doing a hell of a lot of Twelfth Man duty.

I was capped the following year. Or rather, I asked for my county cap. Two or three counties were pestering me to join them so I said to Yardley, "You've seen enough of me now. If you think I'm good enough to play for Yorkshire then they should give me my cap; if not, they should let me leave."

I was capped next match...but I must admit it niggled that I'd had to ask for the bloody thing! I'd been playing since 1951 and held just about every record for an uncapped player. Yet I still had to ask for my cap.

Doug Padgett did even worse. He was 16 and the youngest player to appear for Yorkshire when he made his debut in '51...and he wasn't capped until 1958!

Norman finished in '55, the year Len Hutton retired, and was succeeded by Billy Sutcliffe, son of the great Herbert Sutcliffe. Billy tried hard to move things on a bit. But he was 29 and found himself up against the same seasoned professionals that Norman had found hard to captain.

It wasn't easy for him. And it didn't help that the crowd were on his back, too. We all heard the jeers of 'You're not as good as your dad!' Billy was a good bloke but it was very hard work for him. Looking back, I think he'd have been all right if he'd taken over in 1958, the year Ronnie Burnet succeeded him, instead of two years earlier.

In a way Ronnie was fortunate because I think everyone recognised that there had to be changes and the clear-out of senior players had already begun by the time he took over.

Watson joined Leicestershire in 1957 and then towards the end of the 1958 season, Wardle was told he would not be retained. He was then sacked after criticising the club in a newspaper article and subsequently withdrawn from the England party to tour Australia that winter.

Like all the other younger players, I'd had problems with Wardle. But I always stood up to him. I was strong enough, he spotted that and eventually he was OK with me. But some of the others were frightened to death even to go for a catch because of the reaction if they missed it.

I got the same treatment at first and eventually, after missing a chance in a match at Bramall Lane, I had a real bust-up with him. I said, "Look, when I came into this team I was the best fielder in the side. But you've destroyed everybody's confidence."

I was all right after that. In fact from that point, whenever there was a slog on and the batsmen were attacking Johnny, I was sent into the outfield. I think I got 30-odd catches one season, which was a hell of a lot for an outfielder. But the others were still frightened and you can never play a team game when players are frightened.

Ironically, before the final row that led to his sacking, I think Johnny was trying to do a reasonable job as senior professional. But great bowler that he was – through the fifties he was on his own as a left-arm spinner – it had to happen and we had to start afresh.

Lowson and Appleyard also retired at the end of that summer so Vic Wilson was the only member of the early fifties establishment who was still around at the start of the 1959 season. And Vic was a great bloke.

So with the turmoil of '58 behind him, Ronnie began his second season with a mainly young side featuring several of the players who had played for him in a very successful Second XI. They had won the Minor Counties Championship in 1957.

He knew them and they knew him. And people like Fred, Closey and me were now senior players and, importantly, we all got on. I'm not saying the three of us didn't have our disagreements; we did. But when the dust settled we were still pals and that was important.

Of course, there were concerns about Ronnie. He'd done a good job with the Seconds but he had no background of first-class cricket. And at 39, his fitness was always likely to be a problem. In fact he did break down early in his first season in charge and missed the first seven championship matches.

And how much did he know about the first-class game? He'd captained Baildon to honours in the Bradford league and had played Minor Counties cricket with the second team. But this was going to be a much sterner challenge.

And I don't think Ronnie was totally sure how I felt about him. He perhaps thought one or two of us who were now senior players might not be 100 per cent behind him. But I think it's fair to say we all supported him because he was such a good bloke. He treated everybody honestly and fairly, which in the end is all you can do as a captain.

He was never afraid to ask advice, which he needed to do, and he usually accepted it. And critically, he got the spirit right; after so many difficult years, that was the be-all and end-all. It has to be when you are living in one another's pockets for five months of the year. And throughout the sixties the team spirit was excellent.

The Berni Inn steakhouses played their part, too. They were just starting to open around the country and sometimes in the evenings we'd go out and have a steak and a couple of those great schooners of sherry they used to serve up!

We were Yorkshire lads together and that was always a great advantage. Say what you like about overseas players, I still believe that 11 Yorkshiremen have something no other side could have.

Ronnie came in at the right time...and he finished at the right time, too. I know he didn't want to go after winning the Championship and I can understand that. But he was beginning to struggle physically and we didn't want a skipper who was missing a week here and a week there.

I didn't agree with Brian Sellers very often – in fact I don't think I ever did agree with him again before or after! – but he pushed Ronnie into retiring and it was the right decision.

Vic Wilson took over, retained the title in 1960 and regained it from Hampshire in '62. We won it again under Closey in '63 and after Worcester had won it two years in a row, we collected three on the bounce from 1966. And even when we didn't win it, we were always very close, particularly in '61 when ten of Hampshire's 19 wins came in declaration matches; we had no declaration victories.

Opposing captains were prepared to leave them good targets of around 60 an hour whereas we were set 110 or 120. If we set a side a reasonable target, they wouldn't go for them; if Hampshire did the same, they'd have a go.

So I always say that '61 was really our year as well, although I'll admit Worcester won it fair and square in '64 and '65. They were a good, well-balanced side.

By 1966, though, we were close to being the perfect unit. There were no weak links. We had a formidable batting line-up to choose from in Geoff Boycott, Phil Sharpe, Ken Taylor, Padgett, Closey and John Hampshire. Fred, Tony Nicholson and Richard Hutton were a powerful pace attack, while Don Wilson and I shared the spin. Jimmy Binks was, in the view of my England team-mate Alan Knott, just about the best wicketkeeper in the game.

And there has never been a better fielding side. The close catching was second to none with Sharpe at slip, Closey either in the slips or at bat pad as they call it these days, and Fred at short leg. That lot didn't miss much...and they didn't have helmets.

Ken Taylor at cover and Don Wilson at mid-wicket were world-class. I used to say Wils had telescopic arms...if the ball went past, he seemed to extend his arm a few inches and grab it.

We worked a lot of run-outs together. I used to station my mid-on just that little bit deeper to tempt the batsman into a quick single. When he went for it, Wils would come swooping in from mid-wicket, the telescopic arm would go down and the batsman would be on his way.

All the players were deep thinkers about the game, although I was the only one with a licence to pass on a few words of advice to the skipper. Closey was a brilliant captain and on a day when things were happening out in the middle, he was always in control, directing operations and standing fearlessly close to the batsman at forward short leg.

But on a quiet day, Closey sometimes tended to drift off a bit. Binksy and Sharpey would spot it from behind the stumps and Jim would run over to me and say, "Hey up, t'rudder's gone. Go and have a word with him!" And I'd bring him back into line.

Brian would never have taken that from anyone else, not even Fred. We'd always been close. He was my best man and godfather to Vicky, my elder daughter. And as a captain, he realised I knew what I was talking about and my only interest was the good of the side.

I can still picture Closey at the end of a day's play, sitting in the dressing room surrounded by the Press boys. He'd be saying, "Well, at that stage I decided this...or I did that." And all the lads used to look in my direction and raise their eyebrows. We still have a laugh about it when we get together for one of our reunions

In 1966, when Closey was appointed captain of England for the final Test against the West Indies at The Oval, we travelled down to London together. I'd played in the Third Test at Trent Bridge so I'd had a look at the West Indies, who won three of the first four games.

Garry Sobers was probably at the height of his powers and had already scored 691 runs in seven knocks. But I'd spotted one potential weakness.

So on the way down to London I said to Closey, "Look Brian, the one thing about Sobers is that he'll always go for the hook shot at any stage of his innings, even right at the start.

"We've never really tried him out properly yet. So when he comes in, tell mid-wicket to walk back ten yards instead of walking in and let him have it straight away. He'll definitely go for it."

So John Snow let Sobers have a bouncer first ball, Garry nicked it on to his body and Closey, who had stood his ground at forward short leg, took the catch. It worked a treat.

Afterwards, when I heard him telling the Press how he'd devised the plan that got Sobers first ball, I thought, "Bloody hell, Brian, come on..." But I didn't mind if it made the old boy happy.

To be candid, 1968 marked the beginning of the end. We won the Championship with a 60-run victory over Surrey with five minutes to spare in the final game at Hull but we were just starting to lack a little bit.

Significantly, Fred was beginning to go. He'd lost a yard or two of pace, although we had Chris Old coming through and at that time he was very quick. Maybe we could have got by for another season with Fred bowling fast-medium and Chris operating in short bursts. But Fred decided to call it a day and so did Ken Taylor.

And I left, too.

Basically my departure was down to one man, Brian Sellers. He was the biggest fly in the ointment for me at Yorkshire and he spoiled it for a lot of people. In 1968, I was 36 with a wife and two young children to support.

Yorkshire had only ever given their players a one-year contract but I didn't think it was unreasonable to ask for a bit more security. I wanted a three-year deal.

I'm not a fool and when I went to see John Nash, the secretary, I had five bloody good offers from other counties in my pocket. I said, "Are they going to give me a contract, Mr Nash?"

"No, Raymond, they are not," he replied.

"Well, in that case, I'm afraid I'll have to hand in my resignation."

I gave him my letter during a game at Bradford and in the normal course of events, it would then have gone before the next committee meeting.

Instead, within a quarter of an hour, Bill Bowes, the former Yorkshire and England fast bowler, who covered the county for the Yorkshire Evening Post, came to see me.

"Ray," he said. "I've been asked to talk to you on behalf of the Press about you leaving Yorkshire."

"How do you know about that, Bill?"

"Mr Nash has rung Brian Sellers, who said you could go and any other bugger could go with you."

Ronnie Burnet, who was a committee member by that time, later told me that if my letter had gone before the committee, I would never have been allowed to leave.

I had a lot of sleepless nights before I decided to go and I don't think I would have ever done so but for Sellers and his autocratic approach. But once he had shouted his mouth off like that, there was no way back.

In one way, I suppose, it was the best thing he ever did for me. In 1968, I earned £1,500 as a Yorkshire player...and that included three games for England. I doubled my money at Leicester. And if I'd never gone to Grace Road as captain, I wouldn't have been appointed captain of England in 1969.

It's funny, though, because when I left Yorkshire, Arthur Mitchell, the county coach and a man for whom I had enormous admiration, took Doug Padgett to one side and said, "Illy will captain England."

Now nobody in the country could have seen that at the time because Colin Cowdrey was captain and looked secure...but Arthur sensed it could happen.

And sure enough, when Cowdrey snapped an Achilles tendon before the start of the 1969 series against West Indies, they sent for me. Less than two years later I became only the third England captain to regain the Ashes in Australia.

When I look back at the whole picture, my ten seasons at Leicester was my happiest time. My wife Shirley will confirm that off the field, the atmosphere was like a breath of fresh air after Yorkshire.

Before the first match of my first season, all the players were invited into the committee room for a drink. That had never happened at Yorkshire. The Leicestershire players were made welcome and their wives were properly looked after. We didn't have committee men grumbling if our wives used the same toilet as them.

Leicester had never won a trophy in 90 years. But for a while we were the best side in the country. We won the Championship in 1975, when we also beat the Aussies, the Benson & Hedges Trophy in 1972 and '75 and the John Player League in 1974 and '77.

As John Steele, our opening batsman, once remarked: "It's great to walk on to the field knowing the opposition are frightened of us, rather than the other way round." So over a five-year period, the cricket was as good as anything I'd experienced at Yorkshire. And off the field, in my dealings with officials, it was far better; all in all, the happiest time of my life.

When I say that, however, I'm not talking about the time I spent with the lads. I loved being with the Yorkshire players and a member of a successful Yorkshire side made up of players born and bred in Yorkshire.

From the first Championship year of 1959 to the final title in 1968, we were a team in every sense of the word, on and off the field. Nothing can ever take away those memories. It was a very special time with some very special people. And it all began in that beautiful summer of 1959.

Raymond Illingworth was born in Pudsey, also the birthplace of

Herbert Sutcliffe and Sir Leonard Hutton, on June 8, 1932. An off-spinning all-rounder, he made his Yorkshire debut in 1951 and was capped in 1955. He was a pivotal figure in the side that won seven Championships in ten years and also played in the 1965 Gillette Cup Final. He joined Leicestershire in 1968 and led his new county to one Championship and four one-day trophies before rejoining Yorkshire as team manager in 1979. He made his comeback as a player three years later and when he retired in 1983, he had made 496 first-class appearances for the county, scoring 14,986 runs, with 14 hundreds, at an average of 27.90. He took 1,431 wickets at 18.73. He also played in 40 limited overs games. In all first-class cricket, Illingworth played in 787 matches and scored 24,134 runs, with 22 centuries, at an average of 28.06. He took 2,072 wickets at 20.87 and played in 218 limited overs games. Illingworth made his England debut in 1958 and played in 61 Tests. He was appointed captain in 1969 and in 1970-71 became only the third man to regain the Ashes in Australia. He later served as Chairman of Selectors and in 2010 was elected President of Yorkshire CCC.

1959

April 29, 1959. It Doesn't Matter Anymore, Buddy Holly's posthumous single, has hit the top of the charts and will remain there until mid-May. Ben Hur has won five Oscars at the Academy Awards, Juke Box Jury is the UK television hit and Wolves have retained the Football League Championship.

At Lord's, Yorkshire are preparing to open their season against the MCC, an occasion eagerly anticipated by their players and supporters. Yet to cricket lovers outside the Broad Acres, the title of Holly's classic might seem an apt assessment of the apparently parlous state of Yorkshire cricket.

The previous year was, by the White Rose's lofty standards, calamitous. Under new captain Ronnie Burnet, a 39-year-old former Second XI skipper with no first-class experience, Yorkshire finished 11th in the County Championship, in those days the only domestic competition.

In a dismal, wet summer they won just seven games out of 28. Johnny Wardle, their England left-arm spinner, was summarily sacked for lambasting the county in a national newspaper after being informed he would not be retained in 1959. Two more senior players, Bob Appleyard and Frank Lowson, retired.

Yorkshire, winners of seven Championships in the 1930s, had not won the title outright since 1946, at the time easily the lengthiest hiatus since they won the crown for the first time in 1893.

A shared Championship with Middlesex in 1949 scarcely compensated supporters for such a barren spell. So maybe, after all, Yorkshire cricket didn't really matter any more.

It did matter, though; it mattered a very great deal to a great number of people. It mattered to millions of White Rose supporters inside and outside the county. It mattered to over 11,000 members, every one of whose name and address was listed in the Yorkshire County Cricket Club Year Book, then, as now, a bible for Yorkshire followers. It mattered for the general welfare of English cricket – for isn't it set in stone that a strong Yorkshire means a strong England?

And above all, it mattered to Burnet and his team, many of whom had played under their captain for the Second XI and knew all about the leadership qualities that were to transform the county's fortunes in the summer of '59. In the process, Burnet would establish a dynasty that would bring Yorkshire seven Championships and two Gillette Cup victories in 11 seasons.

The first of those Championships was clinched at Hove on September 1, 1959, when Yorkshire, set to make 215 in 105 minutes, won by five wickets with seven minutes to spare. It was Twenty20 cricket 50 years ahead of its time, a sensational finale to a title race that for some time had threatened to go right down to the wire.

Several players made a telling contribution to Yorkshire's victory beside the seaside. But few would begrudge Bryan Stott pride of place. Stott led the run chase from the front, scoring 96 in 86 minutes and sharing a third-wicket partnership of 141 in just over an hour with Doug Padgett.

It was the high water mark of an 11-year Yorkshire career for Stott, an attacking left-handed opening batsman from Yeadon who at one stage nursed realistic ambitions of a career in professional football.

"Hove was a marvellous experience for everybody," recalls Stott. "And we went from strength to strength over the next ten years. Individuals grew in confidence and ability and the team ethic remained strong.

"The victory over Sussex proved to be the catalyst in producing a Yorkshire side that has not been matched in half a century. I hope one day it will be...and sooner rather than later."

BRYAN STOTT.

THE HERO OF HOVE

William Bryan Stott was born in Yeadon near Leeds on July 18, 1934. A left-handed opening batsman, he made 187 first team appearances between 1952 and 1963. Capped in 1957, he played in four Championship sides and scored 9,168 runs, with 17 centuries, at an average of 31.61. After retiring from the first-class game, Stott played for Harrogate in the Yorkshire League and later served on the Yorkshire committee. In 2005, he was the founding father of the Yorkshire Players' Association, along with Geoff Cope.

My father Harry was a good club cricketer, a hard-hitting left-hand batsman. He taught me from the start. I remember cine films of him standing over me, moving my arms and making me play the shots. He joined Rawdon CC, who played in the Airedale and Wharfedale League, when I was eight or nine so I went along to the junior nets and eventually reached the Third XI. I didn't have any cricket boots so my dad put what we used to call horseshoe nails into a pair of black shoes.

The league had a really good coaching system with a chap called Bert Hinchliffe in charge. He had a bristling moustache and wore a hooped cap. He used to coach eight or nine of us from different clubs and he set me on the path of correct cricket.

When I went to Aireborough Grammar School at the age of eleven, I entered the world of organised schools cricket. Brian Close was at the same school, three or four years ahead of me. I also played football, at left-back. In fact, I was captain of the Airedale and Wharfedale Schools at both cricket and football and progressed to Yorkshire schools at both games.

We played football matches against sides from Lancashire, Birmingham, London and, of course, the professional club scouts were about, too. When I was about 14, we received letters from Leeds United and Sheffield Wednesday, inviting me for trials.

There was a family conference that ended with my father suggesting that I should forget about football and concentrate on cricket and going into the family plumbing business, H & S Stott of Yeadon. I never had any regrets.

There was never really any talk of county cricket, either. Some of the lads in the schools set-up were already dreaming of making it into the Yorkshire side; I never did. County cricket wasn't talked about, it just seemed to evolve.

From the age of 17, I was playing in the Bradford League, first for Yeadon and then Lidget Green. And from representative schools games against Lancashire, Durham and Notts, the next step along the route was an invitation to the Yorkshire nets.

Ken Taylor and Doug Padgett were there, too, and before long we were playing Second XI cricket. We won our Colts caps together but soon afterwards, I came within a whisker of disappearing off the White Rose radar altogether.

Why? Arthur Mitchell, one of two Yorkshire coaches along with Maurice Leyland, had reached the conclusion that I was never going to make it. On a personal level, Arthur was as right as a bobbin with me. But for some reason he didn't want me around any more as a player. I used to flash outside the off stump quite a lot and that wasn't in Arthur's book at all.

Once at the winter nets Arthur hardly said anything as I went in to bat and stood with his back to me at the other end of the net for most of my session. Anything he did say was super-critical. I thought, "I'm struggling here. He's washed his hands of me." I couldn't understand it. I came out of the net, thinking my career could be heading for the rocks.

As I was taking off my pads, Maurice came round the corner of the tarpaulin and said, "Bryan. My net next week." When the time came, he walked into the net with me. "Now then, what about this shot, flashing outside your off stump? Do you think it's worth playing it?"

"Yes. It's a natural stroke for me. All right, I sometimes get out but it makes me a lot of runs. In all honesty, I don't think I can stop playing it."

"Right. Let's see how we go on. But if it starts getting you into trouble, we'll have to do something about it." If Maurice hadn't taken me in hand, I don't think I would have become a regular Yorkshire player. And I think it always amazed Arthur that I ever scored any runs with that stroke.

I made my debut on July 26, 1952, against Middlesex at Bramall Lane, eight days after my 18th birthday, but it wasn't until 1957 that I gained a regular place at the top of the order. By that time, I'd done my National Service and spent a couple of seasons playing for the RAF and the Combined Services against county opposition. A wonderful experience.

I reached 1,000 runs for the first time in '57 and again the following year. But 1958 was a dreadful year on and off the field and quite honestly, when we set off again in '59, nobody inside or outside the county expected anything more than a re-building operation in Ronnie Burnet's second season as captain.

And that's how it looked at the start. Ronnie was great at losing the toss and for the first couple of months we were very inconsistent. Everyone made a contribution but nobody really took hold of the cricket.

Because Ronnie lost the toss so often, we weren't able to control games by making the vital decision whether to bat or bowl. We were more or less at the mercy of opposing skippers. And with Fred Trueman often away at Test matches, we struggled to bowl sides out.

We started to gel as a team against Derbyshire at Chesterfield at the beginning of July. I'm absolutely certain that was the game that changed our fortunes. Donald Carr declared with Derby on top. He wanted to win the game but probably miscalculated by a quarter of an hour. He left the door just a bit too far open.

We were chasing 301 in just over three hours. Ken Taylor was in good nick and got 144 in quick time. Everybody else supported him. I'd been injured in the field and substituted during their second innings so I was obliged to bat lower down the order.

Donald wouldn't let me go in before seven but Ronnie tried to send me in at six. As I was walking out, Donald came running over, shouting, "Go back! Go back!" and I had to do as I was told. But in the end it didn't matter. We got the runs in pretty close order to the close of play. And crucially, that victory proved to us that we could win a game in a run chase. The tide had turned.

After about two-thirds of the season, Gloucester, Surrey, Warwickshire and Lancashire were all there or thereabouts and at the start of August, we had a couple of good wins against Middlesex and also beat Kent at Leeds. So we set off for what our supporters called the Southern Tour well placed.

Traditionally, Yorkshire used to play a few games in the south at the end of the season – this time it was Somerset, Gloucester, Worcester and Sussex – before heading home for the start of the Scarborough Festival at the beginning of September. We'd been doing it for donkey's years. In 1939, Yorkshire were down at Sussex on the day War broke out.

We played Somerset at Bath. It was notoriously a spinner's wicket and Brian Langford was a good steady off-spinner. He bowled very well. Closey could handle spin and suggested that the right-handers should use the sweep against Langford whenever possible. One or two of them took this to heart and swept at everything. It didn't work. Chasing 255 in three and a quarter hours, we were all out 17 runs short.

On to Bristol, always a strange wicket. The ball tended to keep a bit low and there was always a bit of movement for the seamers... and help for the spinners, for that matter. You would really have needed two or three games there to get used to it properly. They made 294 for eight declared and then we were bowled out for 35 with ridiculous ease.

Tony Brown and David Smith were both medium pace, could use the seam very well and Tony, in particular, bowled beautifully. He just went through us, taking seven for 11 from 10.5 overs.

Brian Bolus went in at number five and made 12 not out. And when Brian, or 'Bollus' as Ronnie sometimes called him, came into the dressing room, the skipper said: "Leave your pads on, Bollus, you're opening. You're the only one who can play this lot so you might as well carry on!"

Brian opened with Ken when we followed on, continued where he'd left off and batted four hours for 91. No one gave him any real support and we lost by an innings after an hour's play on the third day. A disaster. Two heavy losses in two games. We'd set off on tour on top and after two games we were third. Worcester became a real muck or nettles game.

I took advantage of the early finish at Bristol to go to the brine baths at Droitwich Spa. I'd been in a lot pain in my shins, particularly the right one which had taken some stick over the season. There was a lot of fluid on the bone. I was determined to go to the baths and relax, to use our extra time off properly.

It was delightful. The bath was the size of an average swimming pool in those days and the water was lovely and warm and so buoyant that you bobbed about like a cork. It was a bit like the Red Sea, I suppose, or like sitting in an armchair.

After a while I was wrapped in warm towels, lay down in one of the cubicles that surrounded the pool and went to sleep. It was the best thing I ever did. It helped take the soreness out of my legs and I felt like playing again.

We always had hard games against Worcester. A good side with the right balance. Jack Flavell and Len Coldwell were top opening bowlers and they had a strong batting line-up, with people like Don Kenyon, Martin Horton, George Dews and Dick Richardson. The arrival of Tom Graveney from Gloucester in 1961 and Basil D'Oliveira three years later made them even stronger and they won the title in 1964 and '65.

We knew we had to win and we knew it would be hard work. They batted first and Ronnie made a lot of bowling changes throughout the innings. Closey, in particular, did well. He'd always had an uncanny knack of coming on and getting a wicket, often with a full toss or a long hop, and he kept nipping in. He finished with four for 34 from 16 overs and we bowled them out for 120.

We knocked up 262 in reply. I carried my bat for 144 in what *Wisden* rather uncharitably described as "a valuable if at times uninspired innings". I preferred to play quite freely but I could get my head down if necessary and on this occasion, the end justified the means. It was the only time I carried my bat, although I came close once or twice more.

Fred Trueman and Closey claimed four apiece in their second knock and we were left needing 160 to win. Ray Illingworth's unbeaten 40 saw us home by five wickets. Not for the first time in 1959, Raymond had a good match. He was 27 by this time and had become a very, very good cricketer. We'd been able to see him steadily improve with nearly every game.

It was one of our best victories of the season. We were absolutely under pressure and everybody contributed. We'd halted the slide and we were back on top of the table. Surrey, now our only challengers, were six points behind.

However we set off for Brighton knowing that they were favourites. They had two games left, both at The Oval, against Middlesex and Northants. We had one. So with 12 points for a win and nothing for a defeat, the equation was straightforward. We simply had to win...and hope that Surrey didn't.

We always had good games against Sussex. They seemed to have batsmen who made runs against us when we didn't expect it. We'd think we were through their batting then someone would pop up and make a score. They were always up for a fight. Mind you, the same applied to just about every side we played.

I think a lot of that stemmed from the fact that so many counties had head coaches who'd played against the great Yorkshire side of the thirties, who won seven championships in nine years.

They were a very strong side but they didn't win graciously. They let it be known how good they were and I was aware that they'd made quite a few enemies on the circuit.

Over 20 years later, there was still very much a feeling of "We're not letting these bloody Yorkshiremen win." Often they'd rather play out a draw than give us a chance and Sussex were absolutely determined that we weren't going to win.

Fred was tired. He'd bowled over 1,000 overs for Yorkshire and England and he couldn't find that zip. Bob Platt had bowled well all year but he wasn't in the side at Hove because of injury.

He used to suffer from sore shins and sometimes he really struggled, even though he was always ready to bowl through it. Raymond, Brian and Don Wilson had also bowled a lot of overs on wickets where there wasn't much for them apart from a lot of hard work.

But everybody was doing a really good job. We were happy. There was never any question of anybody playing for himself. Never. It didn't even enter our heads. Every move, every action was in the best interests of the team. That was accepted and understood.

If you lost your wicket trying to help Yorkshire win the match, fair enough. The feeling and understanding was tremendous although obviously it helped that we were a winning side.

Hove provided beautiful weather and a lovely fast wicket; very straight, very true, good to play on. And big crowds. There were marquees around the boundary and it really was a lovely atmosphere by the seaside. As usual, Ronnie lost the toss and Sussex batted first.

This time it was Ken Taylor, with his little swingers, who nipped in with the important wickets at the top of the order. By the time he'd removed Alan Oakman, Ken Suttle, Ted Dexter and Jim Parks, Sussex were 63 for five. Don Smith and Tiger Pataudi steered them away from real trouble but we would always have settled for a total of 210.

We didn't start well either but Raymond scored a hundred and we recovered from 81 for five to 307 all out. Don Wilson hit his first Championship half-century. But by lunchtime on the third day we still hadn't got them out. Les Lenham and Jim Parks scored fifties and at the interval, they led by 193 and we still had to get three wickets. There was no real prospect of anything other than stalemate. In fact, they could easily have propped and copped, settled for the draw.

The dressing rooms at Hove were quite close together and if you walked down the corridor, it was possible to hear what was going on inside the other team's holy of holies. So during the lunchtime interval, we took the opportunity to listen in.

They were obviously split about what to do next. Some wanted Robin Marlar to declare, thinking they were far enough in front and had enough time to bowl us out if we went for the runs. The other half said they'd give us nowt.

Marlar did not declare. And for me that was absolutely the right decision. I would have done exactly the same thing in his position. He was spot on. Why should he declare? It wouldn't have been fair on Surrey if he'd handed us a realistic chance of winning. He took the view that if we wanted the title we had to go out there and win it.

Even so, the last few batsmen struck out and went for the runs. In fairness, that's how the lower order tended to play in those days: hit out; if we get runs we get 'em, if not we get out.

Jackie Birkenshaw took four fantastic catches in the innings, three of them after lunch. They were all big skyers in the deep. He was only a youngster in his second season and he was under real pressure. He caught them all and played an absolutely vital role in the win.

Jackie joined Leicestershire in 1961 after playing 22 Championship matches in three seasons. With Raymond established as an off-spinning all-rounder, his chances were always going to be limited but no one can deny the role he played in our win at Hove.

They finished with 311, a lead of 214. If they'd added another 20 or 30 in as many minutes, it would have been curtains. But a target of 215 in 105 minutes gave us an outside chance. There were a lot of Yorkshire fans down there and as we walked off the field, two people ran up to me and said, "What are we doing? What are we doing?"

"We're going for them. Obviously."

The first person I spoke to when we reached the dressing room was Philip Sharpe, our stand-in scorer. Philip had been out of the side for the last three games and had travelled down to Worcester to watch the match with his father, who was having a few days' off.

But when Cyril Turner, our regular scorer, was taken ill, Philip stepped into the breach and came down to Hove. I asked him to try and work out how many overs an hour Sussex had bowled in the first innings. Once we knew that we could see how many we were likely to face in the 105 minutes ahead of us.

And I also asked him to put the overs up on the board so we'd know more or less how many would be left. We reckoned we'd need eight or nine an over. Ronnie altered the batting order and Ken, who had batted at six in the first innings, went in with me. We went out with all guns blazing.

Ian Thomson opened the bowling and his first ball gave me a chance to play one of my favourite shots, through the covers off the back foot. Four. We took 15 off the first over, and when Ian came on to bowl the third, I hit the first delivery for six.

It was a purely instinctive stroke and flew dead straight back over his head. I can still see his face now. Pure disbelief. In the space of those first three overs, we were ahead of the rate and on our way.

Closey came in at three and hit a six clean out of the ground. They couldn't find the ball and the umpires didn't have another one. We lost about six minutes waiting for another one to come out of the pavilion.

His departure, with the score on 40, brought Doug Padgett to the crease. Dougie was technically the best batsman in the side, very correct. He could place the ball beautifully but he couldn't slog.

His arrival created a dilemma for Marlar. Closey and I were both left-handers so he'd been able to place a field for both of us without too many alterations when the strike changed. When Doug and I were together, he could easily have packed one side and then changed the field after each single.

That rigmarole might have involved half a minute after every single scored and would have taken a huge amount of time out of our 105 minutes. That was his quandary on that day, not the declaration. But he kept his fields more or less split and very little time was wasted.

To my mind, that was a very brave thing to do and, inevitably, his decision meant there were more gaps than if he'd packed one side of the wicket.

I said to Doug, "Look, we've got to run for everything. If there's any chance at all, we'll make every one into a two." We set off with this in mind. If the ball didn't go straight to the fielder, we were going to back ourselves against the fielders.

Everything was up for grabs and we ran the first run as fast as we possibly could. We got away with murder at times and there were a lot of scrapes, a lot of near misses and some tough decisions for the umpires.

But the vital ingredient, luck, was with us and we got away with it without any real problems apart from tiredness. We ran a phenomenal number of twos and, at times, we were on our knees. Literally.

We kept the score moving, moving, moving all the time and increased the pressure on the fielders, who grew more and more ragged. We put on 141 in just over an hour and they simply couldn't contain us.

It was so thrilling to be involved. Pure exhilaration. I don't think either of us will ever forget it. It was such a wonderful experience. We broke the back of the target and from then on it was just a normal game of cricket.

Dougie got out for 79 with the score on 181 and I followed 18 runs later, caught on the mid-wicket boundary by Pataudi for 96. Funnily enough, when I was in the seventies, Tiger had clung on to a similar chance but stepped over the boundary in making the catch. He signalled immediately that it was not out but nevertheless Marlar walked to the edge of the square to check that Tiger was 100 per cent certain.

The following day there was a picture in the paper of me walking off…and already, Brian Bolus was disappearing into the middle distance to join Raymond and finish the job with seven minutes to spare. We'd scored 218 for five in 28.3 overs and won out of nothing. Surrey were beaten by Middlesex. We were champions!

Champagne appeared from nowhere. Where it came from I do not know because it certainly wasn't there in the morning and it wasn't there at lunchtime! We started to enjoy it.

The BBC camera crews arrived and Fred loved every minute, doing interview after interview. Everybody was going wild. The Sussex lads joined in. It was something we'd never expected at the start of the day.

Nor, it transpired, had the majority of the Press corps. We had our Yorkshire reporters with us throughout the Southern Tour, journalists from the Yorkshire Post, Evening Post, the old Evening News, Bradford Telegraph & Argus and the Sheffield Telegraph and Star. They were our faithful band of reporters.

They were very fair by and large although they used to give us some stick as well as praise. They were good to have about and there was a mutual trust. We never had a problem about chatting to them because we all knew what would be on and off the record.

But not many of the big-name national newspaper boys followed us to Hove, having more or less made up their minds that we weren't going to win it. So it wasn't until nearly lunchtime on the final day that they honoured us with their presence.

They had been at The Oval but when it became likely that Surrey weren't going to pick up any points and we might win, they dashed south to Brighton. Our Press lads told us later how new faces would keep arriving in the press box as the events unfolded.

The game ended at 4.23pm and we knew we had to drive up to Scarborough for the Festival game against MCC the following day. Normally we would have been away within half an hour but it must have been seven o'clock before we left Brighton. So we were celebrating for quite a while!

There were no motorways in those days, of course, so it was quite a journey. We didn't try to travel in convoy so as the hours went by, we became pretty well separated according to the speed of the car and driver.

The two main Festival hotels were the Balmoral and the

Salisbury and it wasn't until two o'clock in the morning that we started to arrive in dribs and drabs. Only to discover that none of the supporters in Scarborough had gone to bed.

They were waiting for the champions to come home. We were dead tired but it was a wonderful reception. Everybody wanted to know what had happened down at Hove.

The following morning we reached North Marine Road to find thousands of people milling around outside the ground. The place was already full and they hadn't been able to get in. But they still waited to see us arrive. I'd never seen as many people at a cricket match in my life.

When we parked the cars, people rushed forward, wanting to carry our bags into the ground. And the path between the main entrance and the pavilion was absolutely jam-packed with people, all smiling and laughing.

The biggest moment of all was when we took the field. The whole crowd had swarmed on to the ground and formed a corridor for us to walk between the pavilion and the square and they gave us a tremendous ovation. People had come to Scarborough just to be there on the day we returned with the Championship.

We won the game after another run chase and then we were on the road again for the final match of the season, Champion County v The Rest at The Oval. Obviously none of us had ever taken part in that one before. Yorkshire decided in advance that they would stick to their tried and trusted formula of only taking 12 players plus the scorer.

As Cyril Turner was still unwell, Philip was taken as scorer. Ken Taylor, who also played football for Huddersfield Town, had been recalled for Second Division duty. But that still left two players, Dickie Bird and Vic Wilson, and only one place in the party.

Dickie had made six appearances while Vic had played 15 games but lost his place after a terrible loss of form. He was 38 and we all thought it was probably going to be his last year.

In 13 years with the club, he'd never played for an outright Championship-winning side and Ronnie wanted him in the team. It was widely seen as a thank you for all his years of service. So Dickie was left out.

Closey responded with the idea that Dickie was one of the boys and we all ought to chip in and pay for his hotel bill for the four days we'd be down there. Ronnie put the idea to the committee, who agreed. Vic scored a hundred in the second innings and pulled us out of the mire before we won by 66 runs after following on.

We owed a lot to Ronnie. He freely admitted he wasn't a county player. He'd been skipper to most of us in the second team and the young lads coming into the side had won the Second XI title with him in 1957.

They knew him well and the spirit in the side was incredible. We didn't always get on, of course, and there were heated moments at times. But it was never allowed to continue beyond the kind of sudden flare-up that happens if one player is disappointed with another or if players are tired.

As well as his limitations as a player, Ronnie had struggled a bit with his fitness. But the team hadn't suffered and Ronnie was the man who had brought it all together. We used to keep our eye on Closey at second slip. He'd be moving fielders about. Ronnie knew and accepted it.

As wicketkeeper, Jimmy Binks was also a great help to Ronnie. He was a very astute cricketer as well as a great wicketkeeper. He could feel how the bowlers were performing from the way the ball landed in his gloves, if they were tiring or not getting much help from the conditions. He'd pass it on to Ronnie.

Raymond was also a close adviser so the skipper was never short of information from senior players. And everybody felt able to join in and make a contribution. That hadn't happened in Yorkshire cricket for a long, long time and we went to work every day looking forward to it.

So the cricket was over and we were presented with our Championship bonus of £100, a very useful amount of money in those days. Then in the autumn, Sir William Worsley, the Yorkshire President, entertained us to a celebration dinner at his stately home, Hovingham Hall, near Malton.

The family were all keen supporters and his daughter Catherine, later the Duchess of Kent, sat between Ken and I. It was a lovely night. We stayed at the Worsley Arms in the village, courtesy of Sir William.

It was the end of the celebrations. But what we didn't know was that even as we were still savouring our Championship, Ronnie's time was running out.

In November, Brian Sellers, the cricket chairman, invited him out to lunch. He put forward a situation that Ronnie hadn't considered but Sellers, and some of the committee, had: that Ronnie should resign and allow Vic Wilson to take over. Ronnie eventually agreed.

The announcement was made soon after Christmas and it was a huge surprise to us all. We had all assumed that Vic would retire. Instead he came in to skipper the side. We retained the Championship in 1960 and after finishing second to Hampshire in 1961, regained it in 1962.

We started that season with 14 capped players. That had never happened before. Vic, Closey, Raymond, Jimmy Binks and Fred were obviously going to start matches when available so that left nine of us fighting for six places, with one or two younger players, like Geoff Boycott, John Hampshire and Tony Nicholson, starting to push from the Second XI.

On the way to a pre-season friendly match at Settle, I asked Maurice Leyland how it would work. He said that four or five players would each be given an extended run in the side on a rota basis but obviously some of us would have to go at the end of the season.

A week before the first game against MCC at Lord's, Vic told Mike Cowan he wouldn't be involved. We assumed that meant 13 players would go south for the game at Lord's and then matches against Oxford and Cambridge Universities.

But as we were walking off the field after nets on the day before we were due to travel, Vic appeared alongside me and said, "Bryan, you're not going down to London."

"What do you mean?"

"You won't be playing at Lord's." He didn't give me any reason. I was shattered. The Second XI didn't have a game for around six weeks so there seemed no prospect of playing myself into the side. I went to see John Nash, the Yorkshire secretary, on the Monday. "What's going on?" I asked him.

"All the players have been allocated to Yorkshire League sides and anyone who isn't involved with the first team will play league cricket at the weekend."

"Fine. I'll go and play for Harrogate."

"Well, no. You've been allocated to Doncaster."

"Doncaster? It's miles away."

"The league has drawn lots and you've been selected to go to Doncaster." I went to Doncaster and got four ducks in four weeks. They weren't impressed. I managed to score a hundred for the Forty Club against St Peter's School, York, and then Second XI cricket started.

The first team had played 13 matches before I was given a chance against Derbyshire at Hull and to be honest, I'd thought my career was over. Apart from a bit of wounded pride, that didn't really worry me because I knew that before too long I would have had to go back into the business anyway. This experience had brought me down to earth.

I was batting at five and went in about 25 minutes before lunch. I scratted about, picked up a run or two off the edge. I'd no idea what I was doing or how I managed to survive until the interval.

There was a sandwich and a cup of tea waiting in the dressing room for the not out batsmen while the rest of the players enjoyed what was traditionally some of the best catering on the circuit in the dining room.

I looked at the sandwiches and the tea and said to myself, "Bugger it! If I'm going to get out straight after lunch I might as well do it on a decent meal." I headed off to the dining room.

The Press table was at the top of a flight of stairs and as I walked past, Ross Jenkins from Sheffield grabbed me and said, "What on earth are you doing out there?"

"I haven't a clue."

"It looks like it. Listen. How did you play when you came into this side?"

"A lot different to that."

"Right. Get out there and do the same thing. Play as you want to play, not as you think you ought to play." I decided I'd nothing to lose, went out and attacked the bowling, everything started to click and I ended up with 145. That put the cat among the pigeons and I stayed around for the rest of the season.

We were down at Bristol at the end of July when we learned that Brian Bolus and Mike Cowan had been released. I'd already made up my mind that I would go, too. I had too much to lose business-wise if I wasn't going to be with the First XI all the time.

But when Closey was appointed captain for 1963, I said to my wife, Sheila, "I just want one more year, playing with Brian as the official captain." For the previous five years, Closey had pulled the strings, first with Ronnie's consent and then, under Vic, in a more subtle way. It had to be like that because Vic had laid down the law to Brian in the second home game of the 1960 season at Hull.

He told Brian to stop interfering. He said, "I'm a professional captain and I don't need a senior professional out there as well." It was an attempt to stop Brian contributing but we all knew that was going to be impossible and it happened just the same.

I took Brian out to dinner during the opening game of the 1963 season against MCC at Lord's. I told him that as I'd be finishing at the end of the year, I was prepared to shuffle up and down the order or play in the Seconds if need be. He was happy with that and said he'd see it as an opportunity to perhaps find another opening partnership.

I must admit it wasn't the same. But I didn't mind. I just wanted to play that year with Brian. Young Geoffrey Boycott appeared on the scene and we both scored centuries in the Whitsuntide Roses Match at Bramall Lane. Batting at four, I scored my last hundred, Boycs, who joined me at 56 for three, scored his first and we put on 249 for the fourth wicket.

I played in 17 Championship games before I developed appendicitis during the game against Warwickshire at Scarborough at the end of July. And that was it. The end.

I watched what would have been my last Roses match at Old Trafford on television from my hospital bed and I'd so been looking forward to playing my farewell game at the Scarborough Festival a month or so later. But it was not to be.

It had been a fantastic experience and a wonderful period of my life. Before I even played a Second XI match, I appeared as Twelfth Man in the Roses Match at Old Trafford.

That was in May, 1951, and a few weeks later I found myself savouring the atmosphere of a Test Match dressing room as England's Twelfth Man in the fourth Test against South Africa at Headingley.

I got the call again the following year, this time for the first Test against India, when Fred took three wickets for no runs at the start of their second innings; the scoreboard read 0 for four. I had to fetch his lunch and a beer during the interval so he could have a rest. It was probably the first time we'd really sat down together and had a chat. Memorable!

And, of course, Len Hutton was in the dressing room in the early years. He was super. One day when I was Twelfth Man at Sheffield, the only ground which had some nets, Len handed me three new bats. "Take these out, Bryan, and tell me which you think is the best one." Len was captain of England at the time so for him to be asking a young lad which bat he should use was incredible.

He was a lovely man and to have his son Richard come into the side in 1962 while I was still playing meant so much. Richard was a good all-round cricketer. We roomed together on one away trip and I recalled to him what a horrible time Billy Sutcliffe had endured with some of the crowd.

Like Richard, Billy was the son of an all-time great and some so-called supporters used to shout some awful things at him. I said to Richard, "Billy had a rough time because they compared him to his dad. You might get the same thing from some idiots in the crowd who think they are being funny. Try and ignore it; just get on and play your game."

He replied: "Bryan, I'm a fast bowler. My father could never bowl fast. So as far as I'm concerned there's never going to be a situation when it's going to bother me." That was his approach throughout what developed into a very successful career.

Great memories, too, of an era when past players were always welcomed in the dressing room for a chat and a cup of tea. Maurice and Arthur Mitchell were with us anyway and we'd also see on a fairly regular basis people like Herbert Sutcliffe, Arthur Wood, Frank Smailes, Bill Bowes, who was with the Press corps, Don Brennan and Ellis Robinson.

Occasionally, Herbert would bring Percy Holmes with him to Bradford. Percy's face would light up and he'd have a smile on his face throughout the day. He wasn't all that well but he enjoyed it so much and the dressing room lit up with him. You don't forget experiences like that. It was a wonderful connection, one era with another era and a World War in between. We just gelled.

After I retired, I used to go back in and have a chat sometimes but during Geoffrey's time as captain, it was decreed that past players were not allowed in any more. All of a sudden, any connection Yorkshire cricketers might have had with players from other eras was stopped. The door was closed.

And for around 30 years, our only regular get-together was the annual Gibson Cup golf competition for past and present players. I was sure we needed something more regular and in 2004, Geoff Cope asked me if I'd be interested in forming a former Players' Association.

We compiled a list of names, addresses and telephone numbers and wrote to them all. The response was excellent. I drafted a few easy by-laws and the following year, we held an AGM to create a stable association.

Initially, qualification for membership was one first-class game for Yorkshire. That has now been amended to include any capped Second XI player.

It's gone very well indeed, particularly with the older players. And Martyn Moxon, Yorkshire's Director of Professional Cricket and the Association's president in 2009, has been working hard to interest his generation. They were the ones who suffered in all the upsets of the past and there have been barriers.

The current team represent the future but it was the lost generation we needed to attract and it was very gratifying that several players from that era, Martyn, Steve Oldham, Kevin Sharp, Ashley Metcalfe, Jim Love, Neil Hartley, Richard Blakey, Peter Hartley, Richard Kettleborough, Chris Shaw and Ian Fisher, attended our annual dinner in 2009

Inevitably, at our annual lunch and dinner, we reminisce about the golden decade; 1959 and that first Championship will always stand out. We had so much confidence, when we took the field we expected to win.

We knew it would take hard work but we left the dressing room absolutely convinced we would win. Of course things went wrong and we failed sometimes. But that never prevented us from starting the next game with exactly the same conviction.

RONNIE BURNET.
OCTOBER 1918 – MARCH 1999

John Ronald Burnet was born in Saltaire on October 11, 1918. A lower order batsman, he made his Yorkshire debut as captain in 1958 after a successful spell as captain of the Second XI. Capped in 1958, he made 54 first-class appearances for the county, scoring 889 runs at an average of 12.88. He played in one Championship side and retired at the end of the 1959 season. Burnet later served on the Yorkshire committee. He died on March 7, 1999.

Bryan Stott remembers: No statistics or analysis can define what Ronnie Burnet did for Yorkshire cricket. In two short years, supported by a group of enthusiastic and variously talented cricketers, he changed the fortunes of Yorkshire CCC.

Yet in 1958, his appointment was the subject of some surprise and unwarranted criticism, some public, some private, even some from senior members of the side. And at the time nobody could begin to realise that, within 18 months, he would be the catalyst for radical change in our fortunes.

Ronnie had no pretensions whatsoever of being described as a first-class cricketer. He had a penchant for fast cars, mixed easily in any company and the tremendous team spirit he generated within the dressing room gradually proved its worth on the field.

Our own confidence in our ability gradually matched our captain's own faith in us and our competitiveness improved. Everybody supported everybody else. And when Test calls took senior players away, others came in from the Second XI and adapted easily to the spirit in the dressing room.

Ron had the good sense to seek the advice of his senior players like Brian Close, Raymond Illingworth and Jimmy Binks. But he wasn't afraid to consult other players if he felt the occasion demanded it.

He wasn't the strict disciplinarian people believed. But he possessed an absolute conviction in his own belief of right and wrong in the dressing room. The team disciplined itself – and very effectively, too.

The side he inherited in 1958 probably had better players than our Championship team but the way they approached their cricket was very confrontational. Man to man in the dressing room.

That wouldn't have gone down well with some of the lads in Ronnie's side. He created a balance. There's no point having a side of superb Test players if they can't get on. They won't get the results.

And within the space of two seasons he transformed his young lions from doubt and disarray to dedicated and determined champions.

He did it with a unique blend of encouragement, persuasion and the occasional reprimand. But above all, he did it by the way he understood how to handle each individual in the side.

1960

It was the year when Elvis Presley was suffering from those hup, two, three, four Occupation G.I. Blues, John F Kennedy was elected President of the USA, a light-heavyweight by the name of Cassius Clay won a Gold Medal at the Rome Olympics and Spartacus, aka Kirk Douglas, was giving the Romans all kinds of grief on the silver screen. The average house price in the UK was £2,350.

The Beatles first hit, Love Me Do, was still more than two years over the horizon. And as the Yorkshire players headed south for their first Championship game of the season, the Everly Brothers and Cathy's Clown were flying the Stateside flag midway through a five-week spell at the top of the charts.

Bizarrely, the fixture list for 1960 decreed that Yorkshire would begin their quest for a second successive title against Sussex at Hove, where they had claimed the Championship in such memorable style six months earlier. And once again the game ended in a run chase.

Déjà vu was not on the agenda, however. This time it was Sussex and their new captain, Ted Dexter, who came out on top, winning by 32 runs.

It was the first of only six defeats Yorkshire would suffer that summer as 17 victories in 32 matches earned them another Championship, finishing a comfortable 32 points ahead of Lancashire.

However, *Wisden* was not wholly impressed by their achievement, pronouncing, "In actual fact, there was no really outstanding side, most of the leading counties going through periods when they looked most ordinary." Can't win 'em all, I suppose.

Like Sussex, Yorkshire had a new captain, Vic Wilson, the first professional to fill the post since Tom Emmett, captain from 1878–'82. From East Yorkshire farming stock, Wilson played for York and Scarborough before making his county debut in 1947.

And the transition from Burnet to Wilson was, apart from two Roses defeats by Lancashire, a smooth one, with no major changes in personnel from the 1959 campaign.

Jimmy Binks became the first Yorkshire wicketkeeper to claim 100 victims in a season and Doug Padgett topped the batting averages with 1,387 Championship runs at 40.79, including five centuries and six fifties.

Padgett, a fixture at number three throughout Yorkshire's golden era, was a stylish, technically correct batsman who, perhaps, never quite fulfilled his early potential.

However, his form in 1960 was good enough to earn him a place in the England side in two of the five Test Matches against South Africa, his only caps. "It took some doing to even get into the side at that time," recalls Padgett.

"Look at the amateurs who were around for starters. Peter May missed the series because of illness but that still left Colin Cowdrey, Ted Dexter, Raman Subba Row and MJK Smith, who all featured regularly that summer.

"Among the professionals, Noddy Pullar opened with Subba Row and Ken Barrington played in four of the five Tests. Tom Graveney never even got a look-in.

"So chances were few and far between and by and large, if you blew it, you were going to have a hell of a job getting back in."

Yet if Padgett's own Test career was short and not particularly sweet, he would, during his time as Yorkshire's coach between 1971 and 1999, have a significant role to play in the development of no fewer than 18 future England players.

And not least the boy he spotted on the outfield during Yorkshire's game against Northants at Abbeydale Park, Sheffield, in August, 1989.

DOUG PADGETT.

AN EYE FOR TALENT

Douglas Ernest Vernon Padgett was born in Idle, Bradford, on July 20, 1934. A top order batsman, he made his debut on June 6, 1951, aged 16 years and 321 days, at the time the youngest player to

*appear for the county, and was capped in 1958. He played in 487
first-class matches, scoring 20,306 runs, with 29 centuries, at an
average of 28.55. He also appeared in 57 limited overs games and
played in seven Championship sides and two Gillette Cup Finals. He
made two England appearances in 1960 and is one of only 12
batsmen to have scored over 20,000 runs for the county. In 1971, he
succeeded Arthur Mitchell as County Coach, a post he held until
1999 when, after a 50-year association with the club, he retired.*

I was sitting on the Abbeydale Park balcony at lunchtime, having a
mug of tea and watching the kids playing cricket on the outfield. I
noticed this young lad batting, he'd be about 14, and straight away,
he stood out. He was different.

I thought, "He's playing like a little pro." His bat was straight,
he'd a good action, balanced, used his feet and got into all the right
positions. So I watched him for a while longer then put my tea down
and wandered out on to the ground.

I asked someone his name and I was told his mother and father
were on the ground as well. I said, "He looks a good little player to
me."

My informant replied, "Aye, Doug, he is. But he was born in
Manchester." Well! I couldn't believe it.

In those days Yorkshire simply didn't even consider anyone who
was born outside the county so our hands were tied. Or so it
seemed. But I made a mental note of the lad's name: Michael
Vaughan.

I was good mates with Graham Saville, the Lancashire coach,
and soon after spotting Michael, we were having a chat on the
phone. I mentioned Michael's name in passing but I don't know
whether Sav did anything about it, although I later heard that
Lancashire had invited Michael to the nets.

Then in 1990 Yorkshire amended the homegrown rule, deciding
that a player would be eligible if he'd been raised in the county and
learned his cricket in Yorkshire, even if he wasn't actually born
here.

Michael had already played for Yorkshire Schools and for various
age group sides so I contacted his club, Sheffield Collegiate, and
arranged for him to come to the nets. He joined the Academy

straight away.

He was a quick learner and had a good head on him. He was very calm and collected. You didn't have to tell him anything twice. He took it all in first time. When he first started playing for the Second XI he wasn't really strong enough to hit the ball off the square but he always played it into the right areas.

I just told people to wait a couple of years until he started piercing the field. I knew he was going to be a good 'un and my only concern was: could he play the quicks? We wouldn't know that until he faced them but of course, he could. No bother.

He took everything in his stride and it didn't surprise me at all that he went on to play for England.

So did I. But unlike Michael, who played in 82 Tests and led England to an Ashes victory in 2005, I never established myself in the side. I played just two Tests in 1960 and then went on an A Tour to New Zealand the following winter.

But I suppose I'd have settled for that when I first started at Idle CC, my village club, in the Bradford League. I always loved my cricket and when I was a little lad, I used to go to the club after school and stay down there until dark, particularly on Tuesday and Thursday practice nights.

For a while, the pro at Idle was C S Dempster, the former New Zealand batsman, and he was always there on a Thursday.

On the Idle ground there's a hill sloping down from the pavilion to the field and when we'd finished practice, he'd stand at the top of the hill, banging balls into the air for me to catch on the field down below. He'd hit 'em for as long as I'd stay out. He was very good for me was C S Dempster.

I was 13 when I played my first game in the first team. It was a league record at the time; it still might be. I'd gone down to Idle to play for the Second XI but one of the first teamers had been called away for some reason so they needed another player at Pudsey St Lawrence. I'm pretty sure Vic Wilson was playing for Pudsey.

The Idle chairman, a chap called Raleigh Hatton, said he'd give me a shilling a run. I got ten and sure enough, he gave me a ten bob note afterwards. The first time I ever got paid playing cricket!

My brother Granville was 14 years older than me and used to open the batting with a chap called Wilf Horner, whose brother

Norman later played for Yorkshire and Warwickshire. Wilf got a lot of runs in the Bradford League and after a while, it was a toss-up as to who went in first with him, Granville or me.

In the end, Granville left and went pro-ing at Lidget Green, Farsley and Brighouse. Then he moved jobs and went to play in the North Staffs and South Cheshire League. He finished second in the league averages in his first year. Who was first? Garry Sobers. So Granville was a fair cricketer.

I opened with Wilf for a while and in June, 1951, we shared a club record opening partnership of 219 against Lightcliffe. The local paper came and took our picture afterwards. The scoreboard shows that Wilf scored 127 of them while I contributed 90 and that summed up our partnerships.

I never could keep up with him. It reached the stage where one or two of the spectators would start giving me stick when they'd had a few pints, telling me to get a move on!

Eventually John Hill, who'd gone to Bradford Grammar School with Granville and was a real stalwart at Bowling Old Lane, came to see my dad, Harry. He wanted me to go and play for Old Lane and said he just wanted me to go out there and bat, no pressure to score quickly.

"If he bats all afternoon, that'll do me," he said. So I went to Bowling Old Lane and stayed there through my two years in the Army and during my early days at Yorkshire.

I was picked for Yorkshire Schools and then England Schools and in 1949, I went to the Yorkshire winter nets for the first time for coaching from Arthur 'Ticker' Mitchell and Maurice Leyland.

Young players weren't driven around in limousines in those days and my father never owned a car; in fact I don't suppose he'd have ridden in many! I had to catch two buses and then carry my bat and bag up Kirkstall Hill to Headingley. Twice a week, Tuesday and Thursday, in the dark.

I made my debut for the Second XI against Northumberland at the Racecourse Ground in Thirsk on July 10, 1950. I was ten days short of my 16th birthday. Raymond Illingworth played, too. So did Norman Horner and Jackie Firth, who later went to Leicester.

I travelled to Thirsk in Jackie's Ford Prefect. The captain was a chap called Geoff Keighley, who played a few first team games in the late forties and early fifties.

Northumberland had a quick bowler -- at least he seemed pretty quick to me at the time -- called Ken Earl and people were saying that if he'd played for a first-class county he'd have been on the boat to Australia on the 1950-51 tour.

I made 29 in our first knock and then me and Illy were together at the end as we won by seven wickets after making them follow on. We only needed twenty-odd but Earl had taken three for 14 by the time we got 'em.

We were paid £5 a man. On the first morning of the match, the captain went to the nearest bank and came back with eleven crisp white fivers. He handed them round, one to each player. I always wished I'd kept that first one!

I stayed in the Second XI from then on but at that stage, I wasn't really thinking about first team cricket. So it was a bit of a surprise, to put it mildly, when I was called up for the game against Somerset at Taunton the following year.

Len Hutton and Willie Watson were playing for England in the first Test against South Africa at Trent Bridge and Norman Yardley was there in his role as Chairman of Selectors.

My debut was on June 6, 1951, but to tell you the truth, it's all a bit of blur. I don't really remember even how I made it to Taunton.

I know that in those days players were only allowed to travel by car in a 100-mile radius from Headingley and while the rule was stretched a bit for one or two places, Taunton certainly wasn't one of them. So we must have gone by train.

Don Brennan, the wicketkeeper, was captain in Yardley's absence and we bowled them out pretty cheaply on the first day. I should have been batting at five but we lost a few early wickets and Don decided to hold me back when the third wicket went down with about 20 minutes left.

So I batted at six the next morning. I got twenty-odd not out and ended up running out of partners. The first ball I received in county cricket was bowled by Ellis Robinson, the old Yorkshire off-spinner who'd moved to Somerset in 1950.

I turned it round the corner for a single and I was on my way, the first of over 20,000 runs for Yorkshire!

I always made a point of reminding Ellis about it when we met afterwards and he'd say, "Aye, I remember it an' all. And if I'd had owt like a leg trap they'd have copped it and tha'd 'ave got nowt!"

I didn't play again that year and went into the Army in October, '52, so I missed the 1953 and '54 seasons with Yorkshire.

But I was playing regular cricket for the Army alongside people like Gordon Barker, who joined Essex, Tom Cartwright, the Warwickshire and England all-rounder and Bomber Wells and John Mortimore from Gloucester. It was a good standard of cricket.

One Sunday we were playing a game at Catterick at the same time as Essex were playing Yorkshire at Hull. Essex had heard about Gordon, who was born in Bramley and had scored a lot of runs in the Bradford League.

They knew Yorkshire weren't showing much interest so Doug Insole and Trevor Bailey came over to have a look. As it happened, Gordon and I both got a hundred.

Bark was due to be demobbed the following year and Trevor asked him if he'd like to go down and play a trial game before the end of the season. Against a Canadian XI, of all things. Then he turned to me. "It's no good asking you, is it?"

"No, I'm all right where I am, thanks."

Bark was a nervous lad and before he set off for Essex, he said, "Do you think I'll get any runs, Doug?"

"Aye, course you will, Bark, lad. Get off and get down there. It's only Canada. You'll be right." And off he went. The morning after the first day, I grabbed a paper to see how he'd got on. Essex batted first and Bark had been bowled for nought!

Anyway, second innings he got a hundred, joined Essex the next year and finished up scoring over 20,000 runs for them. He also played football for Southend United.

Demobbed and back with Yorkshire, I played 14 games in 1955 and scored my first hundred against Warwickshire at Edgbaston. Less than three weeks before, we'd been playing Glamorgan at Harrogate and I'd reached 96.

For some reason I decided to hit Jimmy Pressdee, their slow left-armer, over the top. I don't know why; I very rarely went over the top. I was caught and bowled. I remember thinking, "I'll never get a hundred now," as I walked off.

I appeared pretty regularly in 1956, reaching 1,000 runs for the first time, but I was in and out again in '57 before things started to take off for me the following year after Ronnie Burnet succeeded Billy Sutcliffe as captain.

It was a turbulent first year for Ronnie, with the sacking of Johnny Wardle and retirement of Bob Appleyard and Frank Lowson. But gradually he pulled us all together.

He was a great chap; not the best cricketer in the world but his man management was top drawer. He knew how to handle people and there was never any bother in the dressing room. From the start of '59 we just seemed to go from strength to strength.

And once Ronnie had assembled his own squad, he kept us all together. If one of us was having a thin time, Ronnie stood by him. We all knew where we stood with him and we got results for him.

If he thought we could play and would give 100 per cent for the side, he would back us. Everybody benefited from that approach and it was something that continued for years under Vic Wilson and Brian Close, right through to our last Championship in 1968.

I suppose I was at my best during the four seasons from 1959. In all first-class matches, I scored 2,181 runs at 41.15 in '59 and then passed 1,500 in each of the next three seasons.

In three years under Vic's captaincy, I scored 5,257 runs with 12 hundreds and 23 fifties. Anything over 1,500 runs a season or an average of 40-plus was pretty good going on uncovered pitches. An average over 50 was pretty rare in my time and it was a feat I never achieved.

Even so, I was playing well enough to give the selectors a nudge and I received the call in 1960 when I replaced Mike Smith for the fourth Test against South Africa at Old Trafford.

Smith scored over 2,500 first-class runs that year and hit 54 in the first Test at Edgbaston and 99 at Lord's. But he was left out after getting a duck in the third match at Trent Bridge, even though England won by eight wickets with a day to spare.

These days he'd probably have a central contract and be more or less guaranteed a full series.

The first two days at Old Trafford were wiped out so we found ourselves on a wet 'un in both innings. Anyone could have been rolled over on that pitch and only two players, Roy McLean, who scored 109, and Barrington, who hit 76, passed 50.

I made five and two. But I stayed in the side for the final Test at The Oval on another wet wicket. In the first innings, I made 13 out of 155. Then Pullar and Subba Row put on 290 for the first wicket second time around and when I went in at six, we'd reached 373 for four.

I made it into the thirties and who knows what might have happened if I'd gone on from there and made 70, 80 or a hundred. Instead I was run out by Dave Allen, the Gloucester off-spinner.

However, thanks to Brian Sellers, the Yorkshire chairman, I'd already been given the nod that I'd be on the plane for the winter tour to New Zealand.

We were playing at Sheffield when I spotted Sellers coming up the steps to the Yorkshire dressing room. He looked at me and said, "I want to see you at the close of play."

I thought, "Bloody hell, what's up now?"

But he said: "Now then. Do you want to go to New Zealand this winter on this here A tour?"

"Aye, course I do."

"Well, I'll tell you now, you're going." Apparently, he'd been down at Lord's the previous day. Then he added, "Don't tell anybody, not even the wife. But take it from me, you're going to New Zealand." He was right.

Dennis Silk of Somerset was captain of a 14-man squad that also included my Yorkshire team-mate Don Wilson. And they took former Yorkshire batsman Willie Watson along as senior professional.

Three years earlier, when Willie left Yorkshire, he'd had a word with me. "I'll be going to Leicester next year," he said. "As captain. Will you come with me?"

I still wasn't capped at that time but I said, "No, Willie. I'm going to give it another year here." He tried again afterwards but I was determined to stay with Yorkshire and in fact, I was capped in 1958.

The tour party had a strong batting line-up. As well as me and Watson, there was Roger Prideaux from Northants, Eric Russell of Middlesex, Jim Stewart of Warwickshire, Jim Parks of Sussex and Lancashire all-rounder Bob Barber.

Bob batted in the middle order then but later joined Warwickshire and ended up opening the England innings with

Geoff Boycott.

We hadn't been out of Heathrow long before Willie sidled over. "Have you got any cigs?" he asked.

"No."

"Where do you want to bat on this tour?"

"Three, of course."

"You can't bat three."

"Why not?"

"We've got this fella from Warwick, Stewart. He'll bat three."

"Right then, I'll go in first."

"You can't go in first. There's Prideaux, they think the world of him at Lord's."

"Maybe so. But he can't open on his own, can he?"

"Eric Russell. He plays for Middlesex at Headquarters. And he's a regular opener. He'll be going in first with Prideaux."

"What about four?"

"Bob Barber."

"It looks like five then."

"Jim Parks."

"OK, it'll have to be six."

"Where do you think I'm going to bat?"

"In that case, I might as well get off at bloody New York and go back home."

Sure enough, that was the line-up for the first Representative Match at Dunedin, even though I'd done as well as anyone, apart from Prideaux, in the four warm-up games.

The selection committee was Silk, who was unfit to play because of a hand injury, Watson and Parks and Jim told me afterwards, "Sorry, Doug. It's Willie. He's captain and he wants this team." I often wonder if my refusal to join Leicester three years earlier had anything to do with it.

The game ended in a draw. Prideaux scored a couple of half centuries and Parks hit 82 in the first innings but nobody else made a score.

I scored 125, batting at four, against Central Districts in the game before the second match at Wellington but it didn't do me any good. They kept an unchanged line-up.

This time we were beaten by 133 runs, no one passed 50 and

when I made another century before the third match at Christchurch, they couldn't really leave me out.

I batted at three and scored 54 in the first innings and 13 not out in the second. After the tour I got a letter from Silk saying that I'd been badly done by. He apologised.

In all first-class matches, I scored 446 runs in 13 innings, with two hundreds. Only Prideaux, who scored 710 from five more knocks, scored more. We were the only two players to average over 40. But it wasn't enough and that was it as far as England was concerned.

Instead, I became part of one of the most successful county sides in the history of the game. After winning our first Championship we had eight or nine really good years.

The personnel changed a bit after Vic left and Brian Close took over in 1963. But we'd learned how to win in 1959 and we carried on winning right through the Sixties.

Which was the stronger side? Vic's or Closey's? It's hard to say but on balance, we probably reached our peak during Vic's era, although it has to be said we were pretty useful under Closey as well!

But I think the side Vic Wilson took over in 1960 was probably the best team of the period. The batting was strong with Bryan Stott, Ken Taylor, me, Closey, Phil Sharpe, Brian Bolus and Vic playing for five places.

Illy could be relied on to score either 1,000 runs or take 100 wickets...or both. Fred Trueman would always top the 100 mark as well and he had good support from Bob Platt, Mel Ryan and Mike Cowan. And Don Wilson was getting better all the time.

Jimmy Binks was one of the best keepers around, if not the best. On top of that, we were a bloody good fielding side, too. Either catching or run saving. And above all, we expected to win. OK, we got stuffed now and again but that could happen to any side on uncovered wickets if the weather went against them.

A team might lose the toss on a Saturday, see the opposition score 300-plus and then find themselves on a wet 'un on Monday morning.

So anyone could get done...like we were at Bristol in '59 when we were rolled over by Gloucestershire for 35 and six years later for

23 against Hampshire at Middlesbrough.

But those days were few and far between right through to 1968 and, on balance, the members didn't have too much to complain about.

Neither did I. I enjoyed my career, make no mistake. And I think everybody else at Yorkshire would say the same thing. I played with a great set of lads who, above all else, were a really close-knit team.

We used to have a go at one another in the dressing room but woe betide an outsider if he tried to criticise any member of the side.

We weren't paid much but we never went in and demanded more like they do today. Every year we'd be sent a letter informing us that there'd be a pay rise of two per cent and that was it.

We never asked for it; if we had, they'd have kicked us out. In fact, that's exactly what happened to Illy when he asked for a contract in 1968. Sellers told him where to go.

Before the 1965 Gillette Final against Surrey, we learned that the opposition were on £100 a man if they won. Closey went in to see Sellers, told him about Surrey and said, "So what about us?"

Sellers replied, "Win the bugger first and we'll see." I think we ended up with a tenner. We won seven Championships for Yorkshire but we were never given any kind of memento. It was very poor really.

At one stage, there were nearly 30 committee men at the club and the majority of them were successful businessmen, running big companies. But they didn't look after the players very well.

I don't really think they wanted to know us from September to April. It rankled a bit, of course. But in the end, we just got on with the job of being a professional cricketer.

It wasn't always easy. In my very early days, we had to book our own accommodation and pay for it out of our match fee. The older pros knew where we could stay, although we didn't always use the same hotels or boarding houses. Half the team might stay in the Black Horse and the others in the White Swan, or whatever.

Every night, Herbert Walker, our scorer, and Bright Hayhurst, the masseur, would sit up in the hall and note down what time the players came back in and then they'd report back to the captain next morning.

One night, before my time, they'd waited up long into the night but still there'd been no sign of Ron Aspinall and Alec Coxon, two senior players. In the morning, they told Sellers, "Skipper, we waited up while half past three and Coxon and Aspinall still hadn't come in. Half past three!"

Sellers replied, "Of course they hadn't, you silly buggers, they're stopping down the road in the White Swan!"

And before the days when we stayed at either the Balmoral or the Salisbury, finding a room at Scarborough during Festival time was always a problem. Easy for the amateurs, they stayed at the Grand Hotel, which was very grand indeed in those days.

But all the boarding houses were booked up early and we had to take a chance on whether we'd actually be playing at the Festival or not.

We'd usually be pretty sure about the Yorkshire v MCC match but there was no real way of knowing whether we'd be lining up for the Players against the Gentlemen or for T N Pearce's XI against the tourists.

Our usual lodgings were at Mrs Hogg's boarding house and she did her best to fit us all in. But even so, Fred Trueman and Eddie Leadbeater still had to share a bed one night.

Life on the open road had its problems, too. Cars weren't what they are now and there were no motorways. Me and Raymond travelled together all our careers but our cars weren't high-powered stuff by any means. Illy had a Standard Vanguard first and then a Triumph Herald.

I remember once I was driving Illy's Herald back from the south and we'd made it as far as Bawtry up the A1. We pulled up in a line of traffic at some lights in the town centre and I looked in the mirror to see a wagon bearing down on us.

"This bugger's not going to stop," I said. And he didn't. Bang! Next thing we knew, we were both laid flat out on the floor of the car looking up at the roof.

The front seats were little more than tubular chairs and they'd completely collapsed under the impact. We survived in one piece but Illy swears to this day that it affected his shoulders. He still blames his stiff necks on it.

He was unlucky with that car, was Illy. He'd just got it all mended and good as new when we travelled over for a game at

Scarborough. We were staying at the Balmoral Hotel, where the car park was behind the hotel and you had to drive down a little alleyway to reach it.

Illy was just minding his own business and making his way down the alley when some fella ran into the back of him again! He wasn't very pleased, I tell you.

I had a little Mini to start with and then moved up in the world with a Ford Corsair. Very smart. One day, after a service, the garage delivered it to Park Avenue before we were due to head south; somewhere in the West Country, I think.

Illy jumped into the passenger seat and David Swallow from the Bradford Telegraph and Argus sat in the back. We'd done about 20 miles when all sorts of warning lights started flashing on the dashboard.

"What's going on?" I said to Illy.

"I don't know but it might be an idea to pull over and see." The car was on fire underneath the bonnet – and we'd just filled up with ten gallons of petrol.

Fortunately a lorry was passing and the driver jumped out with a fire extinguisher and put out the blaze. I had to ring my father-in-law and he came over and collected us.

I bought an Austin Cambridge soon afterwards and never had a minute's bother. Best car I ever had.

None of the off-the-field stuff really bothered us, though, and by the end of the 1968 season we'd lifted seven Championships in ten years under Ronnie, Vic and Closey. But when Closey's side started to break up, there weren't half some holes to fill.

In 1968 alone, Fred retired, Illy went to Leicester and Ken Taylor left straight after his benefit to take up a teaching job in South Africa. Jimmy Binks retired in 1969. Then in 1970, Closey was sacked and joined Somerset.

I was appointed coach and second team captain at the same time. So we'd already lost half a team by the time Phil Sharpe, Don Wilson and Dick Hutton left at the end of the 1974 season. No wonder we had some lean times after that.

My switch to the coaching side came totally out of the blue. I'd done all the courses and gained an advanced certificate and helped Arthur Mitchell a bit during the winters. And I realised the time was approaching when I'd have to decide what I was going to do after I finished playing.

If a player wanted to stay in the game – and I really did because I'd known nothing else apart from the odd part-time job in the winter – it was either coaching in some capacity or the umpires' list. If I hadn't opted for coaching I don't know what I'd have done.

When Arthur retired in 1970, the committee asked me if I'd like to become coach and Second XI captain. I didn't really want to finish and I told them I felt I could still play first team cricket.

Geoff Boycott had just been appointed captain and he wanted me in the side. But John Temple, who was cricket chairman at the time, wouldn't have it. In the end, they were holding a gun to my head. Did I want the bloody job or didn't I?

I was 36 with a young family; basically, I had no choice. But I took it on what I thought was the understanding that if I was needed in the first team, I would play. It never happened, although Boycs kept saying he'd asked for me but the committee wouldn't have it.

I didn't know whether to believe him or not but at the start of the 1972 season, I attended a meeting of the cricket committee in my role as coach and second team captain.

Before the business got under way, Boycs said, "Chairman, before we start, I want you to tell Doug that I asked for him to play several times last year."

Temple replied: "Geoffrey, it's a new season let's get on with the business of the day."

"No, chairman. I want you to tell Doug that I asked for him several times last season."

And all credit to Boycs, he wouldn't let it drop. He kept asking and asking until, eventually, Temple said: "All right, yes. Now let's get on with the business..." But I never played again.

I captained the Seconds for the best part of ten years and once it was clear that I wasn't going back into the first team I started to go in at number nine or ten. There was no point me taking up a batting place ahead of one of the young lads, was there?

And it will seem odd in this day and age, when all counties have a big coaching staff, that I hardly ever worked with the first team.

It was the same with Arthur and Maurice when I was a player.

We'd see them at winter nets and then pre-season but that was it. The captain was in charge of the first team and no one else.

That's how it continued until 1979 when Yorkshire decided to appoint a cricket manager and they brought Illy back from Leicestershire.

From the start, I kept an eye on young players who were coming through in the leagues.

I played as pro at Marske in the North Yorkshire and South Durham League for three years and while I was there I spotted Bill Athey and Alan Ramage and first heard about a young quick called Paul Jarvis.

Bill and Paul went on to play for England and Ram would have done if he'd shown a bit more dedication – and if he hadn't also played football for Middlesbrough. He was pretty quick, was Ram, and he could bat. He'd have been a bloody good all-rounder if he'd got stuck into it a bit more.

After leaving Marske, I had one last year with Bowling Old Lane in the Bradford League before calling it a day.

From then on, I used to go round the leagues on a Saturday, looking at players I'd heard about or I'd seen had got wickets or runs. And I developed good connections with the schools

I suppose hundreds of young players came through the Second XI while I was there. Look up who played between 1971 and 1999... I worked with them all. I coached Arnie Sidebottom in the early seventies and his son, Ryan, in the nineties. Same with Richard and Michael Lumb.

In all, 17 of the lads I coached went on to play for England while Steve Oldham, Arnie Sidebottom, Martyn Moxon and Kevin Sharp became involved in the Yorkshire coaching structure in various capacities

Some players fulfilled their potential, others fell by the wayside. Some, like Graham Stevenson, did both. A wonderful cricketer, Stevo. As a bowler, he was quick, with a great outswinger. As a batsman, he could take an attack to bits on his day. And he had a wonderful arm.

His first team debut was against Middlesex at Bradford in 1973 and I remember him saying to me, "When I go down them Park Avenue steps for the first time, my knees'll be knockin'."

I said, "They'll like you at Bradford. If you look as if you can field and you're trying, you'll be all right. First time you get t'ball in t'outfield, make sure it goes back in flat and over the top."

And he did. It went straight as an arrow. He played for England and went on tour but he gradually fell out of love with the game and didn't want to play any more. I never knew why.

Yorkshire kept him on and we talked to him time and again. In the end, after Yorkshire finished him, Steve Coverdale, the Northants chief exec, talked him into going down there for a year. But it didn't work and he packed it in, aged 31. Sad. A great player.

David Byas was always strong and hungry. If he got in, he didn't give it away; he went on and made a big score. All through his Second XI career and on into the first team.

He was a great asset to Yorkshire cricket and in 2001, captained them to their first Championship since '68. Yet in his Second XI days, I didn't really look on him as captaincy material. But I'd never any doubt he'd do well. He was dependable, he'd graft and fight and he had some spirit about him.

I used to watch Anthony McGrath week in and week out when he played for Bankfoot in the Bradford League. He was always going to be a good player and I thought him and Michael Vaughan would be the backbone of Yorkshire's batting for eight or ten years.

Darren Gough whistled through in no time. Barnsley was always a good breeding ground...as Dickie Bird will tell you! I'd already had Stevenson and Oldham from there. Martyn Moxon, too.

Goughie was bubbly, full of life and aggression. You could see he wanted to get on and he just had to play first team cricket. He was a natural.

Ryan Sidebottom was the same. I remember taking Ryan down to Leicester for his Second XI debut and I thought straight away, "Here's a little gem. We'll just have to guide him along and he'll be all right." And he was. It's funny. Bowlers seem to get there quicker. I don't know why.

There were quite a few slow bowlers who came into the Seconds and, for one reason or another, never really played in the first team. Players like Ian Fisher, Gary Keedy, Ian Swallow, Paul Booth, Phil Berry, James Middlebrook and the Batty brothers, Jeremy and Gareth.

They all ended up going elsewhere. Gareth certainly should never have been allowed to leave. What a competitor he was!

It broke my heart when Steve Rhodes left in 1984. We just couldn't hold on to him because David Bairstow was wicketkeeper and captain and the club stood by him.

Steve was made to be a Yorkshire wicketkeeper. He was absolutely brilliant and, of course, after he joined Worcester he went on to play 11 Tests and nine one-dayers for England. I could have cried when he left, I really could.

And then there was another young lad I was sure would go right to the top; a left-hand batter called Neil Lloyd. He really looked to have everything. Tragically he died in September, 1982, when he was just 17.

He'd already played for Young England and the Second XI. Shocking. It was a terrible blow and put everything else into perspective. What a great little player he was going to be.

I suppose the lads saw me as something of a father figure and I liked to be there if they needed a quiet chat or whatever. But I wasn't averse to the odd practical joke at their expense.

Once we were playing a one-day match at York and Texaco must have been the sponsors because they had adverts all round the ground. They also supplied loads of beer mats in the bar.

So just before the match ended, I collected four mats and, in my best handwriting, wrote on each one: "Please supply the bearer with four gallons of petrol."

I went into the dressing room and shouted, "Look, lads, I don't know what to do with these. They're a perk from Texaco but I've only got four so you can't all have one. You'll have to scrap for 'em. Each one's worth four gallon of petrol at that Texaco garage down t' road."

For a few minutes there was mayhem...and then four players emerged from the scrum with their prize. As soon as they were changed, they jumped into their motors and roared off in the direction of the filling station.

They filled up and then presented their beer mats to the cashier, who was understandably less than impressed. They all ended up having to cough up for four gallons of petrol.

I seem to recall Tony Nicholson was one of them...and he had no bloody money in his wallet!

I sometimes used to call the Twelfth Man over and whisper, "Go ask the lads if anyone wants salmon today. T'chef says there's only two portions for each side and it's first come, first served if you order in the kitchen now. The rest'll have to settle for steamed fish."

The lads would stampede into the kitchen to discover the chef was preparing meat and potato pie with not a salmon in sight.

In the end I finished when I was 65. I'd been with Yorkshire for 50 years, man and boy...literally. So perhaps it was time to go.

There was talk of keeping me on in another capacity but they never came up with anything. But they were never very good when players were leaving, weren't Yorkshire.

I've never really been back. The odd day at a Test Match, maybe, but I haven't been to a Yorkshire match. And I've stayed in touch with a few of the players from my era, although I'm not a member of the Players' Association.

But I went back to Headingley for Yorkshire's pre-season lunch in 2009 when the surviving members of the 1959 Championship side were invited as special guests.

There were eleven of us round the table: Closey, Raymond, Bryan Stott, Ken Taylor, me, Phil Sharpe, Brian Bolus, Dickie Bird, Don Wilson, Bob Platt and Mel Ryan.

We were introduced one by one and we were all given a good reception. Then Closey, Raymond and Bryan did a little question and answer session. It was a good day.

1961

Yuri Gagarin, a Russian cosmonaut, beat Yorkshire to the punch. On April 12, 1961, he became the first man to travel in Space, 17 days before Yorkshire opened their season against MCC at Lord's.

Gagarin's historic flight was by no means the only significant event of the year. In March, the Beatles appeared at Liverpool's Cavern Club for the first time, betting shops were legalised a month later and in May, Spurs became the first club to achieve the League Championship and FA Cup double since 1897.

Elvis Presley was on top of the charts with Wooden Heart on that first day of the season and the first edition of Private Eye rolled off the presses in September,

By which time Yorkshire had lost their Championship crown to Hampshire. To players and supporters from that era, 1961 will always be remembered as The One that Got Away.

With two successive Championships under their belt, Yorkshire made a flying start by winning seven of their first eight matches. And they led the race for much of the season.

Hampshire and Middlesex hung on to their coat tails, however, and when, in late August, Yorkshire lost to Kent and Middlesex and drew with Warwickshire, Hampshire pounced to win the first title in their 98-year history.

So it was scant consolation that when Yorkshire faced the new champions at Bournemouth in the final match of the season, they won what had been widely forecast as a Championship decider by 58 runs. Yorkshire lost only five of their 32 Championship matches but a tally of ten draws told its own story.

Once again, Fred Trueman and Ray Illingworth each claimed more than 100 wickets and Fred found valuable support in the shape of Mel Ryan and Bob Platt, proud fast bowling sons of Huddersfield.

Platt played in 18 matches, taking 48 wickets at 21.58, while Ryan appeared in 20 games and took 61 wickets at 22.13, figures that reflected a strong effort from all the bowlers. Indeed, *Wisden* was moved to observe "that it was not the bowlers' fault that the title was lost".

Nearly 50 years down the line, with Ryan and Platt re-united in the baronial splendour of the clubhouse at Woodsome Hall Golf Club on the fringes of Huddersfield, Hampshire's unexpected success became once again a bone of contention.

"Hampshire won the Championship in the same way that Ipswich Town won the Football League in 1962," insisted Platt. "Because no one expected them to do it.

"We beat them down at Bournemouth then drove up to Scarborough for the festival and collected a bollocking from Brian Sellers for finishing second."

"Yes, we did," recalled Ryan. But you have to remember the weather in those days. Generally speaking there was an awful lot of bad weather up here that they didn't get down south.

"There was many a season when we hadn't even practised outside before we went down to Lord's for the first match against MCC. I'm sure Hampshire played more cricket than we did in 1961."

Platt: Mind you, the Championship couldn't have gone to a better man than Colin Ingleby-Mackenzie, their captain. He got everyone to smile about the game.

Ryan: And Hampshire did have Butch White, who was a very good fast bowler, and, of course, Derek Shackleton.

Platt: Ingleby put Shack on in April and didn't take him off till bloody September! In Shack's last full season in 1968, he bowled over 1,000 overs – and he was 44. And not a single half-volley. I'll tell you what, though, he couldn't bowl at Fred, could he? Fred used to smash Shack!

Ryan: But even though we missed out on the Championship in 1961, we were still regarded as the biggest side in the game. We used to just about fill every away ground and lots of our own supporters came, too.

People sometimes ask me if I'd like to be playing today, when there's so much money kicking around. But I always say, No. I never got rich playing cricket but I was around at the best possible time. It was the best ten years of my life. A wonderful experience.

Mel Ryan and Bob Platt.

Made in Huddersfield

Melville Ryan was born in Huddersfield on June 23, 1933. A fast bowler, he made his Yorkshire debut against the Combined Services in 1954 and played in his first Championship game the following year. He was capped in 1962 and went on to make 150 appearances for the county, claiming 413 wickets at an average of 22.92. He also appeared in three limited overs games. Ryan played in four Championship sides and later served on the Yorkshire committee.

Robert Kenworthy Platt was born in Holmfirth on December 26, 1932. A fast bowler, he made his Yorkshire debut in 1955 and was capped in 1959. He made 96 first-class appearances and played in four Championship sides before joining Northamptonshire in 1964, where he played for one more season. One of the few inswing bowlers to make his mark with Yorkshire, he took 282 wickets at 22.65. He later served on the Yorkshire committee and was cricket chairman when Yorkshire won the championship in 2001.

So you are two proud sons of Huddersfield whose careers as Yorkshire fast bowlers ran more or less in tandem. Where did it all begin?

Platt: We learned our cricket in the Huddersfield League, Melville at Bradley Mills and me at Holmfirth.

Ryan: Which is not part of Huddersfield at all...they're a bit different there! In actual fact, the first time I ever played against R K Platt was at football. He was in goal for Holmfirth and they were a superb side.

Platt: We were, we won everything.

Ryan: I played for Paddock, an inside-forward as we were called in those days. We were a rough lot! Anyway against Holmfirth, we won a corner and I caught it perfectly on the volley. Bang! A goal.

Not many people did that against Holmfirth. And I remember Bob picking the ball out of the back of the net and turning to this big stocky lad who played wing-half. I forget what they called him.

Platt: Oliver Woodhouse.

Ryan: That's it, Oliver Woodhouse. He kicked anything that moved. Bob just pointed at me and said to Woodhouse, "Watch him!" Oliver watched me all right but I managed to steer well clear of him for the rest of the match and escaped in one piece. My goal gave us a 2-1 lead but we lost 6-2.

Platt: We played in the old Red Triangle League, didn't we? Holmfirth won the Under-16s two years running and then the Under-18s straight away.

But you must have faced one another on the cricket field, too.

Platt: No. Mel and I never really played cricket against one another at all because when we were juniors, Bradley Mills and Holmfirth were in different sections of the league. We didn't play against one another at school either.

Ryan: I went to Huddersfield College. They weren't too bothered about sport there and I wasn't very good at schoolwork. I was more interested in cricket and football and I knew that in the long term, I would go into the family newsagent business. We eventually had shops in Huddersfield, Halifax and Leeds and I ran the business with my brother, Granville, until we sold out six or seven years ago. In my last summer at school, when I was 15, they chose me as second reserve for the second team. I said I'm sorry, I'm not doing that. I was playing in the Huddersfield League for Bradley Mills second eleven at the time and the following year I was picked for Yorkshire Under-16s. I was very tempted to go back and say to the headmaster, "Twelve months ago I was second reserve for your second team; now I'm playing for Yorkshire. Do you think you might just have got it wrong?"

Platt: That sounds familiar. One Friday morning at Holme Valley Grammar School, as it was called in those days, my younger brother, Stuart, crossed our names off the teamsheet for a school match on the Saturday afternoon because we knew we'd be playing for Holmfirth first team. The headmaster, K R Brain, found out and we were hauled in on the Monday morning. "I don't know who you think you are," he said. "Do you think you're going to play for Yorkshire or something?" I never forgot those words. And as a punishment, he banned us from playing sport at school. Wednesday afternoon was the official sports afternoon but as we were banned, Stuart and I went into the geography room, did our homework and then went off to play for Holmfirth juniors. Soon afterwards I was picked for the Huddersfield League Under-18s against the Bradford League at Fartown. It was part of the cricket week that was held every year during the textile factory holidays. Brain's ban had been lifted by then and I was supposed to be playing for the school on the same day. I was in a bit of a quandary but as it happened, the maths master, a chap called John Barron, played in the Huddersfield League for Hall Bower and took an interest in my cricket. So I asked him what I should do, play for school or the league. Barron said, "The headmaster won't even know about this game at Fartown. So cross your name off the teamsheet and write 'ill' alongside. He'll never know any different." In cricket terms, it was probably the best thing that ever happened to me. Ken Taylor was also in the Huddersfield team and the Bradford side included Raymond Illingworth, Bryan Stott and Barry Stead, the pace bowler who moved from Yorkshire to Notts in 1959. I still have the scorecard.

Ryan: And I've still got my first invitations to the Yorkshire nets. When you received one of those it was the big-time. It meant a mention in the Huddersfield Examiner. I'd probably be 14 at the time. What's more, it was the great Yorkshire and England all-rounder George Herbert Hirst who recommended me...as a batsman. He'd spotted me in the indoor nets that were held during the winter in a Nissen hut in the village of Marsh on the outskirts of Huddersfield. It was the only winter net in the area and anyone could go along.

Platt: A batsman? Impossible, Melville! What was your highest score in first-class cricket? I seem to have forgotten...

Ryan: I made 26 not out against Worcestershire at New Road in July, 1963...and I also made 26 against Essex at Clacton a few weeks later. But we won't go into that if you don't mind because next thing you'll be reminding us that you once scored 57 not out.

Platt: Too right I will! Against Derbyshire at Chesterfield in a three-day match starting on July 4, 1959. I put on 43 for the ninth wicket with Jimmy Binks and 41 for the last wicket with Chris Wood, another pace bowler who played four games that year. And if I hadn't run out of partners, I'd have gone on to score a hundred.

Ryan: But seriously...

Platt: I am serious.

Ryan: When I played for Bradley Mills, I used to bat at number three and I did well. I also opened the bowling. Then we signed a guy – I forget his name – as captain and he refused to let me bat so high because I was also the opening bowler. He shoved me down to number seven. That's why I left and moved to Eccleshill in the Bradford League in the early fifties. And in my first match against Saltaire, I scored 46. A match report in the local paper read, "Ryan did not trouble the opponents with his bowling, earning a return of two for 48. But he did surprise the crowd and his club officials by showing that he is also useful with the bat, he was unbeaten with 46." But of course once I started playing for Yorkshire Seconds, I was in there alongside top-class specialist batsman and as a bowler, I was down there at the bottom of the order with the nog-enders. Bowlers were never pushed forward as batsmen at all. They are now but not in our day. You started at number eleven whether you liked it or not and you didn't really have much opportunity to show what you could do. You were either going in to slog because they needed quick runs or to block it to save the match.

Platt: Doug Padgett used to go on about the responsibility and stress involved in batting at number three. But I used to tell him, "Come on, Doug, I'm under more pressure than you, batting at ten or eleven. When I have to bat, I'm either trying to save t'game or win it. You never experience that at number three!" But I never knew you had aspirations as a batsman, Melville.

Ryan: Well, you learn something every day, don't you?

Platt: I was supposed to be a footballer really and I had one or two offers of trials with professional clubs. My younger brother Stuart was the cricketer in the family. He was opening the batting for Holmfirth when he was 14 and I only moved up the ladder at cricket because one day I had to drive him to Headingley. When he was 16, he decided to leave Holmfirth to go and play for Leeds in the Yorkshire League. But when it came to his first game, my father, who established the family electrical business in Holmfirth in 1928, was ill and couldn't drive. So I was going to take over as the chauffeur. Even though Stuart was leaving, I expected to stay at Holmfirth but as it happened, the previous week against Linthwaite, I'd been reduced to bowling third change. Herbert Sills, our old pro, wasn't happy about that and said to me, "This is ridiculous. You get off to Leeds as well. I know they want you." So I did. I was fully expecting to play for their Leeds League side but instead they bunged me straight into the Yorkshire League against Castleford at Headingley. That's when I discovered first-class wickets and realised I wasn't quite as quick as I thought I was.

Did you play anywhere else apart from your clubs at that stage?

Platt: In the early fifties, we also played Sunday cricket for the Yorkshire Owls and Yorkshire Corinthians. They were two friendly sides made up mainly of older players from the Bradford and Yorkshire Leagues with a few up and coming youngsters thrown in as well. Ronnie Burnet played and so did Derek Blackburn, who captained the Yorkshire Seconds. Neither side had a ground of their own but instead played games all over the country. We learned a lot with them.

Ryan: And we learned a lot on the Corinthians' 1955 trip to Paris as well...and not all of it cricket! You don't normally associate the French capital with the sound of willow on leather but we went over and played two games against the Standard Athletic Club of Paris, made up mainly of players from the British Embassy. The Owls also used to go on a southern tour and one year, we played at the Vine CC in Sevenoaks, one of the oldest clubs in the world. They first played there in 1734. I took four wickets in four balls, three of them clean bowled. A few of the Owls players were captains in the Bradford League and if they thought a young player had a bit of talent, they poached him for their own club. And realistically, if you were going to make the grade, you had to be playing in the Bradford League. The Yorkshire League was supposedly superior but Bradford was more competitive and you really learned what the game was all about.

Platt: Very true. I played very good cricket for Leeds in the Yorkshire League but soon after joining the RAF in 1954, I went to play for Bradford in the Bradford League. Mel joined us from Eccleshill soon afterwards. That was a real awakening because it was as near as you could get to the way Yorkshire played.

You both made your Championship debut in 1955, within four weeks of one another, and over the next decade, you spent a lot of time operating from the opposite end to 't'finest bloody fast bowler that ever drew breath'. Otherwise known as Frederick Sewards Trueman.

Ryan: It's startling when you look at the length of Fred's career and how many overs he bowled. Between 1949 and 1968, he bowled over 16,000 overs in first-class cricket. He frequently bowled more than 1,000 in a season. Bob and I were average county cricketers and if we played in say 20 out of 28 Championship games we'd bowl something like 500 overs. But Fred was a star, a top international fast bowler – and I mean fast, not fast-medium – and for England and Yorkshire, he could expect to bowl around 1,000 overs a season as a matter of course.

Platt: And to do that for so long and only be injured twice says everything about his fitness. When Fred said he was injured, nobody believed him. He was incredible. As soon as I try to tell people just how good he was, they say, "Oh, you're off again about Trueman." But I'll tell you this. Over the last 60 years I've seen a lot of fast bowlers and the only ones I would put in remotely the same category for durability are Joel Garner, Courtney Walsh and Malcolm Marshall. And even they didn't perform for 17 seasons, week in, week out.

Ryan: Unfortunately in those days, Yorkshire and Fred were not appreciated at Lord's. I played there several times and I could always sense that people in the establishment disliked us, especially when we were winning. And Fred would have taken a lot more than his 304 Test wickets if his face had fitted at Lord's. They didn't take him to Australia in 1954-55 or to South Africa in 1955-

56, not to mention tours to India and Pakistan. And he missed quite a few home Tests as well. They said it was because he was a naughty boy. Well in his early days, he could be. But nothing like as bad as people tried to make out.

Platt: No, nothing like. And another myth about Fred was his sledging, as they call it today. Not long ago, I was talking cricket with my accountant and insurance broker and the conversation turned to all this sledging and bad language business. One of them said, "Well, it's always gone on. Fred was at it as well, wasn't he?" I said, "He bloody well wasn't. He daren't...because the umpires were in control of it. They were all ex-players and knew what was going on."

Ryan: No, Fred wasn't abusive, he was funny. He could make an off the cuff remark that would have everybody laughing, including the batsmen and umpires. Like the time we were playing Surrey at The Oval when Bernard Constable came in to bat. Bernard was only a little fella but he was very military in his bearing and was ramrod straight as he walked. Fred watched Bernard's progress from the pavilion and when he reached the crease, he said, "Morning, Bernard. I see you've still got that pick-axe handle up you're arse!" Everybody just collapsed.

Platt: He was hardly ever in our dressing room. He spent his time in with the opposition, having a laugh with them. I once took his bags into the visitors' dressing room on the first morning at Harrogate because I knew he'd be spending most of his time there. They all loved him and sometimes we didn't see him until quarter past eleven.

Ryan: Fred always had the last word. If ever we were having a joke at his expense, he would find an instant one-liner to finish it off. Always. The only person who ever caught him out was Richard Hutton. Once Fred had been regaling us with the details of one of his great performances, in which every ball either took a wicket, pitched leg stump and missed off by a whisker or had the batsman playing and missing outside the off stick. And when he'd finally finished, Richard's cultured tones floated over from a distant corner of the dressing room. "Would you call yourself a modest man, Fred?" Not even Fred had an answer to that one.

Platt: He could have the dressing room in stitches within seconds of walking in. And for years after we retired, he used to phone me once a fortnight and he'd always have a new joke. I can't remember them, of course, there were so many.

Ryan: It says everything that I don't think I ever had a wrong word with him in ten years. He just wasn't that sort of guy.

Platt: The only time I saw the other side of him was at the end of the 1954 season when he wasn't chosen for the winter tour to Australia. They took Frank Tyson, Brian Statham, Alec Bedser and Peter Loader and left Fred behind. He was in a real bad mood over that and rightly so. They were all good bowlers but not as good as Fred. He really could bowl and he was so strong. The rest of us would be flogging around, bowling 30 overs a day, sometimes more. And halfway through the last session we'd had enough. Not Fred. Chuck him the new ball at 5.30 and he'd be coming in like it was half past eleven.

Ryan: He had the best end, though. It was uphill and against the wind for the rest of us! Up the steps from the football end at Bradford Park Avenue, as we used to call it, while Fred launched himself from the Pavilion End. The only time it would change was if we were getting wickets and he wasn't.

Platt: It worked out OK for me, though. Fred bowled outswingers, I bowled inswing so if there was a bit of a cross wind it would help us both.

Ryan: And Fred used to just rip through the tail. I took 400 first-class wickets and I always say 390 were batsmen one to six. I would probably have taken another 100 wickets if I'd been able to bowl at nine, ten and eleven and from the right end. And no question, I would have been more successful if Fred hadn't been at the other end.

Platt: I'm not so sure. I only had three ten-fers, ten wickets in a match, in my career, against Surrey, Middlesex and Worcester. And Fred played in all three games. When I look back at the scorecards from those games, I see that I knocked down more early batsmen than Fred did. Maybe that was because they were so relieved to get away from Fred that they didn't mind taking me on. Who knows? But yes, he'd have nine, ten and jack bowled out before you could even get your sweater off. And, of course, if you believed everything he said, he never bowled a straight ball in his life. Every delivery did a bit for Fred. Once we played down at Worcester and I'd been having a bit of a rough patch in the previous matches. After my first couple of overs, I had a word with Jimmy Binks. I said, "Am I doing a bit?"

"Aye, just a bit." It was the same after the third over but then, after the fourth, Jimmy said, "There's not as much happening now."

I replied, "How do you mean? I've just been talking to Fred and he says it's pitching leg stump and missing off for him."

"Don't believe it. He hasn't got one to move off line all morning!" But that was Fred. And how he used to wind up the batsman! I remember once he was bowling to Arthur Milton, the Gloucestershire and England opener, who went back and played the ball defensively with the middle of the bat. Fred let out a staggering groan and growled, "If you'd missed that, you'd have been lbw!" But Arthur had simply middled a straight one.

Ryan: I'll tell you what, though. We had the best part of ten seasons opposite Fred but it might have been a very different story if David Pickles had stayed around. He would have been the best partner of all for Fred. David came from Halifax and was only 21 when he started in 1957. But he really was quick, as quick as Fred. And he had steep bounce, which Fred didn't. Fred skidded the ball more.

Platt: I agree. Neither of us would have played much if David hadn't disappeared off the scene so suddenly in 1960. I'll tell you what, there was a game against Notts at Trent Bridge one year when Fred and David were operating in tandem and the batsmen didn't know which end to run to!

Ryan: David could have been a great bowler. But his action meant he used to bowl from halfway out on the crease and Bill Bowes tried to change him, make him bowl stump to stump. Bill was right in his way but trying to get David bowling wicket to wicket finished him. It really was a shame.

So was Fred the greatest cricketer you ever played with?

Ryan: The three greatest were Len Hutton, Fred and Bob Appleyard. Hutton was a master batsman in every sense of the word. He scored 163 when I made my debut against Combined

Services at Harrogate in 1954 and I'll never forget that innings. They simply couldn't set a field to him. And on uncovered wickets, Appleyard was unplayable. I reckon he would still take 100 wickets a season today...from 16 games and on covered wickets.

Platt: I wouldn't argue with those three. Appleyard was the best all-round bowler I've ever seen. Given half a chance he'd have changed the rules of the game so that he could have bowled at both ends.

Ryan: There's never been another like him. He was equally at home opening the attack and bowling outswingers at fast medium or cutting his pace and bowling off cutters. I have never seen a bowler as good as Appleyard at his best and a lot of ex-first-class cricketers would say the same.

Platt: Mind you, Bob could be difficult. Once, long after we gave up playing and when we were both serving on the general committee, I was leaving a meeting with another committee man. He said, "By, that Appleyard can be an awkward bugger!"

I replied, "You didn't play with him!" Once at Chesterfield, when Billy Sutcliffe was captain, Johnny Wardle and Appleyard were arguing all day about which end they should bowl. Bill kept swapping them round but in the end, he'd had enough. He came over to me and said, 'Bugger 'em, I'm going to put Raymond on.' And Illy took five or six wickets while Wardle and Appleyard were still arguing over which end to bowl.

Ryan: I was at Bramall Lane on the day in 1958 when Johnny was told he was not being retained for the following year. Fred and I were in the dressing room with Wardle at lunchtime when John Nash, the secretary, came in and said Brian Sellers wanted to see him. Fred and I had our boots off, having a cup of tea and when Johnny came back, Fred said, "Well, what's they want thee for?"

Johnny replied, "I've been sacked."

"Don't be so bloody daft," said Fred. But he had. Johnny was a funny man to the crowd and a great bowler but he didn't get on very well with Ronnie Burnet. Or the rest of the team, come to think of it.

Platt: A great bowler but he could be very caustic.

You mention Brian Sellers there. Another larger than life personality?

Ryan: People talk about A B Sellers as captain of the great Yorkshire side of the Thirties. About A B Sellers, the autocratic chairman of cricket from 1959 to 1972. But basically, like Margaret Thatcher, he went on for too long. Right up until his retirement, he tried to run Yorkshire County Cricket Club as a one-man band. But if you analyse Yorkshire's history, things went downhill from the moment they lost Raymond Illingworth in 1968 because Sellers wouldn't give him the security of a long-term contract. Then Sellers sacked Brian Close in 1970. The whole character of the side went with Illy and Close. Yorkshire were left with nobody, and I mean nobody, of anything like the same stature, apart from one man, G Boycott. Geoffrey realised that. But if Closey or Raymond had not left, Boycott would not have gone on to occupy the place in the history of Yorkshire cricket that he eventually did. So I look at that situation and say that OK, Sellers may have had his good years, particularly when he was skipper, but as chairman, he went on too long.

Platt: And as a captain, Sellers could apparently be very pig-headed, too. Ellis Robinson, who played in the Thirties, once told me how Sellers would look at the wicket before the toss and then always have a word with Hedley Verity and Bill Bowes about what to do. But there was a spell when Hedley and Bill stopped talking to him. Hedley had turned up for a Roses Match at Old Trafford and declared himself unfit. Sellers wasn't having that and made him play. Hedley didn't bowl so well and the committee were on to him wanting to know why. He told them he'd reported unfit but Sellers had made him play. That put the cat among the pigeons with Sellers and the outcome was that there was no conversation between them for a season and a half. Sellers had to use Arthur Mitchell, who later became the county coach, as a go-between. That was an example of Sellers' pig-headedness. But while he had a reputation for being abrasive he could also be as soft as a brush if you stood up to him. That's how I found him, although I think it helped that I had a job outside the game.

Ryan: Yes, because of that, we did receive a bit more deference from Sellers. But even though we both had a business outside cricket, it would be wrong to say that we weren't professional in our approach; we were very professional indeed. However we also had something to fall back on unlike people who just played professional cricket for a living and nothing else. Apart from the odd part-time job in the winter, cricket was their livelihood and the build-up to July 1 and the announcement about who was being retained for the following season must have been pure hell. If you didn't receive a letter, you knew you were OK.

Platt: One year we were playing Surrey at Bramall Lane and I was in the bar with Bryan Stott at the close of play. We were having a chat with Ellis Robinson, when we were interrupted by Chris Furness, a vice president of the club. He said, "Congratulations, Stott."

Stotty wasn't actually playing in the match so we were all a bit bemused. He said, "Thank you very much, Mr Furness. But why?"

"Well at yesterday's meeting, you would have been sacked but for one vote." That's God's truth, it was the only intimation he received that he would be playing for Yorkshire the following year.

Ryan: Under Sellers, the cricket committee had no real say whatsoever, even though it consisted of 12 people. Decisions went through John Nash and Sellers. End of story. Those two thought the committee were superfluous. Unfortunately after Sellers went in 1972, the committee didn't want another strong character in charge. They elected John Temple as chairman, a very nice guy but he couldn't make a decision.

Platt: And, of course, Sellers thought he should pick the team as well. I was in the hotel bar with Ronnie Burnet the night after we'd been bowled out for 35 at Bristol in '59. In those days there were no telephones in the bedrooms and a messenger boy kept wandering into the bar holding up a board that read, 'Mr Burnet, phone call.' He must have come in three or four times. Eventually, I asked Ron if he'd seen it. He said, "Aye. It'll be Sellers picking t'team and I'm not answering it." And that's why we won the Championship...because Ronnie stuck with us while Sellers would have wanted to change the lot of us. The calls kept coming next morning but Ronnie didn't answer.

Ryan: When Vic was captain, Sellers ruled the roost. No matter how well you were playing, if Sellers wanted someone else in, that was it. Like Dickie Bird being left out after his famous 181 against Glamorgan at Park Avenue in 1959.

In this day and age, it seems hard to imagine anyone being left out after scoring 181.

Ryan: Dickie had come in for Ken Taylor, who was away playing for MCC against India at Lord's, which was seen as a Test trial in those days. When he returned, Dickie was left out.

Platt: Having said that, Mel, Glamorgan did drop Dickie a few times on the way to his 181. Doug Padgett was batting at three and he was halfway down the pavilion steps about four times in the first half hour before he realised the catches had gone down. After Yorkshire, Glamorgan had the best close fielders in the game in those days: Wilf Wooller, Alan Watkins and Peter Walker. And they kept putting him down off Don Shepherd. It was unbelievable.

Ryan: I could tell a tale or two about Wooller! Once we were playing against Glamorgan at Cardiff Arms Park when Billy Sutcliffe was captain. It was turning square and Yorkshire only picked Fred and me to take the shine off the ball. Glamorgan didn't even bother with a quick bowler and before the start of our innings, Wooller took the new ball over to the rugby terraces and rubbed it on the concrete. Neither of the umpires tried to stop him and Billy never said a word.

Platt: Well he and Wooller were at school together weren't they? Wrekin College. The umpires knew what Wooller was up to but they used to turn a blind eye to that sort of thing.

Ryan: Aye...and it's a good job they did because you would never have played so many times for Yorkshire if they knew you picked the seam like you did! It came back like a razor blade after you'd been to work on it.

Platt: I wouldn't argue with that! A while back, one of my dogs took a lump out my thumb and it was pretty sore for a couple of weeks. A pal rang up to see how I was and I told him, "It's a good job I'm not still playing for Yorkshire because with my thumb in this condition, I wouldn't have been able to work the seam!" Everybody was at it. There was even a tale about the time Bill Alley was umpiring a Lancashire game in the Seventies. After Peter Lee had taken four early wickets, Bill took a close look at the ball. Then he called Peter over and said, "Lee, if you don't take seven wickets with this, I'll report you to Lord's!'

Alley often gets a mention when cricketers wax lyrical about great characters on and off the field but clearly, you lived in a more relaxed era.

Ryan: It couldn't possibly happen nowadays but sometimes we actually played golf before the start of a day's play. Wherever we went, we were given the courtesy of the course and we'd make an early start, play nine holes, often with one or two of the Press corps who followed us around, and then go off to work. It loosened us up, relaxed us and for my money it was a lot better than risking a serious leg injury by playing football as a warm-up like they do today. Having said that, we did play a bit of football as well. I once turned out at Old Trafford, the football ground that is, in a benefit match for Brian Statham. And there was another game when Tommy Steele played against us for the Showbiz XI at Odsal Stadium in Bradford. He was at the height of his fame and brought along a young actor he tipped for stardom – as an actor, not a footballer. His name was Sean Connery. He wasn't a bad footballer either. Millicent Martin, from the satirical show That Was The Week That Was, was there, too – although she didn't play! But Ronnie Carroll, her husband, did and there were a couple of ex-pro footballers as well: Billy Wright, the former England captain, and Wally Barnes.

Platt: And before the Sunday League was introduced in 1969, we played Sunday charity matches at cricket as well. I once played in a game at Whitkirk, on the outskirts of Leeds, and Derek Ibbotson, the Huddersfield runner who held the world mile record at the time, was in our line-up. After we'd fielded for a couple of hours or so, Derek was completely knackered. "I don't know how you manage to stick at it this long," he said as we left the field at tea.

I replied, "Well I don't know how you manage to run a bloody mile in four minutes!" But he was staggered at the way so much running and fielding had affected his legs.

How much cricket do you watch these days?

Platt: I'm afraid I only go to cricket to meet my friends. County Championship cricket is puerile. You know exactly what's going to happen as soon as you arrive on the first day. At Headingley it might dobble about a bit for about an hour on the first morning but by the fourth day, it's as dead as sponge. And say what you like, apart from Durham no side has got what I would call a good class county bowling attack.

Ryan: I'll turn out to watch a Test Match, although I have to admit that despite all the hype, the standard of the Ashes in 2009 was not high. At the start of the series, that Mitchell Johnson chap couldn't bowl a hoop down a hill.

Platt: No, he wouldn't have got into Yorkshire Seconds in our day. He'd have gone to the nets and been told to go home.

Ryan: I'm convinced the game has been plagued by limited overs cricket. I played my first Gillette Cup tie against Notts at Middlesbrough in 1963. It was 65 overs a side in those days. And I honestly thought people were joking when they said we could only bowl 15 overs and that it didn't matter if we didn't get anybody out. I'd been brought up – as we all had – to take wickets. I remember saying, "Do you mean to tell me that if I bowl a maiden over it's as good as taking a wicket?" And I was told it was. As a result of that attitude, we've ended up with a load of mediocre medium-paced bowlers. One-day cricket has ruined the first-class game.

Platt: But I'll tell you what, Melville, wouldn't it have been nice to drive from Huddersfield to Headingley knowing you were playing in a 40-over match and you'd only be bowling eight overs maximum?

Ryan: In Twenty20 they only have four! I don't mind Twenty20, I just wish they wouldn't call it cricket.

Platt: I've every sympathy with Test players because there is far too much Test cricket played today. But county players think they've had a heavy season if they bowl 400 overs. They should have a look at Fred's workload over the best part of 20 years.

After winning the Championship in 1959, Ronnie Burnet left and Vic Wilson took over as captain in 1960. Did you expect

that to happen?

Platt: Not really, no. In 1959, Vic wasn't in the side after mid-July. He'd struggled all season and when we travelled south to play our final game against the Rest of England at The Oval, we more or less assumed he wasn't going to be around in 1960. It was a case of dear old Vic, he's 38, he's past his best, let him play his last game for the Champion County at The Oval. The committee took that on board and picked him. But we made a mess of it in the first innings, followed on and Vic pulled us round with his only hundred of the season. We won the game and all of a sudden Vic was back in the frame if they were going to have a new captain for 1960.

Ryan: I don't think they wanted to risk Ronnie Burnet for another year. He was 41 and there were worries about his fitness. Brian Sellers, the cricket chairman, didn't like Ray Illingworth and he didn't like Brian Close. So Vic was the only choice. The great thing about Vic as a captain was that he was a good listener. I don't mean in the sense of asking advice, more in absorbing information from the conversations going on around him. And in our dressing room of that era, the cricket talk was incredible. We talked about the game, the people who played it and our own approach. I remember Raymond once saying to me, "Mel, what do you think about on that long walk back to your mark?" I mumbled something about looking round the ground and how I didn't really think about anything until I turned and started my run-up. He wasn't impressed. "Well, you shouldn't be looking at that bird sat in the corner, you should be thinking on where you're going to put your next ball. Nothing else. Just that one thing." He was so meticulous. He talked cricket, cricket, cricket all the time. We all did. We absorbed it all...or most of it, anyway! And Vic absorbed more than most.

Platt: You're absolutely right about Raymond. He more or less ran the show right through from 1959 to 1968.

Ryan: Yes, he was the brains behind all three captains. But let's not forget that Closey was a great man manager. He led from the front and for me he was a superb captain. He was a dominant character; even Fred Trueman was frightened of Closey, and he got the best out of people. He'd say, "You're playing for Yorkshire, you're the best." He meant it and we believed him. He allied himself to Raymond and they were a perfect combination under Vic and again when Brian took over. I loved Closey. He had his ups and his downs but he was a lovely man.

VIC WILSON.
JANUARY 1921 – JUNE 2008

John Victor Wilson was born in Scampston near Malton on January 17, 1921. A left-handed top order batsman, he made his debut in 1946 and was capped two years later. Wilson played in 477 first-class matches for the county, scoring 20,548 runs, including 29 centuries, at an average of 31.66. In all first-class cricket, he totalled 21,650 runs. He took 520 catches for Yorkshire, a figure exceeded by only four players, and was a member of the 1954-55 MCC side who regained the Ashes in Australia under the captaincy of his Yorkshire team-mate, Len Hutton. Wilson led Yorkshire from 1960 to 1962, winning the County Championship twice. He died on June 4, 2008.

Bob Platt remembers: Vic Wilson was a thoroughly decent man. He was quiet, modest, dependable and intensely loyal to Yorkshire cricket and to the East Riding, where he lived all his life.

As a captain Vic had a natural way of earning his players' respect and their loyalty. He didn't upset his players and he didn't shout and lay down the law. He didn't have to because we all knew that he set high standards for himself and for everyone else. He was only interested in what was good for the team.

And perhaps it's fair to say that to some extent, he was under-estimated as a leader. Yes, he had Brian Close and Raymond Illingworth in his ears and he inherited a very talented young side from Ronnie Burnet. They were only going to get better.

But he was only in charge for three years and in that time he won two County Championships for Yorkshire. That record speaks for itself.

As a fielder, he was genuinely world-class, particularly at short leg. He had massive hands and could catch anything. In fact Len Hutton took him to Australia in 1954-55 purely because of his fielding.

Vic didn't play in any of the five Tests – in fact, he never played for England – but if England needed a substitute fielder at any time, they had the perfect man in the squad. In any position.

And as a batsman, he was tough and determined. He scored nearly 22,000 runs in first-class cricket and only ten Yorkshire players have scored more runs for the county.

His only real weakness was against leg-spin bowling. But he wasn't alone in that where players from the East Riding were concerned. It must have been something to do with the wickets at Scarborough.

And one of my fondest memories of Vic is how another son of East Yorkshire, Jimmy Binks, exposed his frailties against leg-spin in the Headingley nets.

Now Jimmy had a lot of qualities as a wicketkeeper – there haven't been many better – and a cricketer but leg-spin would not normally be regarded as one of them.

But on this occasion, he trotted in and clean bowled Vic. It brought the house down, it really did.

As Raymond Illingworth said when Vic died, "He was totally reliable, a man who gave 100 per cent and never gave up fighting. If you have eleven players like Vic Wilson in your team, you will never be a bad side."

1962

It was the year of the first James Bond film, Dr No. The year when the Beatles were turned down by Decca Records and released their first hit single, Love Me Do, on Parlophone.

The year when Presidents Kennedy and Kruschev confronted one another over the Soviet Union's missile base in Cuba, when Hollywood icon Marilyn Monroe died from a drug overdose, when the satirical television programme That Was The Week That Was prompted outrage among the British Establishment and when a new Ford Cortina cost £591.

The Shadows were top of the UK charts with Wonderful Land when Yorkshire took the field for their opening match of the season against MCC at Lord's on April 28.

And a wonderful land it was for White Rose supporters as Vic Wilson, in his third and final year as captain, led the side to their third Championship in four years

Wilson's reign ended in emphatic style with a seven-wicket victory over Glamorgan at Harrogate despite the second day being completely washed out.

The ground staff, helped by supporters, began the mopping-up operations before dawn on the third and final day; Yorkshire completed them with over two hours to spare.

The guard was changing, however, and with 14 capped players on the books and a trio of young hopefuls pushing for a regular place, the Yorkshire players knew only too well that Wilson would not be the only player to leave.

And when the retained list was announced in July, the axe fell on Mike Cowan, a left-arm pace bowler from Doncaster, and Brian Bolus, an opening batsman from Leeds.

Cowan and Bolus had gone to school together, they were capped together and now they were sacked on the same day.

"The disenchantment began to set in during the 1962 season," recalls Cowan. "I wasn't playing regularly and I wasn't as good a bowler once I started worrying about not being in the side and about the money I was missing.

"Nine years earlier, I'd have taken everything in my stride. But when a cricketer is a bit older and married with kids and a mortgage, things take a different turn. Their way of life depends on him playing regularly."

The following year, when Cowan was playing as professional for Rochdale in the Central Lancashire League, Bolus began a ten-year stint with Nottinghamshire, winning the first of his seven England caps.

"I didn't play in any of Yorkshire's last 14 Championship matches in 1962," he remembers. "I asked if I could make one final appearance at the Scarborough Festival but the committee decided against that.

"Perhaps they feared I might make a hundred. Who knows?"

MIKE COWAN.

THE ENTERTAINER

Michael Joseph Cowan was born in Leeds on June 10, 1933. A left-arm pace bowler, he was capped in 1960 and made 91 first team appearances between 1953 and 1962. He played in two Championship sides and took 266 first-class wickets for the county at an average of 24.01. He toured Pakistan with the MCC A team in 1955-56 but was forced to return home early after sustaining a serious back injury. After retiring from the first-class game, Cowan played league cricket on both sides of the Pennines and since 1959, he has been a familiar figure on the after dinner circuit.

I was born in Leeds but Doncaster is all I've known. I came here when I was four. It's been my place, they are my kind of people.

As a kid, I went to Lord Street Junior School, where I was taught by Sister Mary Oliver. Much later on, she also taught Kevin Keegan, the England footballer, who was born in Donny.

I grew up in the same era as Alick Jeffrey, another wonderful footballer whose career was wrecked when he broke a leg playing for England Under-23s in 1956. He was only 17 at the time and already the big clubs, including Manchester United, were falling over themselves to sign him.

Doncaster was also the birthplace of Bruce Woodcock, the former British and European heavyweight champion. After he retired, he ran a pub and we often used to enjoy a round of golf together.

And above all, I've seen Doncaster Town, my cricket club, win the National Club Championship at Lord's. Captained by my son Nick. It doesn't get much better than that, does it?

The family home was in Harrowden Road, a bike ride away from the racecourse and the old football ground at Belle Vue, and Roy Clarke, the creator of Last of the Summer Wine, lived in the corner house at the top of the road.

We lived at number 190. There was a lamp post right outside our house with another road running off at right angles. That gave me plenty of room for a run-up to bowl at the lamp post. In the summer, I used to be out there bowling at my lamp post every night.

At the beginning of April, my father used to fix a piece of hardboard over two of the front window panes because if the ball hit the kerb, it took off and flew through the window. It stayed there 'til September.

When I was 12, I started going to St Michael's College in Leeds. In Headingley as it happened. We were taught by Jesuits. My father had gone to the same school. Lads came from York, Wakefield and all over.

We caught the 7.20am train from Doncaster to Leeds and then it was a 20-minute walk up to St Michael's. If the train was delayed we had to ring up from a phone box but I don't recall being late too often.

The first stop was Carcroft, just outside the town. That's where the two Henigan sisters got on to go to Notre Dame School, also in Leeds. One of them later became Mary Parkinson, wife of the journalist and broadcaster, Sir Michael.

For the return trip, we caught the 4.40pm train and I got home about 6.15. If it was foggy we were given permission to leave early. So in the winter we'd go up to one of the priests and try to convince him there was going to be a real pea souper within the next half hour.

Francis Matthews, the actor who played Paul Temple in the TV series of the late Sixties, went to St Michael's as well. So did Brian Bolus, who was playing for Yorkshire with me ten years later.

He was a clever lad was Brian and a good all-round sportsman. He captained the school at cricket and football. He was godfather to Nick, my eldest lad. We were capped by Yorkshire on the same day and we left on the same day when we were released at the end of 1962.

I was taught cricket by the Jesuits, mainly by a chap called Father Lynch, but I never got into the school team on a regular basis.

I wanted to bowl fast but after Father Lynch had spotted that I was a left-arm bowler, he used to say, "Use the gifts God has given you, Cowan." And he made me bowl spinners. But I was never that good.

So instead of playing for the school, I started playing here in Doncaster for a works team from Bembergs, textile manufacturers who later became British Nylon Spinners and then ICI. I'd probably be 16 at the time.

Bembergs was originally a German company and the story did the rounds that during the War, the authorities caught a couple of German spies hiding down the chimney of a pub called the Reindeer in High Street. The two men had connections with Bembergs, apparently.

My father used to tell that tale -- and he should have known because he was a regular at the Reindeer, a gents-only pub. He would only ever go in those but as the years went by he kept having to change his local as more and more pubs allowed women in.

In Doncaster there was a big evening knock-out competition and Bembergs were drawn against British Ropes, who had a very strong side. They played in the Yorkshire Council. But we beat them and went on to reach the final, which was a hell of an achievement for a small works side.

British Ropes signed me on soon afterwards and I was playing for them one Saturday in June, 1952, when I received a telegram from Yorkshire asking me to report for the Second XI the following week.

I was Twelfth Man in that game and made my debut in the two-day match against Lincolnshire at Barnsley on June 18 and 19. I played in four more Minor Counties Championship games and during the winter I went to the indoor nets.

I started at the outdoor nets at the beginning of April, 1953. Four weeks later, I was playing for Yorkshire against MCC at Lord's.

I think Len Hutton played a part in me being picked. He was captain of England at the time and led us to victory over Australia later that summer. I was totally in awe of Len.

I was bowling in one net when Maurice Leyland, one of the coaches, said, "Go and bowl in the other net, lad."

I'd already seen who was batting in there and couldn't really believe what Maurice was saying. "What, at Len Hutton?" I asked

"Aye", he replied. "Len Hutton in the other net."

I didn't get Len out but looking back, those few deliveries were massively important for me. Maurice must have seen something and put me in the other net so Len could have a look, too.

As it happened, Len took a bit of a shine to me, probably because I was a left-arm fast bowler and there weren't many around.

I bowled round the wicket at the time but Len encouraged me to bowl over the wicket like Alan Davidson, the Australian all-rounder, who finished up with 186 wickets in 44 Tests.

I went to the annual pre-season lunch at Headingley a couple of weeks later and Brian Sellers, the cricket chairman, stood up and said the usual stuff about what good things Yorkshire were going to do in the coming season.

Afterwards, the young lads went off into one of the dressing rooms and we hadn't been in there many minutes when a group of pressmen arrived. One of them asked, "Which is Cowan?"

I stood up. "Me, why?"

"Don't you know?"

"No."

"You've been picked for the first three games." I thought he was joking, I really did and looking back, it seems odd that no one from the club thought to tell me first. Those three games were against MCC, Lindsey Hassett's Australians at Bradford and then Essex at Hull in the first Championship match.

There were a couple of gaps in the attack because Fred Trueman was away in the RAF for most of the season and only played in ten Championship matches. Bob Appleyard ended up missing the whole season because of tuberculosis and Brian Close hardly played at all because of injury.

I never dreamed I had a chance but I finished up playing 12 first-class games and taking 39 wickets.

At Lord's, I opened the bowling with Eric Burgin, who was from Sheffield and had made his debut the previous year. And the first time I touched the ball in first-class cricket was to catch David Sheppard off Eric for two. I was fielding at mid-off.

My first wicket was Nigel Howard, the captain of Lancashire. Caught and bowled. In the second innings, I took four for 34 and we won in two days.

Next up, the Aussies at Park Avenue. I was 18 years old and I'd taken four wickets at Lord's so it was a case of "Bring on the Aussies!" I could see the headlines in my mind: Doncaster Boy destroys Hassett's Men..."

I took none for 105 and bagged a pair. Keith Miller scored 159 not out and as we were walking off after the Aussies had declared on 453 for six, he tapped me on the shoulder and said, "Well bowled, son."

"Well bowled?" I replied.

"You beat me five times on the front foot."

I was more bothered about the number of times I'd seen the ball disappearing to the boundary but I suppose that gesture summed up Miller and his approach to the game

In those early days, I used to look around the Yorkshire dressing room and it seemed just about everyone was a Test cricketer: Hutton, Frank Lowson, Johnny Wardle, Willie Watson, Norman Yardley, Don Brennan and Brian Close and Fred, when they were available. I sometimes wondered what I was doing there.

Wardle was a great influence. I travelled with John and we'd talk cricket all the time. The journeys sometimes took hours and hours and we'd stop off a couple of times on the way.

If you didn't learn something from an experience like that you were bloody thick and it's something that's lacking today with motorways and high-speed travel.

He was a great bowler, and I mean great. And so knowledgeable. It's no fluke that Brian Close and Ray Illingworth became good captains because they used to go out to the middle with John and look at the wicket before play began. He knew the game backwards.

Of course it's no secret that he could be difficult and in one game, he dropped two catches off me on purpose. Willie Watson had a right go at him but Johnny replied, "Well, he dropped one off me."

Nevertheless, I will always think of him as a great bowler and of how willing he was to help anybody. If you asked him, he loved helping.

After he retired, he opened a night club, The Ponderosa at Thorne, near Doncaster. There were also a couple of indoor nets on the site, where he did a bit of coaching.

And for a while, he was groundsman here at Doncaster Town. He loved grounds did John and what he didn't know about grass wasn't worth knowing. Keith Boyce, the groundsman at Headingley, used to ring him up regularly. I spoke at Johnny's funeral in 1985.

I played five matches in the first few weeks of that season and then returned to British Ropes before being called up again in July. That was not good news for Mr Whittington, inevitably known to everyone as Dick, who ran the side at British Ropes.

Yorkshire had invited him to Park Avenue for the match against the Aussies and feted him a bit in the pavilion. But he still wasn't too keen on the idea of his star bowler missing a load of league matches and I wasn't quite sure about how I stood with Ropes for the rest of the season.

I found out soon enough. One evening, after I'd been playing for Yorkshire against Derbyshire at Chesterfield, I got off the train at Doncaster station and the first thing I saw was a billboard for the Evening Post, Doncaster's local paper.

It read, "Cowan Sacked." Whittington had decided enough was enough and signed another bowler.

I was called up for the RAF in 1954 and didn't play at all for Yorkshire. Instead, I joined Bingley in the Bradford League and every week I used to hitch a lift from my base at Driffield on the back of my sergeant's motor bike.

I also played regularly for the RAF, including two games at Lord's, against the Army in 1954 and the Navy 12 months later, when the selectors were watching because MCC were taking an A tour to Pakistan the following winter.

I took 13 wickets in the match and afterwards Sir Pelham

Warner, the Grand Old Man of English cricket, came up to me and said, "Well bowled, Cowan. One day you could be a great bowler."

And he must have had some influence with the selectors because when the party to tour Pakistan was named, I was in there. I came out of the RAF in October, 1955 and set off for Pakistan at the beginning of December.

We went by ship and I shared a cabin with Closey. I don't remember exactly how long it took but it was a bloody long time.

Donald Carr was the captain and we had some good players in the side like Closey, Peter Richardson, Jim Parks, Ken Barrington, Fred Titmus and Tony Lock.They went on to play in a few Tests between them, didn't they? Lockey bowled so many overs out there that he wore out his left boot.

It was one of the first official overseas tours to Pakistan, who had only been playing Test cricket since 1952, and the food was awful. We lived on boiled eggs and chips.

And because it was a Muslim country, alcohol wasn't allowed. The only way we could get round that was for each player to have a certificate saying he was an alcoholic. That enabled us to justify our big trunk full of bottles of beer.

One night, during the third Representative Game against Pakistan at Peshawar we were having a party. The beer was flowing and before long water started flying around, too.

Idris Begh, one of the umpires in the match, was there and although he obviously wasn't drinking, he was loving every minute.

Eventually some of the lads chased Begh out into the corridor. He was laughing his head off but just at that moment, some of the Pakistan players came back into the hotel after their evening meal.

They saw what was happening and they cracked out laughing, too. But of course Begh couldn't afford to be the laughing stock of Pakistan cricket and complained about our behaviour.

All of a sudden we were at the centre of an international incident and at one stage there was a strong chance we'd be sent home. What a load of rubbish! It was just a bit of fun that was blown up out of all proportion.

From a cricketing point of view, the tour was a complete disaster for me. I only played four matches and suffered the back injury that was to change my career.

It happened when I was bowling in the game against Combined Universities at Lahore. I caught my foot in the matting wicket as I followed through and immediately felt a searing pain in my lower back.

The physio thought it was sciatica caused by a muscle slipping and hitting the sciatic nerve. I had treatment for three weeks and tried bowling in the nets. How was I to know I should have been resting, that I'd cracked my bottom two vertebrae?

Inevitably, I kept breaking down and eventually I was flown home from Lahore. Billy Griffith, one of the assistant secretaries at the MCC, met me at Heathrow.

I spent a month in Harrogate, having intensive treatment at the Royal Baths, and I was declared fit to start the 1956 season. I played in Yorkshire's first five games and I was really flying. Then damn me, my back went again, at Northampton in May.

This time I went to see a specialist, Mr Broomhead, in Leeds. He'd also operated on Len Hutton after he broke his left arm during an Army training exercise in 1941. He diagnosed my problem and suggested a bone graft, which was a very big operation in those days.

He took some bone out of my backside and made my last two vertebrae into one big one. I didn't play again until late in the 1957 season and I had to change my action because of the injury.

I wasn't quite as sideways on as I'd been before but I was still quick, although not as fast as I was before. I played a bit in 1958 but it wasn't working out for me and in 1959, I played for Bingley again.

They paid me a lot of money, I topped the Bradford League averages and we won the Championship. So did Yorkshire, for the first time in 13 years. Without me.

I'd more or less resigned myself to never playing for Yorkshire again when, during the winter, I had a call from Vic Wilson, Yorkshire's new captain, asking me to think about going back.

He didn't have to ask twice, I was back in the side more or less straight away and we won the Championship again in 1960. I took 77 wickets at 22.67, including nine for 43 against Warwickshire at Edgbaston, the best figures of my career.

It was their second innings and I took my first two wickets on the Monday evening. But as we were walking out the following morning, Vic came over and said, "You'll be going with the Seconds tomorrow, Mike." How was that for man management? I was totally deflated.

Mel Ryan nicked in and picked up a wicket early on but then, when we took the second new ball, everything clicked and I took seven for 11 from 10.2 overs. And afterwards, Vic said, "Perhaps you'd better come with us to Somerset after all."

They used to pick the team for three or four games in advance but he took that decision off his own bat without calling the committee. But not even Yorkshire could have dropped me after I'd taken nine for 43.

I was capped at the end of the season...although I had to ask Brian Sellers personally.

He was a very dictatorial man but I was determined to tell him what I wanted and made an appointment to see him during the lunch interval on the first day of our match against MCC at the Scarborough Festival.

The rest of the lads couldn't believe I was going to take him on and they kept saying, "Are you really going to see him, then?"

"Too bloody right I am!"

Sellers didn't waste time with small talk. "Now then, what's this about?" he said.

"I'm married now, Mr Sellers, and I've got a young boy. I'd like more money. I've been tapped up by other counties but I want to play for Yorkshire."

"Who's tapped you up?"

"I'm not telling you. I'd just like more money."

He looked at me for a while and then said, "You've got it."

"Thank you." When I got back to the dressing room the lads were all waiting. "What's he say? What's he say?"

"He says I've got more money." It didn't happen straight away, though.

After winning the Championship we had to travel down to the Oval for the annual Champion County v The Rest match. I'd already booked a holiday on a farm near Newquay that week but I had to cancel and instead, we went in late September...when Newquay had shut down for the winter.

There wasn't a lot to do and one morning when we went into a café for a cup of tea, I picked up the Daily Telegraph, turned to the cricket page and there was a headline reading, 'Yorkshire award four caps.'

It was Phil Sharpe, Brian Bolus, Don Wilson and me. I rang home. "Where the hell have you been?" said my dad. "I've had Press men all over the place."

So I was finally a fully-fledged Yorkshire player. But if I hadn't taken nine wickets at Edgbaston I might easily have been out on my ear. My reward for playing in that Championship side was a Parker pen with my name on.

That was about par for the course. Ken Barrington once told me that his reward for winning one of Surrey's seven successive championships in the Fifties was a wallet with his initials on it.

When I started, we were paid a fiver for a win. Less tax. Later on, for a three-day game away from home, we received £22 less tax. The club paid our bed and breakfast but we had to find the money for our evening meal and travel. And £22 less tax wasn't a lot for a three-day game involving a four-night stay in London.

I remember me and Dougie Padgett once went into a restaurant in King's Cross, just across the road from the station. It was a three-course meal and when it came to the dessert we were asked if we wanted a sweet or the fruit basket. We opted for the fruit.

There was a pineapple sitting on top of the basket so I cut off the top, cut a slice for me and another one for Doug. When the bill came, they'd charged extra for the pineapple.

I called the waiter over. "What's all this then?"

"Well, you've had the pineapple."

"Of course we've had the pineapple. It was in the fruit basket."

"Yes, but the pineapple was extra."

"It doesn't say so on the menu."

"And you've sliced it the wrong way as well. We won't be able to use it again."

"I don't care. That's how we slice pineapples in Yorkshire and we're not paying extra for it." And we didn't. It was a matter of principle."

It was also a matter of looking after the pennies. It's no good being envious about the sponsored cars and things they have these days but we were struggling to afford a second hand old banger, never mind being given a fancy sponsored car.

Having said that, though, I remember Closey turning up for his Benefit Match against Surrey in 1961, driving an open-topped Mercedes coupe. He'd hired it specially.

Johnny Wardle, who was at the match, couldn't believe it. He said, "What the bloody hell are you doing?"

Closey didn't see what he was getting at. "How do you mean?" he replied.

"It's your benefit, there are people going round wi t'buckets for you and you turn up in an open-topped Mercedes. What are they going to think?" He was dead right there, was Johnny.

Then at the end of the 1962 season, after our third Championship in four years, Yorkshire told me and Brian Bolus we weren't being retained.

Brian went to Notts and played for England the following year. I signed on as professional at Rochdale in the Central Lancashire League and started looking for a job.

And I soon discovered that when you finish professional sport, the hardest thing is getting into another job. I was never mollycoddled like they are today but even so, I was looked after pretty well.

Then all of a sudden I had to wake up in the morning, realise I had a family and a mortgage and that I was playing a different game.

Over the years, quite a few ex-pros haven't adapted; they have thought the world owes them a living because they've played pro sport. But if you go in with that idea, you'll finish up skint.

I got myself a job as a salesman for Horlicks – I lost it because I kept falling asleep! Next I worked for Unichem and then for Penguin Books, who actually head-hunted me. I loved working for them.

I enjoyed selling. It enabled me to get around, meet people and have a natter. And for the first few years after leaving Yorkshire, I was able to carry on playing to a decent standard.

At Rochdale, the money wasn't a lot worse than Yorkshire had been paying and I also played a few games for Northumberland in the Minor Counties as well.

The Central Lancashire League was very competitive and there were same damn good pros around. People like Sonny Ramadhin, Clairmonte Depeiza, Cec Abrahams, Reg Scarlett and Cec Wright, who was still turning out in the Saddleworth League over 40 years later at the age of 73!

There was also a young South African by the name of Basil D'Oliveira, who was in his fourth and last season with Middleton before joining Worcestershire in 1964. At the time, we weren't really aware of how Dolly had been unable to play first-class cricket in his homeland because of his colour. He was just another league pro.

And it certainly never crossed our minds that five years later, his selection for England's tour of South Africa would spark a row that played a crucial role in the end of apartheid in South African sport.

All we knew was that he was a hell of a good cricketer and a lovely man. I did him at our place but he scored 50 against us at Middleton.

That year I took 73 wickets at 12.45 but Rochdale said that even though I'd done them proud, they couldn't afford to keep me. So I moved to Littleborough, who played in the same league.

The following year, I took another 57 wickets at 12.63, including all ten against Werneth. They were great times but towards the end of the season, I pulled a thigh muscle and that was that. Ken Shuttleworth, the Lancashire and England bowler who had made his county debut that year, took over.

After that, I played for Wakefield in the Yorkshire Council alongside Vic Wilson and Sonny Ramadhin. We were a decent side. Then I turned out for Brodsworth, a pit village near Doncaster. Richard Lumb, who later played for Yorkshire, learned his cricket there. So did his brother John.

And finally I came home to play for Doncaster Town in the Yorkshire League in 1967. I've been here ever since.

I started as captain and then served on the committee. And the first thing I did when I joined the club was to make junior membership free. A few people didn't like that but I said, "How else are we going to encourage kids to come here?"

And do you know, we've never looked back. We've got a great junior section now, one of the best in the county.

In fact, two young lads who played for us in the 1998 National

Club Championship final at Lord's, Richard Dawson and Simon Widdup, went on to play for Yorkshire. So did Simon Guy, who was our wicketkeeper for a while.

My three grandsons all play: Jonathan in the Under-14s, James and George in the Under-9s. James is my daughter Joanne's boy and Jonathan and George are my eldest son Shaun's lads. Shaun runs the Under-14s.

My other son, Nick, has played at Doncaster for years and still captains the Third XI. His knees are knackered but he'll never give up. He coaches three of the junior sides on a Friday night.

I don't have an official role these days, although I help with fund raising and finding players. But I go along every Saturday, first and second team. Three of us sit together: Mike Lynes is a retired headmaster and Peter Musk a retired knicker maker.

People say we're like the Last of the Summer Wine but it's terrific, especially when it's warm, just talking and reminiscing. We don't booze, just a few cups of tea. And anyone is free to join in.

Winning the National Club Championship was a brilliant experience. The town was going through a bad time. All the collieries had shut down and there was a lot of bad Press about the way the Council was being run.

Doncaster Rovers had just been relegated from the Football League and then all of a sudden, the town's cricket team came along and people had something to smile about again. It was unbelievable.

We beat Harrogate at their place in the semi-final and met Bath in the final. The night before the final there was a dinner, with John Carr, son of Donald Carr, my captain in Pakistan 43 years earlier, the Master of Ceremonies.

One person from each club had to say a few words and when it was my turn, I reminded the Bath people of the culture difference between the two places.

I told them, "In Bath, when you hear the William Tell Overture you know it's by Rossini; in Doncaster, we look out for the Lone Ranger!" I presented their chairman with an inscribed glass bowl to commemorate the occasion.

And there was a really nice touch on the day of the final when I discovered that a lad called Rupert Swetman would be keeping wicket for Bath. His dad, Roy, had kept wicket to me in Pakistan.

Lord's will always be special. In my first three games there, I was applauded off and while the pitch is a bit flat now, there was always something in it for the quicks in my day, courtesy of the famous Lord's "Ridge" that was flattened out in the Sixties.

Alan Moss, the Middlesex quickie, used to take a load of wickets every season and I always remember Fred saying, "If bloody Mossy can get 100 wickets a year, how many would I get?"

Since I began my public speaking, I've been lucky enough to speak at one or two functions there and I always make a point of going out and sitting on the balcony and just gazing around.

It really is a special place and anyone who claims it isn't doesn't have an ounce of romance in his soul. I'd pay to go just to watch the grass grow.

A dinner there is certainly quite a contrast from my first venture into the world of public speaking at Carlton Towers Cricket Club near Selby in 1959.

They asked me to make the speech at their annual prize presentation and as Fred was usually the only Yorkshire player who received invitations like that, I was quite flattered.

I went with my late wife Judy. We were married in 1959 and on our honeymoon we finished up playing Beat the Clock on Sunday Night at the London Palladium, the weekly variety show on TV.

Bruce Forsyth should have been the compere but he was ill, the only time he missed the show. His replacement was Arthur Haynes, the actor and comedian. We won a washer and a spin dryer!

What's more I copped a Yorkshire committee man staying at the same hotel...and he wasn't with his missus. He's dead now but I won't name names.

When he spotted me in reception, he whispered, "You haven't seen me, have you?"

I replied, "No, I haven't. But I know I've got at least one vote on the selection committee now!"

Judy and I always used to laugh about my first speaking engagement at Carlton Towers because before I started I had five gin and tonics to settle the nerves.

Judy said that I fell off my chair halfway through the evening. I don't remember it actually – but then again, after all those G&Ts, I don't suppose I would, would I?

But things seemed to go all right. Soon afterwards, the Doncaster Round Table invited me to speak and then I had an invitation from the Rotary Club.

Next I received a call from Newark Cricket Club. "We've got Fred Trueman coming along to our dinner. Will you join him?"

Fred was to make the main speech and then the plan was for him to do a question and answer session with me. Instead, he cleared off and left me to handle the Q&A. I went down well.

Fred and I went along to his next engagement together and as we were driving home, he said, "You know, you ought to start charging."

"Don't be daft. I'm not a big name like you."

"No but you make people laugh. Start charging."

I wasn't playing for Yorkshire at the time so when the next call came, I said tentatively, "I'd like a bit of petrol money if that's OK."

"How much would you like?"

"Twenty-five pounds?"

"No problem."

I carried on like that until one night a while later the phone rang just as I was putting my coat on to go and watch Doncaster Rovers. A voice with a thick Scottish accent said, "Hello, is that Mr Cowan?"

"Speaking."

"This is Stenhousemuir Cricket Club. We'd like you to come and speak at our annual dinner and we'll pay you a hundred pounds."

I thought it was one of my pals taking the mick. I said, "Right, I'll tell you what. Give me your number and I'll ring you back." I thought that had stuffed him.

Anyway I rang back and the same voice said, "Stenhousemuir Cricket Club." It wasn't a wind-up after all.

When I put the phone down I said to Judy, "You won't believe this but somebody wants to give me a hundred quid to go and speak." It just grew from there and before long the invitations were coming in from all over. In 1980 I did 15 Benefit dinners for Jack Simmons, the Lancashire all-rounder,

These days it tends to be more business dinners like the one I did for a big insurance company at King's College, Cambridge, in 2009.

As I walked into the college beforehand, I could hear the choir rehearsing for the Christmas service of Nine Lessons and Carols and I just stood there transfixed. I must have listened for fully ten minutes.

Before the dinner started, six men from the St John's College Choir sang the Grace in Latin. It was a memorable evening.

I speak regularly on cruises, often run by Saga where the audience is more my age group! And I've been to Dubai, Kenya, Hamburg, all over. Not to mention Stenhousemuir...four times!

One particular dinner sticks in my mind more than most – and I hope this doesn't sound as if I'm trying to show off.

Barbara Kelly, the television and radio personality who used to appear on the quiz show What's My Line?, ran a speakers' agency called Right Address and I was on her books.

She had a very deep voice did Barbara. One day, she called and said, "Michael, I'd like you to go and speak to the Association of Directors at the Savoy Hotel in London.

"It includes overnight accommodation but I'm sorry, we haven't been able to find you a room at The Savoy. We've had to book you in at The Waldorf instead."

I thought, "Oh what a shame!"

I went to the dinner and without bragging, I did very well. You see southern audiences love the northern accent. I don't know why. A southerner can come up here and die on his arse but it's not the same the other way round.

It was a terrific night. And afterwards, I collected my mac from the cloakroom, walked through the reception at the Savoy and across the road to the Waldorf. I paused in the entrance, looked back and saw the Savoy all lit up. It looked magnificent. So did the Waldorf.

And I remember thinking, "I just wish my dad was still alive. For a lad from Doncaster to be doing this can't be bad."

Through the Right Address agency, I also had a call from a chap at Luton Golf Club, inviting me to talk at their annual dinner.

When he began by saying, "Eric Morecambe is unable to speak at our dinner...," the jackpot signs started whizzing round in my head. "And we're wondering if you could do it instead."

"When is it?" He gave me a date.

"Yes' I'm free that night."

"Oh, splendid, I'll put your name down now."

"Just a second…"

"Yes?"

"What's the fee?"

"The fee?"

"Yes, the fee."

"Eric Morecambe wasn't charging a fee."

"Oh well, that's all right then. I won't charge a fee either because I'm not coming!"

I've done the Lord's Taverners Dinner, sat between Terry Wogan and David Frost, and three dinners with Tim Rice. I love him. In 2009, we spoke together at the Ashes dinner at Rudding Park near Harrogate on the night before the Leeds Test.

The next day, I spotted Tim in the car park behind the pavilion. He called me over and said, "I hope you don't mind, Mike. I've been telling some of your stories to my friends."

I replied, "Why should I worry, Tim? I sing your songs every day."

I used to get a bit uptight at mixed dinners because when I first started, I did swear a bit and I never knew quite how far I should go.

As soon as I stood up I was thinking, "Should I say that or not?" and it distracted me. Nowadays I never swear. There's no call for it.

And to be honest, it sickens me when I hear about some of the so-called celebrities who charge a fortune and all they do is eff and blind.

After Judy died in 2002, I started going to the Rotary Club. We meet every Monday and I've made some cracking pals. I play Father Christmas every year.

Sheila, my partner, is in Rotary, too. She was the first lady president in 2008 and did a brilliant job. She likes going to my dinners and I once said to her, "Why do you come when you've heard it all before?"

She replied, "I enjoy watching the other people and seeing how you make them laugh." I enjoy it, too. I certainly don't have any complaints about the way things have worked out.

Regrets? Not really. Although I wish the back injury had never happened. I'd like to have known how good I might have been.

At Johnny Wardle's funeral, I had a chat with Len Hutton and he told me, "You know, Michael, I had great hopes for you."

And if Len thought that, I must have been some good, mustn't I?

BRIAN BOLUS.

MARATHON MAN

John Brian Bolus was born in Whitkirk, Leeds, on January 31, 1934. An opening or middle order batsman, he made his Yorkshire debut in 1956 and was capped four years later. He appeared in 107 first-class matches for the county and scored 4,712 runs, with seven centuries, at an average of 29.26. He played in three Championship sides before joining Nottinghamshire in 1963. He moved to Derbyshire in 1973 and retired three years later after playing in a total of 469 first-class matches and scoring 25,598 runs, with 39 centuries, at an average of 34.03. He also played 143 limited overs games. Bolus, who won seven England caps after leaving Yorkshire, became an England selector in 1994 and later served on the ECB's England Management Advisory Committee for six years, four of them as chairman.

I have never been able to calculate accurately whether I extracted every last ounce out of my talent or whether I should have done a lot better. What I can say, though, is that I enjoyed almost every moment of my 20 seasons in first-class cricket.

I suppose that is why I was still fighting an uphill battle against the red ball when many of my contemporaries were doing well in their chosen careers away from the game.

I just wanted to keep going...I was never one for giving up. And I was still playing in the leagues at the age of 52, eleven years after leaving county cricket.

I hit my first ball in first-class cricket for four. It was bowled, on April 30, 1956, by Edwin Smith, the Derbyshire off-spinner, playing for MCC against Yorkshire at Lord's.

I also hit my first ball in Test cricket for four. That one was delivered by Wesley Hall in the fourth Test between England and the West Indies at Headingley on July 26, 1963. I didn't make many more on either occasion.

I played seven times for England, scored 496 runs and finished with a highly respectable average of 41.33.

And in a 20-year first-class career, I played in 469 matches for three different counties and scored over 25,000 runs, this time with the slightly less impressive average of 34.03. But I'll settle for that.

It all started at Whitkirk CC, my local club on the outskirts of Leeds, and then at St Michael's College in Headingley, where my Yorkshire team-mate Michael Cowan was also a pupil.

I have to say that while Michael and I distinguished ourselves on the cricket field on behalf of the Jesuits who taught us at St Michael's, we certainly failed to do so in the classroom. I must also set the record straight on his positive comments about my football prowess.

The reality is that in my twenties, I played three games for Yorkshire Amateurs, who were based in Leeds and regarded as the best amateur side in the West Riding. My performances were described as "utter rubbish".

I never had any ambitions to play the game professionally, although I was OK in the local leagues. I played anywhere on the left side, enjoyed it, always gave it my very best and carried on playing until I was 46.

Cricket was different and Whitkirk played a major part in my development. A lot of people helped me, including Eddie McKinna, who had played for Yorkshire Colts, Don Ashworth and Len Bannister.

And I was able to watch George Wilson, who had played for Yorkshire as an amateur for three years before the War, from 1936 to 1939, and lived nearby. He had started at Whitkirk before joining Leeds and eventually returned to the club in his later years.

However he had retired by the time I started playing regularly for the First XI. People used to tell me that George was a fine player and in the Thirties there was very little to choose between him and Len Hutton.

Master at work. Illingworth honing his craft during a net session at Headingley. (Yorkshire Post)

Pipe of peace. Ronnie Burnet, the amateur captain who brought harmony to the dressing room and laid the foundation stone for a White Rose dynasty. (YP)

Changing of the guard. Bob Appleyard (left) and Johnny Wardle (second right), who left the club in 1958, pictured with Close and Trueman. Headingley's legendary winter shed is in the background. (Ron Deaton Collection)

Back row : Left to right : Mitchell, Birkenshaw, Bird, D. Wilson, Pickles, Ryan, Bolus, Binks, Sharpe, Leyland.
Sitting : Trueman, Wilson, Burnet, Close, Illingworth.
Sitting on Ground : Taylor, Padgett, Stott.

The Boys of '59. Burnet's squad pictured before a practice match at
Headingley in April, 1959. Five months later they were Champions.
Coaches Arthur Mitchell (back row left) and Maurice Leyland are the
umpires.

Deal me in! Masseur George Alcock (left), Binks, Ryan and Bolus
enjoy a game of cards under the watchful eye of Don Wilson (back
left) and Jackie Birkenshaw.

A vote of thanks. A card from Burnet and his players to acknowledge the plaudits from supporters. (Ron Deaton)

The heroes' return. Stott (left) and Padgett at Scarborough two days after their Championship-winning stand against Sussex at Hove. (Ron Deaton)

Open for business. Stott at work in his hardware store in Horsforth. (YP)

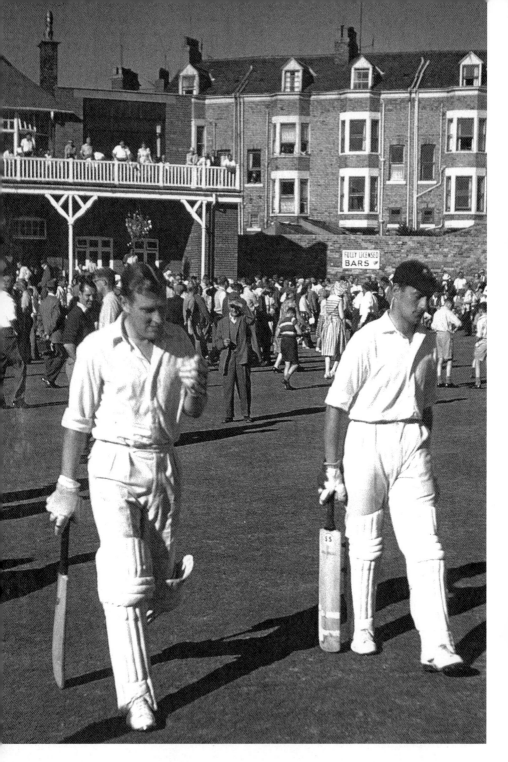

Scarborough fair. Bolus (right) and Illingworth take the field at Scarborough following the 1959 Championship finale at Hove. (Colin Abba)

Yorkshire at
Scarborough,
1960. (From
the left) Close,
Sharpe,
Cowan, Stott,
Vic Wilson,
Illingworth,
Padgett, Binks,
Bolus, Don
Wilson,
Trueman.

Record breakers.
Padgett (right) and
Wilf Horner after their
Bradford League
record first-wicket
partnership of 219 for
Idle against Lightcliffe
in 1951.

Putting on the Ritz. The players and their wives at a celebration dinner to mark victory in the 1960 Championship.

Name game. An autograph sheet signed by the members of the MCC A Tour to New Zealand, 1960-61. Padgett and Don Wilson flew the flag for the White Rose.

Padgett took over as county coach in 1971 and is seen (above) leading out the Yorkshire Second X1 at Headingley and (below) sharing a joke with rising stars (from the left) Ashley Metcalfe, Martyn Moxon and Simon Dennis. (YP)

Yorkshire v MCC at Lord's 1961. Back row (from left) George Alcock (masseur), Sharpe, Padgett, Cowan, Don Wilson, Platt, Bolus, Cyril Turner (scorer). Front Stott, Illingworth, Trueman, Vic Wilson, Close, Binks.

TELEPHONE LEEDS 24260
TELEGRAPHIC ADDRESS "CRICKET LEEDS 1"

THE YORKSHIRE COUNTY CRICKET CLUB

Old Bank Chambers

J. H. NASH
SECRETARY

Leeds 1

RESIDENCE
TELEPHONE PUDSEY 3458   24th March,   51.*19*

Dear *Ryan,*

        Practices, Headingley Ground,
                    Leeds.

You are invited to attend the Practices on

    4, 9, 11 & 13th April, 1961

Your train or bus fare will be paid together
with a fee of 10/-.

You should bring your bat, pads, batting gloves
etc., and also bring a pair of shoes with rubber soles
in the case the practices are in the Practice Shed.

Start at 1.30 p.m.

Please reply accepting.

                    Yours faithfully,

                    Assistant Secretary.

'Dear Ryan...'
Yorkshire's invitation
to pre-season nets at
Headingley in 1961.

Another satisfied customer! Ryan on duty in the family newsagents business in Huddersfield. (YP)

High-fliers. The Yorkshire Corinthians, with Platt (third from right) and Ryan (fifth from right) prepare to leave Manchester airport, known in those days as Ringway, en route to Paris in 1955. Future Yorkshire skipper Ronnie Burnet is on the extreme left.

Pavilioned in splendour. Trueman goes out to bat at Bramall Lane amid a sea of smiling faces. (YP)

Festival Fashions. Sue Platt (left), Shirley Illingworth, Enid Trueman, Sue Ryan and Avril Taylor take to the catwalk at Scarborough. (YP)

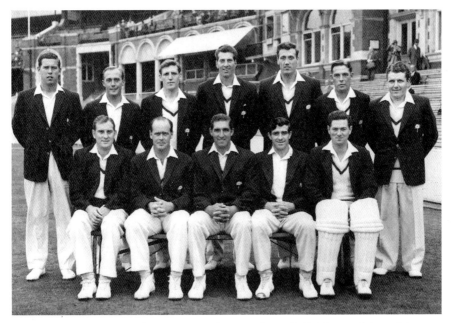

Yorkshire at The Oval, 1962. Back row (from left) Hampshire, Stott, Taylor, Don Wilson, Ryan, Padgett, Sharpe. Front Illingworth, Close, Vic Wilson, Trueman, Binks.

Pause for thought. Nicholson (left) and Cowan take a breather on the pavilion balcony. (YP)

All-star line-up. The programme for Yorkshire's football match against a Showbiz XI at Odsal Stadium in March, 1960. The Showbiz line-up included Tommy Steele (bottom left) and a pre-James Bond Sean Connery (top row, second from right). The game was watched by almost 20,000 fans.

SHIPLEY ROUND TABLE

present a

CHARITY
SOCCER MATCH

SHOWBIZ XI
— V —
YORKSHIRE
C.C. XI

Odsal Stadium, Bradford

Sunday, 27th March, 1960
KICK-OFF NOW 2-45 p.m.

Nº 6458   *Proceeds in Aid of*
World Refugee Year

SOUVENIR
PROGRAMME
2/6 D.

Sign please! Cowan (left), Platt and Ryan put pen to paper for three young supporters.

All together now! Lancashire's Alan Wharton (back left) joins a White Rose chorus featuring Nicholson, Padgett, Don Wilson, fast bowler Peter Stringer and (front from right) Binks, Sharpe and Hampshire (K & J Jelley).

YORKSHIRE COUNTY CRICKET CLUB. 1963

Back row: Left to right: G. Alcock, D. E. V. Padgett, J. H. Hampshire, D. Wilson, M. Ryan, A. G. Nicholson, W. B. Stott, P. J. Sharpe, E. R. Lester.
Front row: Left to right: J. G. Binks, F. S. Trueman, D. B. Close, R. Illingworth, K. Taylor.

The Yorkshire squad at the pre-season photo-shoot, 1963.

Read all about it! The front page of the Scarborough Mercury's four-page Festival special in 1963. (Scarborough Evening News)

Hampshire was one of the few players from the Championship years to enjoy a long career in the Seventies. Here he is seen (above) hitting out against Warwickshire and (below) with the Yorkshire Player of the Year Trophy in 1973. (YP)

YORKSHIRE COUNTY CRICKET CLUB. 1964
Back row: Left to right: G. Boycott, D. E. V. Padgett, M. Ryan, D. Wilson, J. H. Hampshire, A. G. Nicholson, P. J. Sharpe.
Front row: Left to right: J. G. Binks, F. S. Trueman, D. B. Close, R. Illingworth, K. Taylor.

The Yorkshire side pictured at Bradford Park Avenue in 1964.

Happy
families. Binks
with his wife
Jean and
daughters
Jane (right)
and Clare. (YP)

They said he had a natural gift for the game. I often felt as if I was bashing the ball with half a bat or a thick edge while people like George just stroked it around. Dougie Padgett had the same talent.

In the winter of 1951-52, my family moved house to Headingley so the obvious thing was to join Leeds, who played in the Yorkshire League. I had two seasons there before my National Service in Egypt and Cyprus but I didn't play very well.

I don't know why but like quite a few young players, I'd spent hours in the winter practice shed with the Yorkshire coaches, Arthur Mitchell, Arthur Booth and Maurice Leyland, and I became consumed with theory.

It reached the point where I was concentrating so hard on whether my hands and feet were doing the right thing that I hardly saw the ball coming down the wicket.

But my two years in the Army took me away from all that and when I came back I started to play far more freely, both in the leagues and during my early years with Yorkshire.

After National Service, I joined Bradford and had a couple of seasons there before going back to Leeds, where this time I did bat well. As a matter of interest, I actually played for the Yorkshire first team before I had appeared in the Second XI.

I'd gone to the Yorkshire nets in April and when the committee came to name the team for the opening games against MCC and Oxford and Cambridge Universities, Ken Taylor was playing football for Huddersfield Town and Frank Lowson was injured.

That left a hole in the batting order and I was selected and went off down to Lord's with a team that included five England players: Willie Watson, Fred Trueman, Johnny Wardle, Bob Appleyard and Brian Close. I scored nine and nought, the match was drawn and we all headed off to Cambridge.

Billy Sutcliffe had just succeeded Norman Yardley as captain and when we arrived at our hotel, Derek Blackburn was sitting in the reception area.

Derek was a batsman and captain of Bradford, my club at the time, and he eventually became Second XI captain. We were good friends and he helped me secure my first job after National Service with Cornhill Insurance.

Billy was clearly surprised to see him and said, "What are you doing here?"

"I've been sent down by the committee to play against Cambridge," said Derek. So he played and I didn't. It turned out to be his only appearance for the county.

I had to wait until August to play my second and last game of that season, against Worcestershire at Bradford. Then I made just a single appearance in 1957 and eight more, without significant success, the following year.

So it wasn't until the second half of 1959, when Philip Sharpe and Vic Wilson were both having a bad run and had been left out, that I started to play regularly in the build-up to the Championship decider against Sussex at Hove.

A couple of games before we'd lost by an innings in the infamous game against Gloucestershire at Bristol where we were bowled out for 35 in the first innings. I made 12 not out, batting at five, and Tony Brown took seven for 11.

Before the start of our innings on the Monday morning there was a low mist around and we claimed we wouldn't be able to see the ball in what we described as a thick fog. But Tony dismissed it as "just a bit of atmosphere". But he would, wouldn't he?

We were asked to follow on and our captain, Ronnie Burnet, said, not without a touch of humour, that as I was the man in form, I had better open. Numbers six to 11 had all failed to score and the second highest score was extras with eight.

During the second innings, Dai Davies, a kindly Welsh umpire, said to me, "Boy, never hook or cut at Bristol, the wicket is low and slow."

I followed his advice diligently but on 91, just nine runs short of my maiden hundred for Yorkshire, I forgot myself, tried to hook Brown, missed and was lbw.

None of the last six batsmen bagged a pair, although Bob Platt, batting at number 11, accused Ronnie Burnet of trying to run him out for nought. The captain just smiled.

Bristol was a disaster but after beating Worcestershire in our next match, we headed off to Hove for the game that clinched our first outright Championship for 13 years. By pure coincidence, I scored the winning runs.

For years it was the only time I saw myself on telly when they kept showing a little five-second snip of me nudging a ball from Ted Dexter away on the leg side. Yet it was a game in which I had played virtually no significant part. The great performances came from Raymond Illingworth, Bryan Stott and Dougie Padgett.

I remember that when we started our second innings, not many of us thought we had much chance. But Stotty did, he really believed we could do it. And we did.

In 1960, I played in 31 matches and scored over 1,000 first-class runs for the first time. But even so, when the committee met to discuss contracts in July, there was a lot of speculation in the Press about who may or may not be staying.

By that time, my wife Gloria and I had two children, Martin and David, and our daughter Julia was born later in 1961. I needed security so I asked if I could see Brian Sellers, the chairman of the cricket committee. He entertained me to lunch at the Midland Hotel in Bradford.

I put forward the case that much as I wanted to play for Yorkshire, if they didn't feel they could give me my county cap it would perhaps be time for me to move on. Would they sanction that?

To be honest, I'm not 100 per cent sure whether I actually needed their permission to leave because I didn't have a contract – I never signed one in all the time I was there so we were basically on two weeks' notice or whatever.

Anyway all that became academic when I was capped a couple of days later, along with Philip Sharpe, Don Wilson and my old schoolmate Mike Cowan.

I played well again the following year in what was my best season with Yorkshire and scored 1,970 runs, just 30 short of the magical 2,000. And it was a magical target. We had lots of innings, of course, and in 1961, I scored my runs from 61 knocks. But even so, 2,000 runs was always a significant feat.

However, scoring heavily did have its drawbacks, which were pointed out to me in no uncertain terms by Gordon Barker. He was a long-standing friend of Dougie Padgett and had come to attend a day's play at the Scarborough Festival, which always took place at the end of the season.

He was a formidable Essex opening bat, a great theorist, the butt of much humour in and around the Essex dressing room and a fully paid-up member of the county cricket social club.

And while the three of us were together at the festival, Gordon leaned across and told me, "You've got too many runs this year, Bolly."

I said, "You what? How can anyone score too many runs?"

But he was unmoved and insisted, "No, you've got too many... because they'll expect that every year now. When I get to 1,500, I call it off." And there was I with my ambitions of reaching the magical 2,000!

If only I could have maintained my form in 1962, when Yorkshire had too many capped players. We all knew there were certain to be changes and they were creeping up on us throughout the season.

Vic Wilson was expected to retire and for a while it looked as if Bryan Stott would be leaving, too, because he wasn't in the side early on. But when he was given a chance, he did well.

To be fair, I was given plenty of opportunities but I just didn't perform. And when decision day came in July, I was given the elbow, along with Mike Cowan. We'd played together at school, we were capped on the same day and now we'd been sacked together. That can't have happened very often.

In my four years as a first team player we won the Championship three times and finished second once. But perhaps there were people who, in their wisdom, didn't think we were quite what they wanted.

And in fairness, John Hampshire and Geoffrey Boycott were coming along and there was always a belief that good young players should be given a chance.

John and Geoffrey established themselves in 1963 and the following year Boycott took my place in the England side. So time proved that Yorkshire's decision to release me was right and I have no regrets about it.

Given my form in 1962, the sack wasn't exactly a bolt out of the blue and I soon had three offers. First from Nottinghamshire, then from Trevor Bailey at Essex and finally from Leslie Ames at Kent.

"Don't sign for anyone south of the Trent," was the advice of the aforementioned Brian Sellers so I joined Notts.

Of course, I was disappointed to be leaving Yorkshire and people have said that my good form in 1963, when I won the first of my seven England caps, was a case of "Right, I'll show you lot..."

Yes and no. Yes because I wanted to pursue my career and I was determined to do well. No because I never had any animosity towards the county club. I like to think I have a lot of friends in Yorkshire.

The first time I played against my old team-mates was in the first round of the new Gillette Cup competition at Middlesbrough in May.

I batted through the Notts innings and scored an unbeaten 100 out of 159 in 65 overs. The next highest score was 23 from Mervyn Winfield, the only other player to reach double figures.

We lost by four wickets and Cyril Washbrook gave me the Man of the Match award...reluctantly. He said I should have scored a lot more runs as the innings wore on.

Fred Trueman always thought he should have won the award because he took four wickets and scored 20-odd runs. But I don't think he was a serious contender, or not on that occasion anyway.

The next time I played in Yorkshire was in our second Championship match of the season against them, at Bradford in August. I scored a hundred in our second innings and played well until I was caught aiming to slog Don Wilson over extra cover.

It was a habit I never lost. I remember once getting out in the nineties against Lancashire, trying to smash David Hughes' left-arm spin and holing out to Barry Wood on the boundary.

And even at the grand old age of 50, I was still at it, caught at long-off in the nineties again off the bowling of Omar Henry, playing for MCC against Scotland at Lord's.

But throughout that first season with Notts, I played really well. This time I reached the magical 2,000 runs and did enough to be selected for the fourth Test against the West Indies. At Headingley.

They say that Brian Sellers' response was that while I might be good enough to play for England, I wasn't good enough for Yorkshire.

After the West Indies had made 397, I walked out to bat on the Friday afternoon. I took ten off Wes Hall's first over, although it has to be said that there weren't too many fielders in front of the wicket for Hall and Charlie Griffith.

Before Hall's second over, their captain Frank Worrell strolled over and whispered something in his ear. I added just four more runs before departing, caught at slip by Conrad Hunte, bowled Hall.

The following winter, we toured India and in the first Test at Madras, I made 88, the highest score of my short Test career. I batted for six hours 45 minutes and featured for many years in Wisden's list of the slowest individual Test Match innings.

I was batting with Ken Barrington and with about 20 minutes to go he strolled down the wicket at the end of an over. Time for chat.

"Not long to go, Brian," he said. "Waste a bit o' time, son. Take a fresh guard, prod the wicket a bit." Being the junior pro, I did as I was told.

Next time the ball hit me on the pad, the umpire's finger shot up...and they'd been hitting me on the pad all day and none had been given out. The foolhardiness of thinking you can slide one past the umpire!

I played in all five Tests in India and passed 50 four times. Perhaps if I'd converted that 88 in Madras into a hundred, I might have gone on to bigger things.

Nevertheless I finished the series with 391 runs at an average of 48.87 and early in the 1964 season, I was given ample opportunity by the selectors to cement my place.

In the first two months of the season, I played for MCC against Yorkshire and Surrey, for Notts against the Australians and for MCC against the Aussies in what was virtually a Test trial.

In eight innings, I scored a century and two fifties, including 63, opening with Boycott, against the Australians at Lord's. We put on 124 for the first wicket but Boycott was chosen for the first Ashes Test.

He played in all five matches and scored his first Test century in the final game of the series at The Oval. I had no complaints because I hadn't made the most of my chances.

Instead, I returned to the county circuit, completed a ten-year stay at Notts and in the process went from free-flowing strokemaker to blocker. Why? The theory started to kick in again, just as it had in my early days at Headingley.

I used to watch people like Colin Cowdrey, Mike Smith and, to a lesser extent, Peter May playing with bat and pad close together and tried to follow their example. It did not work. Instead of playing my natural game, I became bogged down with technical issues.

Years later, when I was talking about it to Brian Close, he growled, "I'd have stopped you bat-padding, Bolly. I'd have sent you into the nets to bat against the fast bowlers...with no pads. That would have made you get your left leg out of the way. Ouch!"

In self defence, I didn't always play that way but did so too much and too often and frequently made Eddie Phillipson a happy man.

He was a long-serving Test and county umpire and many was the time when, after a vociferous appeal against me for lbw, he would smile, raise his right finger and say, "That's out, Brian."

Between 1963 and 1967, while Yorkshire were winning three Championships, Notts struggled along at the wrong end of the table, finishing bottom twice.

In 1967, with Norman Hill as captain, we didn't win a single Championship game, although ironically we weren't bottom this time because Gloucestershire were just a little bit worse than we were.

The only game we won was the first round of the Gillette Cup against Durham, then a Minor County, at Chester-le-Street. And it was a damn close finish; we won by 11 runs.

Then in 1968, the first year when counties were allowed to play overseas players without a five-year residential qualification, along came Garfield Sobers.

It was the year when big names like Rohan Kanhai, Barry Richards and Mike Procter all came over to play county cricket. But we got the best, no question about it.

Garry lifted the whole team. He was an extraordinary man and in that first season under his captaincy we went from no wins to seven wins, with just three defeats, and finished fourth. And it could easily have been even better.

Garry was incredible. There has always been a notion that players as talented as him don't really have to try; that they can produce the goods without putting in maximum effort.

Well I've seen Garry Sobers absolutely exhausted in the home dressing room at Trent Bridge. Playing for us. Not for the West

Indies, not for himself but for us. He gave everything.

Garry used to bowl himself into the ground at times. A wiser man would not have done so and had I been his captain, I would have taken him off long before he finally stopped. "You have a blow, Garry, and we'll let someone else have a chance."

Trent Bridge was a pretty hot place in mid-afternoon on a sunny day but Garry chose not to notice. And it was in that first season that he hit Malcolm Nash for six sixes in an over in the game against Glamorgan at Swansea. It was an astonishing feat.

I also hit six sixes that day. However it took me three hours and 50 minutes before I was out for 140, caught sub, bowled Nash. At that point Malcolm must have thought the day was going pretty well...and then the Great Man arrived on the scene.

I think Notts paid Garry £5,000 in 1968, plus various expenses, like a car, accommodation and so on. And one committee member said we'd saved £3,000...they had been expecting to pay £8,000.

His failing, if that's the word, as a captain was that he thought that we – that was the other ten of us mere mortals who made up the supporting cast – could play as well as him. And because of that he tended to make declarations that were simply too generous.

One of them was against Warwickshire at Edgbaston in 1970, Garry's third season, on the very sad day that Syd Buller, one of the finest umpires at the time, collapsed and died during a break for rain. This delayed the restart by at least 15 minutes.

Garry had already set Warwickshire a target of 241 in three hours and even though five overs were washed out in the last hour, they still won with 14 balls to spare. Garry had certainly over-estimated our ability on that occasion.

In 1972, he picked up a knee injury early on and only played six Championship matches. He asked to be relieved of the captaincy and I took over.

We struggled a bit and before the start of our last Championship match at Trent Bridge against Warwickshire, I was told I would not be retained for 1973.

That was on a Saturday and over the weekend I had a call from Derbyshire. Would I go and meet their committee on Monday night?

I said certainly, drove across to Derby, accepted their offer to take over as captain the following season and next day enjoyed the distinction of being captain of two county sides on the same day.

Warwickshire had already won the Championship, and maybe I was feeling a bit more generous than usual because after rain had washed out the first day, I left them a target of 154. Then I could only look on as Kanhai and Alvin Kallicharran knocked spots off us and we lost by a long time.

When I made my debut for Derbyshire the following year, I occupied a unique position of being capped by three counties and captain of two.

There's more movement on the circuit these days but in my time, it was very rare, mainly because professionals preferred to struggle on, if necessary, for ten years as a capped player and be awarded a benefit.

Derbyshire was a friendly, family club with a completely different atmosphere from Yorkshire and Nottinghamshire, who were based at Test grounds, and a club who have often punched well above their weight over the years.

They'd finished bottom the previous season but even though we only moved up one place in my first year, I felt we made quite a lot of progress.

It was also the year in which I became only the third captain, after Lord Hawke of Yorkshire and the Hon Lionel Tennyson of Hampshire, to send off one of his own players.

It happened after tea on the first day of our match against Yorkshire at Chesterfield in June.

Alan Ward, our England fast bowler, had bowled well, if a little erratically, in the first two sessions and I needed him to come back after tea. But for some reason when I asked him to bowl, his elastic had broken and he refused to do so.

I persisted for about 40 minutes, but he kept saying no and in the end, I went off the field and told the club secretary what I was likely to do. I gave Alan one more chance and when he refused, I sent him off.

Needless to say, the Press corps spotted what was going on and as we were leaving the field at the close of play, I spotted a group of journalists, led by Peter Johnson of the Daily Mail, sprinting across the field to interview me.

Inevitably it was a big story. Alan apologised straight away but five days later announced his retirement at the age of 25.

Thankfully, he had a re-think over the winter and returned the following year, eventually going on to regain his England place. And once the dust had settled we became good friends again.

I continued as captain in 1974 but early on in the following season, I was having one or two personal business problems and I decided to give up the captaincy. Bob Taylor, the England wicketkeeper, took over.

His fourth game in charge was against Lancashire at Buxton and on the first day, two of our bowlers, Keith Stevenson and Michael Glenn, were taken ill. We were already without Mike Hendrick and Ward so Lancashire took full advantage and piled up 477 for five declared.

We were due to resume on Bank Holiday Monday, June 2, but when we arrived the ground was covered by an inch of snow. No one had seen anything like it.

The following day the snow had gone, we were caught on what *Wisden* described as "a difficult drying pitch" and bowled out twice in three hours.

One of the few moments of light relief came in our first innings when Ashley Harvey-Walker, who was batting at five, took one look at the pitch and handed his false teeth to the square leg umpire for safe keeping.

When I resigned as captain I was 41 but even so the club paid me the great compliment of offering me a two-year contract at the end of the season. But I knew it was time to go.

I retired but went on to play eleven more seasons in league cricket, starting at Bradford, who were playing in the Yorkshire League at the time. From there I moved into the Bradford League, first with Brighouse then with Cleckheaton and finally I had a year at Farsley, Ray Illingworth's club.

We won the Priestley Cup, the Bradford League's knock-out competition, for the first time for 20 years and Farsley wanted me to stay on for another season. But it was 80 miles each way and the travel was starting to get to me.

So in 1984, I came back nearer home to play for Heanor in the Derbyshire League. I had three years there and finally decided to call it a day in 1986 when I was 52.

Sometimes I look back and wonder why I carried on for so long and the moment of truth came when I gave chase for the ball along with a little lad of 15 or 16 and within a few yards, he had left me stranded.

It had been a similar situation in county cricket, really. If the opposition didn't get me out in the first ten minutes, I took a lot of moving; the only problem was that I couldn't get the ball off the square.

So I took up golf instead. I got my handicap down to eight, briefly, but it has always been more of a way to keep fit and in a normal week, I'll play four times, Monday, Wednesday, Friday and Saturday.

It's been very good for me. I play on a hilly course and it's helped me retain my sanity and a reasonable state of fitness.

I was elected to the Nottinghamshire committee in 1993 and the following year, when Ray Illingworth was appointed England's Chairman of Selectors, I joined his team, along with Fred Titmus.

David Graveney replaced me after one season but I stayed on for another two years, acting as a scout on Illy's behalf. Then in 1996, I was elected to the ECB's new committee, the England Management Advisory Committee, which was responsible for all England affairs.

I was chairman from 1998 until 2002, by which time it had become the International Teams Management Group.

There were quite a few changes while I was in charge, including the introduction of central contracts for England players and the appointment of Duncan Fletcher as England coach. It was one of the few jobs I wasn't sacked from!

In fact, when England regained the Ashes in 2005, one or two people were kind enough to say I'd played a part with my earlier work behind the scenes.

But at the end of 2002, I was coming up to my 69th birthday and when I used to arrive at the London-bound platform at Nottingham station at seven o'clock in the morning, I'd be the only person there over 60.

The platform was full of earnest young women in suits, carrying briefcases in one hand and a laptop in the other. I thought, "What am I doing here? I've been at it long enough."

I could have stayed on without any question but I decided to retire from my committee role and as a director of the ECB.

And almost directly as a result of leaving the ECB, in 2004 I became the first former professional player to be made president of Nottinghamshire and while still serving as a member of the county committee. So I had a good run for my money, even though I saw my fair share of P45s!

After I retired from first-class cricket, I went into local government, running the Recreation and Amenities Department at Gedling Borough Council in the Nottingham suburbs.

And my appointment finally enabled me to answer the plaintive cry of "When is our Brian going to get a proper job?" from my Auntie Flo when I was struggling to win a place in the Yorkshire side almost 20 years earlier.

I eventually became chief officer in the department and stayed with the council for 16 and a half years before in March, 1991, aged 57, I was given the chance to retire early and commenced my new life in cricket administration.

One day, when I'd been with Gedling for a while, I was having a chat with Bill Brown, the council's chief executive, and he asked me if, when I looked back, I had any regrets.

I replied, "Yes, I wish I'd played better more often." Then after a moment's pause for thought, I added, "And I wish I could sing really well."

"Sing?" he asked.

"Yes. I don't know why but I've always wanted to sing." I suppose there was no answer to that.

Actually Gloria thinks I'm quite a good singer but I'm not. I can hum along a bit if need be but I certainly wouldn't dare sing when there were people around. If I was in a good mood I might whistle!

1963

The assassination of President John F Kennedy in Dallas, Texas, on November 22, 1963, stopped the world in its tracks. We all know exactly where we were when we heard the news.

It was the year when Harold Wilson, a Huddersfield Town supporter, was elected leader of the Labour Party and when John Profumo, the Secretary of State for War, resigned after his dalliance with a call girl, Christine Keeler, was exposed.

The year when Spurs became the first British side to win a European trophy, the Cup-Winners Cup, and when an armed gang hi-jacked a Royal Mail train in Buckinghamshire.

The Great Train Robbers made off with £2.6m and the bulk of the money was never found; the robbers were, however, and seven of the gang received a sentence of 30 years' imprisonment.

The new cricket season opened as Britain emerged from the worst winter since 1947...not a single frost-free night between December 21 and March 5.

And Gerry and the Pacemakers were on top of the UK charts with How Do You Do It? when Yorkshire, now under the captaincy of Brian Close, played MCC at Lord's in the opening fixture of the first-class season.

By the end of another Championship-winning campaign, Close and his team-mates had demonstrated that they knew exactly how to do it.

The start of the second phase of Yorkshire's Championship years was marked with three players, Geoffrey Boycott, John Hampshire and Tony Nicholson, being awarded county caps.

All three would play a significant role in the side that, under Close's captaincy, won the title four times and the Gillette Cup twice before the end of the decade.

Hampshire has no doubts about the side's quality. "How good were we? After I retired in 1984, I became a first-class umpire and watched county cricket on a regular basis for another 21 years.

"And I have absolutely no doubt that the Yorkshire side I played in was one of the finest county teams the game has seen.

"Only two sides of the modern era approached us: Middlesex, who won three Championships under Mike Brearley between 1971 and 1982, and Adam Hollioake's Surrey, who won three titles in four years from 1999.

"Our record speaks for itself and on top of our success in the Championship and Gillette Cup, we also had an outstanding record against touring sides.

"Between 1963 and 1968, I only finished on the losing side twice: in the second of two games against the 1963 West Indians at Sheffield and in our second match against the Australians at Bradford in 1964

"We won four of the other seven matches, three of them by an innings, including our victory over the Australians at Bramall Lane in 1968.

"For some reason we never quite received the credit we deserved but throughout the Sixties there were very few sides who could get near to us.

"We were as friendly as we were volatile and one outstanding memory of my early years is how the senior players seemed more likely to fall out over a win than a defeat. They'd argue on and on about why we hadn't won more easily!"

JOHN HAMPSHIRE.

ROTHERHAM'S FINEST

John Harry Hampshire was born in Thurnscoe, Rotherham, on February 10, 1941. A middle order batsman, he made his Championship debut in 1961 and was capped in 1963. Hampshire played in 456 first-class matches for Yorkshire and scored 21,979 runs, including 34 centuries, at an average of 34.61. He also made 231 appearances in limited overs games. He played in five Championship sides and two Gillette Cup Finals. Capped eight times by England, he hit a century on debut against the West Indies at Lord's in 1969, the first England batsman to achieve the feat. He captained Yorkshire from 1979 to 1981 before joining Derbyshire, for whom he played in 57 first-class matches, scoring 2,533 runs, with two centuries, at an average of 33.77. He appeared in 32 limited overs games for his new county. After retiring in 1984, Hampshire joined the list of first-class umpires, standing in 21 Tests and 20 One-Day Internationals. Since 2007, he has been on the panel of umpires' mentors.

Sport was always a big thing in the family. My father, Jack, was a fast bowler and played three games for Yorkshire in 1937. He also won a Second XI cap, which was quite an achievement before the War.

He played soccer as well, a centre-half, and in 1937, he was transferred from Mexborough Town, who were in the Midland League, to Manchester City. He played in the same era as people like Matt Busby, Alex Herd and Frank Swift.

But soon afterwards, he broke his collarbone. It was a bad injury in those days and it also affected his cricket career. He moved on to Bristol City and that's where he met my mother, Vera.

After he finished at Bristol City he had about six weeks at non-league Bath, where he became a bit disillusioned, so he moved back up here and joined the Police Force, although he'd actually started his working life as a blacksmith at Hickleton Main Colliery. So he was lucky. Because he was good at sport, he was able to get out of the pits.

I played football as well. I was an inside-forward with Rotherham YMCA and at one stage some pretty high-profile managers were trying to sign me: The one and only Bill Shankly at Huddersfield, Peter Doherty at Doncaster, Reg Freeman at Rotherham and Major Frank Buckley at Wolves, who always had a strong scouting network in south Yorkshire.

I suppose if I'd joined Huddersfield I might have gone on and played for both Yorkshire and Huddersfield at the same time, like Ken Taylor and Chris Balderstone.

I first went to Rotherham Town Cricket Club when I was in a pram because the old man played there. He'd been at one or two other clubs when he was younger but after the War, he never played anywhere but Rotherham. Neither did I and I'm a life member now.

There wasn't too much formal coaching. There was a coach when

I first started as a kid but he left, probably for economic reasons. But of course the old man was a massive help and I had a bit of coaching when I played for Rotherham Boys.

At first, I was a batsman, that was all. But by the time I started playing for Rotherham seconds when I was 14, I'd started bowling a bit of leg spin, too.

In fact in my first game against Monk Bretton on a really wet day, I batted at ten and bowled leg spin. I took five for 30 and scored 20-odd not out.

As time went by I still kept my bowling on but my batting became more recognised and in the end, I finished up opening for the seconds. And when I reached the first team I was a batsman pure and simple and hardly ever bowled.

In fact, I never really bowled again with any serious intent – apart from a certain game against Glamorgan at Cardiff in 1963; of which more later!

I was on the Yorkshire radar fairly early on and played for the Under-15s and Under-18s, while I was also playing football for the YMCA and training with Rotherham United. So a career in both games was still in my sights.

But the old man in his wisdom – and I think he was right – had other ideas. One day, he took me on one side and said, "Look, you've seen what's happened to me. Don't try and play both, do one or the other and get a job outside sport as well."

It wasn't an easy choice. But in the end, I opted for cricket and it was entirely my own decision. And why? Because in those days I could earn more money from cricket than football.

When I first started playing with Yorkshire seconds we were paid £6 a match plus expenses. We played two matches a week so that was 12 quid and a few expenses for starters.

And when I was 17 or 18, I turned professional with Rotherham in the Yorkshire League and was paid another ten quid a match. So in the summer I was picking up 24 or 25 pounds a week, which was a lot of money in those days.

More than my father was earning in the Police and more than your average pro footballer in the early stages of his career.

On top of that, I'd also enrolled for a full apprenticeship as a printer. During the summer, I had a lot of time off for cricket but still worked at the printers when I could. And even though I was only an apprentice, it was still money.

And in the winter, the printers was very, very busy and we worked two or three nights a week overtime, Saturday morning and all day Sunday.

So I was in the money all year round and when I was awarded my Second XI cap in 1959 I picked up another two quid a week. It was the absolute bee's knees; heady days...and I was courting as well!

My printing apprenticeship was at a small shop in Rotherham and I trained as a compositor. But in the end I could also operate monotype and linotype machines as well. I enjoyed it.

Before long, though, I was having a hell of a lot of time off for cricket and because it was a small firm, things were becoming a bit awkward.

So Jack Dickinson, a Yorkshire committee man who was also the managing director of Henry Garnett & Co, who produced the Rotherham Advertiser, got my credentials, the terms of my apprenticeship, swapped over to their place.

That meant I could have as much time off for cricket as I wanted and I was still working there when I was capped in 1963.

I stayed on for another two years but eventually the directors must have decided enough was enough and I was given an ultimatum: either play cricket or work for us. It was no contest.

As it happened, in 1966 I was given the opportunity to go and coach Tasmania, who were not a Sheffield Shield side at that stage, so I never missed out. And I spent the next three winters there. Brilliant.

On the way up, I played for Yorkshire Under-15s, Under-18s and then the Second XI. It was a wonderful experience, both playing and being coached by people like Arthur Mitchell, Maurice Leyland, Arthur Booth and Cyril Turner.

We really looked up to them. They had a no-nonsense approach, no bullshit. None of this putting an arm round your shoulder and saying, "Better luck next time, son."

If you played a crap shot, they said so; if you dropped a catch or fielded badly you were told. It was a very, very hard school and you almost daren't put a foot wrong. It was the same with off-the-field discipline. You always had to be smart and tidy, wear your blazer for lunch and tea.

Even though one or two people thought I would have been better off moving away from Rotherham to play in the Bradford League, I never had any intention of leaving the club.

After all, we played in the Yorkshire League, which covered the entire county anyway, and I played on county grounds like Headingley, Scarborough and Harrogate. Big grounds, good pitches. And we also played at Second XI grounds like Barnsley, Doncaster and York.

It was an immensely strong league but you could say the same about a lot of other leagues as well. Huddersfield, Bradford, North Yorkshire & South Durham.

There were a lot of bloomin' good cricketers around and I would go as far as to say that out of each of the major leagues you could have picked a team good enough to play in county cricket.

But I always felt that if I did well on a Saturday I might just have a chance of playing for Yorkshire seconds. So I got stuck in as much as I possibly could and that's where the recognition came from.

There was no academy, although I think some of the players in the West Riding were cherry-picked. But with Ted Lester, who played for Scarborough, as captain of the Second XI, there was always going to be an opportunity for kids from the provinces.

He could spot up and coming lads in our league and he gave us a chance. I was one of them and I found myself singled out as one of the great white hopes. I never felt comfortable with that.

In fact I never felt at ease at any stage of my career, mainly because I never really thought I was good enough. People always said I was but I was never particularly confident and I always played with a fear of failure.

I played one first team game in 1961, against Leicester at Grace Road, and started playing regularly in July of the following year.

First I played against Notts at Headingley then travelled down to Taunton and the game against Somerset when Fred Trueman was dropped and sent home by Vic Wilson, the captain, for turning up late.

For a young lad, that was something to savour, my all-time hero sent home! But it was an example of the discipline within the side.

Apart from a couple of games in the second team when the first eleven didn't have a match, I was never out of the side again until I left the club in 1981.

And each of those Second XI games came after I'd scored a hundred for the first team. But people hadn't been too happy with my form. That's what we were up against.

I don't like to use the word awesome but when you realised you were playing in the same side as people like Brian Close, Fred, Raymond Illingworth and Jimmy Binks, it was an amazing experience.

It was also a pleasure. I hung back and watched but I was made to feel welcome from the start. So was every other young player. There was never a case of us and them. Not from the players, anyway.

And when Geoff Boycott, Tony Nicholson and myself were capped in October, 1963 we went straight on to the same money as everybody else. There was no suggestion that anyone should be paid more, no matter how famous they were, because all capped players were equal.

That brought everybody either up or down to the level Yorkshire wanted and created a rounded atmosphere in the dressing room. There was never any resentment among the senior players, mainly because they had been brought up the same way.

I got more pleasure out of being capped by Yorkshire than winning an England cap. I had always wanted to play for Yorkshire and when I was awarded my Second XI cap, I thought that was the be all and end all.

But to go on and get my first team cap was something else, particularly when I found out about it in the paper. The statement gave the announcement of the three names alphabetically, Boycott, Hampshire and Nicholson, and a letter from the club arrived in the next day's post.

Being capped also gave us a change of identity within the club hierarchy. When Mr Nash, the secretary, invited me to the nets or to play for the Second XI, he always started the letter, "Dear Hampshire..."

As soon as I was capped, I became, "Dear John..." Along with the letter notifying me about my cap and my remuneration the following season came my Yorkshire first team tie. When I saw that tie with the White Rose, I knew I'd cracked it.

The next letter came in the New Year, asking me to report for pre-season nets and to collect my cap from the county offices in Old Bank Chambers, Park Row, Leeds 1.

I also had to collect my sweaters from Herbert Sutcliffe, the sports shop run by Herbert's son Billy Sutcliffe, and to be measured for my blazer at Burton's Tailors.

You could park your car anywhere in Leeds in those days, so I parked right outside the offices, marched up the stairs and was greeted by John Nash's secretary, Miss Coates.

These days you would describe her as being very far back. I said, "Hello, Miss Coates, I've come for my county cap."

She replied, "There's a full box up there on the shelf. Reach up and pick one." These days, when a player is capped, there is a formal ceremony out on the pitch when the captain hands over a cap and sweater to the newly-capped player.

In comparison, Miss Coates' terse instruction was quite a let-down, really. But it didn't matter. I'd been awarded my county cap and nobody could take it away.

Ironically, though, my career might easily have ended five months earlier when I was hit on the side of the head by a ball from Charlie Griffith in our game against the West Indians at Middlesbrough.

It happened at around 11.40am on May 15, 1963, in the third over of the day -- we started at 11.30 in those days – and in one split second, my life changed for ever. It must have been a short ball but I never actually saw it. There was no sightscreen at Acklam Park, just black slate roofs.

And without being in any way racist, a black hand delivering a dark red ball from the background of a black roof is not conducive to seeing the ball properly. And there was a lot of controversy over whether Griffith bowled or threw his yorker and bouncer.

George Alcock was our physio. He used to play centre-forward for Bradford Park Avenue and had later trained as a chiropodist. So if we had an ingrowing toenail, he was the man to see. But he wasn't too strong in some other areas.

We used to call him Rivetfingers because when he used to rub you there was more electricity in his fingers than in any of the newfangled equipment they have these days.

George was a fabulous bloke, though, and once play had started he invariably used to nip round the back of the pavilion and have a Guinness and a cigarette. He suffered quite badly from emphysema.

After I'd been hit, the search was on for George and eventually he was tracked down to the back of the pavilion, Guinness in one hand, cigarette in the other.

He ran into the dressing room, grabbed a wet flannel and came tottering out towards the middle. Halfway to the middle the emphysema took hold and he ground to a halt, coughing violently.

So a couple of the West Indies players had to pick him up and bring him to me. I was sitting on the ground feeling decidedly groggy and George came and sat down beside me, panting.

"How are you?" he said, between breaths.

"I've got a bloody headache."

"Do you want me to rub it?"

"Christ, no. It's killing me."

So there was nothing else for it...more players moved in and we were both carried back to the pavilion and into the sanctuary of the dressing room, by which time George had recovered his breath.

"I'll have to rub it," he said.

"George, you're not bloody rubbing it. Just get me a cold drink."

"Do you want a beer?"

I went out to bat again in the afternoon, with the strict instructions of my captain ringing in my ears.

"Look," said Closey, "if you get hit again, make sure you don't fall outside the crease, because they'll definitely run you out next time."

That night, even though I was still feeling a bit groggy, I joined one or two of the lads and some of the West Indies players for a pint in the Corporation Taps, the pub we used in Middlesbrough.

I seem to remember Jimmy Binks, Phil Sharpe, Don Wilson and Tony Nicholson were there along with Rohan Kanhai and Lance Gibbs from the opposition camp. I've always got on well with Kanhai since that day, a good man.

"How are you?" he asked.

"Not so bloody good," I admitted. "I've got a headache and I don't feel too clever to be honest."

He replied, "You're a very lucky man, Hamp. If we'd been playing in the West Indies you'd have been dead. The pitches are a lot quicker over there." The consolation prize.

I wouldn't say my career went backwards from that day but it didn't go full tilt forwards. I didn't really kick on as I should have done.

And while there may have been other reasons, essentially I blame that blow on the head. It has had a bigger effect on my life than anything else that has ever happened to me.

That summer, I never slept at all. When we were playing away from home, I found myself walking around the streets near our hotels at all hours of the night.

I suffered violent headaches and eventually I finished up in hospital in October. These days I would have been rushed off to hospital straight away. I had an x-ray which revealed that my brain was still bruised.

From the day I was hit, I wasn't able to concentrate like I should. I never lost confidence, I was never afraid of fast bowling or backed away, which was a blessing. But I always knew what might happen.

Thankfully, I was more or less back in shape when we arrived at Cardiff for our game against Glamorgan ten weeks later. My proudest moment.

If Bob Platt can tell the world about his half century at Chesterfield in 1959, what about my seven for 52 at Cardiff four years later to win the match before lunch on the third day?

In fact, I always tell Bob that the only reason Ray Illingworth, who was captaining the side, put me on was because I'd be quicker than him! But in fairness, I think he'd broken down during their first innings and wasn't fit to bowl.

It was magical, the only performance in my whole career that I ever really talk about.

We made a good score in the first innings, bowled them out for 88 and enforced the follow-on. And late on the second day, when we were struggling to make a breakthrough, Illy called over, "Hamp, come and have a bowl."

I picked up two, Alwyn Harris and Alun Rees, that night and next morning before the start of play, Raymond said, "You're opening the bowling."

I thought to myself, "Bloody fantastic! Opening the bowling for Yorkshire! Get on!" I took another five wickets and we wound it up by an innings and 66 runs before lunch.

As it happened, our travelling Press corps arrived late that morning, just as we were walking out of the gates to set off on the journey north for our next match at Worcester.

I think it was Alan Thompson from the Daily Express who asked what was happening. "Oh Hamp's bowled 'em out," replied one of the lads.

"Don't be so bloody daft. What's going on?"

"You'll have to wait for the evening paper to find out!"

Unfortunately, despite my finest hour in Cardiff, my leg spin did not go on to feature as a regular part of Yorkshire's spin armoury and in my entire career, I only bowled 423.1 overs and took 30 wickets at an average of 50-plus.

I suppose that with Raymond, Don Wilson, Closey and later Geoff Cope taking between 250 and 300 wickets a season between them, I couldn't have any complaints. And Yorkshire never did trust leg spinners anyway.

But no one will ever take away the memory of that day in Cardiff and in some ways, it overshadows my first Test against the West Indies in June,1969, when I became the first player to score a century on debut at Lord's.

The facts are set in stone in the record books but to this day Donald Carr, who was assistant secretary of MCC at the time, jokes that it's just about the worst knock he's ever seen. And I agree with him!

The one thing that can be said about that innings is that I didn't give any chances...because I wasn't playing well enough to get a touch.

During the following winter I had a bad do with the flu or something and was feeling a bit sorry for myself. After a while, Judy, my late first wife, had had enough and said, "For God's sake read this, it might buck you up."

I hadn't really read any reports of my Test hundred and this was Jim Swanton's version in the Daily Telegraph. He wrote that to reach my century, I glided one down to Third Man. Glided? I nicked it...and I nicked it all through my innings. It was horrendous.

In mitigation, I had broken the little finger of my left hand 12 days earlier when I was hit by a ball from Mike Procter in our innings win against Gloucestershire at Middlesbrough. It was a mess and I can't shift the knuckles properly to this day.

Our next match was against Essex at Bramall Lane and before the game, Closey said, "You're probably not fit but I'd like you to play because I think you'll be in the 12 for Lord's. So just go out there and make the best of it."

Closey was right about Lord's and I reported with the rest of the players on the Wednesday. Illy was skipper and knew I'd been bashed so the first thing he said was, "Are you fit?"

I said, "Yes, I am."

"Right, get in those bloody nets!" I padded up and John Snow, David Brown and Barry Knight, England's pace attack, were waiting for me along with Alan Smith, a selector, who could bowl a bit, too. They all had a new ball and they gave me a real peppering.

"How do you feel?" said Illy afterwards.

"All right," I replied through gritted teeth.

"OK, let's see about the fielding." And he and Smith pounded away at me with all sorts of ground shots and catches for another ten minutes or more.

"How's that feel then?"

I said, "I'm all right, I'll be OK," even though I was pretty well pissed off by that stage. But I thought all along that if I didn't play, I might never ever get another chance.

And much as I thought I was lucky to be in the Twelve in the first place, I knew that if I could win just one England cap, I would have it for ever.

I didn't find out I was actually in the side until about half an hour before the start when I passed Geoff Boycott on the outfield. "Well done!" he said. "You're playing."

I thought, "Oh, Christ!" On the one hand I was delighted and elated to be playing for England. On the other hand, I was terrified in case I failed and because of my broken finger.

We lost the toss and had to field. And even though it was a cold day, I didn't put my England sweater on. Instead, I walked out in my shirt sleeves because I was so embarrassed about being picked.

The West Indies made 380 and when I went out to join Phil Sharpe with 35 minutes to play on the second evening, we were four down for 37.

Somehow I survived, although Donald Carr told me afterwards, "Hamp, after that first over I had to go and have a large gin and tonic!"

The following morning, Sharpey went fairly early but I hung on. I was hit twice on my left arm by short balls from Vanburn Holder and learned after the match that I had sustained a hairline fracture.

And finally, after around five hours of hard labour, I reached my hundred...or as Wisden rather euphemistically put it, "He went on nobly to his hundred before Shepherd dismissed him leg before".

I played in the next Test at Headingley, scoring one and 22, and was then left out for the three-match series against New Zealand that followed. I deserved a more extended run after scoring a century on debut.

My next opportunity came when I was selected for the 1970-71 Ashes tour of Australia and New Zealand under Ray Illingworth. That was the icing on the cake.

I played in two Ashes Tests, including the decider at Sydney, and scored one half century. I scored two more fifties in New Zealand in the second half of the tour.

I played one Test against the Aussies in 1972 and then had to wait three years for another chance, also against Australia, in the third Test at Headingley.

The match was abandoned on the final morning after the pitch had been damaged during the night by protestors from the Free George Davis campaign. Davis had been convicted of an armed robbery in London the previous year and was eventually released on appeal.

I was a far better player in 1975 than I had been in 1969 but whereas my captain six years earlier and in all my previous Tests was Illingworth, an Englishman, this time it was Tony Greig, a South African.

Now let me make it clear, I had absolutely nothing against Greigy as a man or as a cricketer. But I felt quite simply that a South African should not have been leading England and made my feelings known. I was left out after that match and never played again.

I plodded along fairly well on the county circuit after that and scored a lot of seventies, eighties and nineties. I never had a problem with that but statistics always matter most to some people and centuries count.

I don't talk about my last few years at Yorkshire and my time as captain after Boycott had lost the job. But by 1975, Philip Sharpe, Don Wilson and Richard Hutton had left the club and on reflection, maybe I should have gone, too, when Derbyshire approached me in 1979.

In fact I would have left if John Temple, Yorkshire's cricket chairman, hadn't asked me to take on the captaincy. That's something you don't turn down. But with hindsight, I should really have left there and then.

Instead, I was captain for two years and embroiled in the in-fighting that almost tore the club apart. It was a terrible time for Yorkshire. Terrible.

In the end, I did move to Derbyshire in 1982 and had three happy seasons there. We had a decent side in the first couple of years but then my legs started to give me problems and I had to have a couple of operations.

I didn't recover quite as quickly as I would have when I was younger and once I stopped enjoying my fielding, I knew it was time to go. I'd always loved fielding, it was the only area of the game in which I felt confident.

I was 43 and a qualified coach but at that time there was no possibility of a coaching job anywhere.

And while I had never really considered umpiring before, I thought, "Well, I've been in the game for a while, I'll take it on." After all, I knew a little bit about cricket and nowt about owt else, as they say.

I was elected to the panel immediately and it was the best thing I ever did. I took to it straight away and enjoyed it immensely. I suppose I must have been good at it, otherwise I wouldn't have done as many big games as I did.

And I found that whereas I sometimes had problems concentrating as a batsman, I had no problem at all with concentration when I umpired. I was out there for six, seven hours a day but I seemed to be on the ball all the time.

There was always a camaraderie among the umpires and the only drawback was that after being involved in a team game for so long, I was very much on my own on long journeys home after a match and there was nobody else to talk to.

Other than that, I thoroughly enjoyed it and I had a better Test career as an umpire than I did as a player, 21 matches against eight. And I also stood in 20 limited overs internationals.

I loved being involved in Test matches. One of the things you don't really appreciate as a player or spectator is that when the teams walk out on the first morning of a Test, the umpires are already there.

So as an umpire you are one of the first two people to walk out on to the pitch and that's the moment when the game starts. It's a fantastic feeling. A full house and an expectant hush. It's spine-tingling at times, particularly at Lord's. Marvellous!

My first Test was between England and Australia at Old Trafford in 1989 and that autumn John Holder and I were chosen as the first two neutral umpires to stand in Tests between India and Pakistan.

If I'd wanted to learn how it felt to walk out into the bullring, those Test matches in Pakistan taught me. If ever I had to prove myself and my ability to handle pressure, that was it.

We played four Tests back to back with just two days off between each one. It was probably the best cricket tour I've ever been on, an exhilarating experience. I was absolutely on fire from the word go. I enjoyed it immensely and I think John and I came out of it very well.

I went on to feature in some real nail-biters, like England v Pakistan at Lord's in 1992, when Barry Dudleston was my colleague.

At the start of the last over, bowled by Ian Salisbury, Pakistan needed one to win with two wickets standing. It was a full house and the crowd were going absolutely berserk

Before the series started, however, the Pakistanis had rejected the provision of an extra half hour at the end of a day's play if a result was possible.

So if Ian Salisbury's final over of the day had been a maiden, we should, strictly speaking, have all walked off and started again the following morning. Imagine the crowd's reaction to that!

Before the last over, Barry and I met halfway down the wicket. We looked at each other and Barry said, "We're not going off, are we?"

"We're bloody not," I replied. "We'd get lynched." Fortunately Wasim Akram drove Salisbury's first ball through the covers and Pakistan had won by two wickets.

In one of my first Tests as an umpire, I strolled into the dining room at lunchtime and joined the players for lunch. "Isn't there any beer?" I asked. They looked at me as if I was mad.

But in my playing days, there was always beer on the table at lunchtime all round the country. I think Northants and Yorkshire were the last counties to discontinue it.

I had a bottle of beer at lunchtime on every playing day of my career...and sometimes if I was out before lunch, I'd have two. Pale Ale, something I'd never have dreamed of drinking in the pub.

But that's what I drank, even in Test matches. And when Illy was captain at Leicester, he sat at the top table and there was always a bottle of red wine.

Nobody abused it and as far as I know it never did anyone any harm. A lot of us went on playing for a very long time...and Illy was still going strong at the age of 50!

TONY NICHOLSON.
JUNE, 1938 – NOVEMBER, 1985

Anthony George Nicholson was born in Dewsbury on June 23, 1938. A former policeman in what was then Rhodesia, he made his debut for Yorkshire in 1962 and was capped the following year. A right-arm fast-medium bowler, he played in 282 first-class matches for the county, claiming 876 wickets at an average of 19.76. He also appeared in 119 limited overs matches, taking 173 wickets at 17.01. He retired in 1975. Nicholson died in hospital in Harrogate on November 4, 1985.

John Hampshire remembers: Nick was the most charismatic man in the side. He'd been to school in Dewsbury and played in the leagues to a decent standard. But when he was 18 he went off to Rhodesia, or Zimbabwe as it is today, to be a policeman.

He was there for six years but in the early Sixties, he decided to come back to have another go at cricket and try his hand with Yorkshire. I first played with him in the second team and right from the start, he was an absolutely top drawer fellow.

He was totally honest, a bit of a Jack the Lad, and the laughs he created! He was a very funny bloke.

It sometimes seemed there was nothing that Nick couldn't do or didn't know – or that's what he led us to believe, anyway! And one of his nicknames was The Book, as in The Book Of Knowledge.

One night we'd been out with one or two of the lads and I know for a fact that he didn't watch a minute's television. But the following day, when people were discussing what had been on the box the night before, Nick seemed to know more about it than anyone!

He didn't have a great action and people might have said he was a player of reasonably limited ability. But he moved the ball through the air and off the pitch at a fairly good pace.

And he bowled straight. He would have been a fabulous bowler today and he was a fabulous bowler then.

His heart was in Yorkshire and in Yorkshire cricket in particular. From his arrival in the dressing room until his death in 1985, we were always great pals.

Geoff Boycott, Nick and myself more or less started in the side together, although Boycott and I had played through from the Under-15s. But we all met up in the Second XI.

And during his time in Yorkshire's Championship sides, Nick was the only member of the team who didn't win an England cap. But for me, he was quite simply the best bowler never to play for England. Far worse bowlers won quite a few caps.

The closest he came was being selected for the MCC tour of South Africa in 1964-65 but he had a back problem and Yorkshire wouldn't let him go; they wanted him back 100 per cent for the 1965 season. That was the way Yorkshire ran the cricket in those days.

Nick was wholly Yorkshire, he didn't think of anything else. He started to have health problems later in his career after he damaged a leg in a benefit game at Ben Rhydding. He suffered with circulation problems from then on.

His death after he'd gone into hospital for a routine operation was a terrible shock to everyone. I broke down crying when I heard. We thought people as strong as Nick were immortal and when he went it was awful. His funeral at Ripon Cathedral was massive.

To die in hospital must have been awful for him. If Nick had to die, it should have been on the way in to bowl for Yorkshire.

1964

It was the year when Beatlemania took over the planet. Here, we'd known about the Fab Four for some time; now it was the turn of the United States and the rest of the world to tune into the Mersey Beat.

In April, John, Paul, George and Ringo occupied the top five slots in the Billboard 100, the US pop chart. Here, they had three number one hits and their first film, a Hard Day's Night, broke box office records.

World Without Love, a Lennon & McCartney song performed by Peter and Gordon, was top of the charts when Yorkshire began their defence of the County Championship against MCC at Lord's on April 29.

It was 14th in a sequence of 17 number one hits by UK artists, dating back to August, 1963, and it would not be until June 28 that the US finally hit back and Roy Orbison topped the charts with It's Over.

For Yorkshire cricket, it was over, too, as they failed to retain their Championship. However, unlike 1961 and 'The One That Got Away' to Hampshire, few had any complaints about a powerful Worcestershire side winning the title for the first time.

In fact, Yorkshire slipped down the table from first to fifth, although, like the new champions, they lost only three matches. However 14 of their 28 matches were drawn, including a sequence of seven successive draws between mid-May and mid-June.

It was not all gloom. 1964 was the year in which Jimmy Binks, widely acknowledged as the finest wicketkeeper in Yorkshire's history, won his only two Test caps on England's tour of India.

Those two caps were scant reward for Binks who, between his debut in June 1955 and his final game in September 1969, played in 412 successive Championship matches and missed just one of his county's 492 first-class games.

He was a pivotal figure throughout the Championship decade but nine years after his retirement in 1969, he left the country and went to live and work in the United States.

"In the mid-Seventies, Britain wasn't my sort of country any more," he says. "The unions seemed to be in control and there were strikes all the time. I had become a bit disillusioned.

"I'd been working for J H Fenner, a Hull-based company, since 1955, starting in the work study department. I think my father wrote to Sydney Hainsworth, the chairman at Fenner who was on the Yorkshire committee, asking if there might be an opportunity for me.

"Fenner's were a worldwide company and in fact, after I'd toured India with England in 1964, I stayed on and worked in their Calcutta office for a month.

"They were power transmission manufacturers, producing things like conveyor belts for coal mines, pulleys and gearboxes, and in 1978, I was the marketing manager in hydraulics, importing power units from the USA.

"One day I asked Herb Stone, who was the president and owner of Stone Hydraulics in the USA, if there might be any vacancies with his company in Europe, preferably Spain. Instead, he offered me a post in the American mid-West.

"We lived in Iowa for four years and moved to southern California four years later. I retired in 2005 by which time my daughters, Jane and Clare, were both living in San Francisco, three or four hundred miles away.

"So Jean and I decided to move north to Grass Valley near Sacramento to be closer to the girls. Jane now lives in Abu Dhabi and Clare in Singapore!

"We've been back to England a few times: I was over in 2006 for the inaugural meeting of the Yorkshire Players' Association and I was elected their first President. And we came over again early in 2009.

"It was wonderful to see some of the boys and remember the old days but I'm not really in touch with many of them on a regular basis.

David Pickles is a buddy and he's been over to see us, Bryan Stott keeps me up to date with news of the Players' Association and John Hampshire sends emails every now and then. But obviously I don't see much cricket over here!

"I will always have my memories, though."

Jimmy Binks.

Letters from America

James Graham Binks was born in Hull on October 5, 1935. A wicketkeeper, he made his Yorkshire debut in 1955 and was capped two years later. Binks played in 491 first-class matches for the county and 501 in all. He played in seven Championship sides and in two Gillette Cup Finals and when he retired at the end of the 1969 season had claimed 1044 victims for Yorkshire. He also appeared in 30 limited overs games. Binks played two Test matches against India in 1964 and was the third in a succession of six post-War first-choice Yorkshire wicketkeepers, whose name begins with the letter B: Brennan, Booth, Binks, Bairstow, Blakey and Brophy. Will the next in line also be a Bairstow?

Hebden Bridge, West Yorkshire, September 30, 2009. email.

Dear Jim,

Thanks for your time on the phone yesterday. As I explained, the book is the story of the Yorkshire side between 1959 and 1969, seen through the eyes of the most important people…the players. As you're unlikely to be in the UK in the foreseeable future, I'm sure we can put the piece together on the telephone and via email. Hope that will be OK.

Best wishes,

Andrew

Grass Valley, California, October 1, 2009. email.

Andrew.

It will be a pleasure. I'll try and answer anything you fire at me, although my memories are fairly dimmed these days…I can't understand why!

Best regards,

Jim

Hebden Bridge, December 10. email.

Dear Jim,

I realise Christmas is just around the corner but if you are OK for one telephone interview before December 25, that would be fine by me.

Best wishes,

Andrew

Grass Valley, December 10. email.

Andrew,

I should be OK, although Wednesday is always a bad one as that's when I hit a little white ball all over the place. Best time would be between 8 am and 10 am our time. A heads up before we talk would give me time to take my memory tablets.

Regards,

Jim

Hebden Bridge, December 17. email

Dear Jim,

Can we start by talking about how you became a wicketkeeper, your early career and your progress into the Yorkshire side?

Andrew

Grass Valley, December 18. email

Fine. Let's make it Monday, 9am my time.

Jim

Hebden Bridge, December 21. Telephone.

My father kept wicket for Hull GPO and, like father, like son, I followed his example. He was a very good keeper. He also gave me my first bat and that's something anyone who's ever played cricket will remember.

I was playing in East Park in Hull with one or two friends and spotted my father and mother walking over towards us. She was carrying the bat and when they gave it to me, I thought, "Wow, a cricket bat of my own!" It was a Len Hutton autograph, although I don't remember the manufacturer.

It was a big hit with my friends because it meant we could finally play cricket properly. We already had a ball, sticking a piece of wood into the grass as a wicket was no problem and we used whatever was available as an impromptu bat.

But now we had a proper bat as well, autographed by the great Len Hutton! I'd probably have been 11 at the time so obviously it never crossed my mind that I would be playing in the same Yorkshire side as Hutton eight years later

I suppose I just took to wicketkeeping naturally. I never really had any serious coaching apart from the advice my father gave me. And Charlie Flood, one of the best keepers in Hull CC's history, was always there to talk about this and that.

I learned about the correct stance, how to keep my fingers pointed either up or down but never in the direction of the ball – that way you break a finger if it hits in the wrong spot. And from there it just evolved.

I never really had heroes or idols in the professional game. Don Brennan, who was Yorkshire's wicketkeeper as I was developing my own game, was the nearest thing to that.

He was a superb wicketkeeper and I suppose I modelled myself on him to some extent. He was unobtrusive, went about his job without any fuss and he was excellent standing up to the wicket against quicker bowlers. I always rated a keeper on how well he could do that.

At school I was an opening batsman as well as a wicketkeeper, first at Maybury High School and then Riley High School, and I made it into the Hull CC fourth team while I was there.

I started playing for the Second XI when I was 16 but I couldn't see any way of making the first team because they already had Stuart Reed, who was a very good keeper and a fixture in the side.

The following winter, I attended the nets at Madley Street Baths in east Hull for coaching from Johnny Lawrence, the Somerset all-rounder who lived at Rothwell, near Leeds, and later set up his own coaching centre there.

My dad came with me and watched while I kept wicket in one of the nets. After a while, Johnny took my dad to one side and said he thought I looked as if I had some idea about keeping wicket.

Dad explained the situation with Stuart Reed at Hull and Johnny said he'd heard that J & S Rhodes, a side representing a woollen mill between Wakefield and Bradford, had a team in the Leeds League and were looking for a keeper.

Leeds was a long way from Hull in those days because there was no M62. But I agreed straight away to play for them the following year, by which time I'd also been to the Headingley nets a couple of times.

Every Saturday morning my father used to drive me to Paragon Station in Hull, where I caught the train to Leeds. When I arrived, Patrick Rhodes, the managing director of the company, would be waiting for me in his Allard sports car and he'd drive me to wherever the team were playing.

Then after the game, he'd take me back to the station, put me on an eastbound train and I'd be back home in Hull at around 9pm. He was great to me and it's one of my biggest regrets that I never really told him then or later in my career just how grateful I was.

Looking back, going to play in the West Riding was an absolutely vital part of my development. If I'd stayed in Hull I don't know whether I would have made it into the Yorkshire side – after all, there haven't been many first-class cricketers from East Yorkshire.

It's a vast area and the cricket is very widespread so it's harder for a young player to be noticed. Everything is much more focused in the West Riding, where there are so many leagues in a relatively small area.

As soon as a young player shows a bit of potential, word starts to get around. That certainly happened to me at J & S Rhodes. The Leeds League was a decent standard and pretty soon, umpires started asking me if I'd been to the Yorkshire nets.

That would never have happened in the East Riding but it was part and parcel of the game in West Yorkshire.

I played regularly for J & S Rhodes in 1952 and the following season I moved up into the Yorkshire League with Leeds CC, who played at Headingley. I was there for one and a half years and while I was playing for them, I made my first appearance for a Yorkshire side, against Hull University in a friendly match.

I made my Second XI debut in a Minor Counties Championship match against Durham at Bishop Auckland on July 8, 1953. Only 38.2 overs were possible on the first day and the remaining two days were washed out.

I played one more game that season and four times in 1954, the year I left Hull Technical College, where I had been studying mechanical engineering. I'd taken my first National Diploma while I was at college and then I studied for my Higher National Certificate at night school during my early days in the first team.

I actually took three of the tests for the certificate in the evening after I'd played for Yorkshire: at Middlesbrough, Cardiff and in London. I can't imagine that happening today.

As soon as I left college, I was drafted into the RAF and expected to be doing National Service for the next two years rather than pursuing my cricket career. Instead, I was discharged after ten days after my medical examination revealed I was suffering from Tuberculosis.

It felt like the end of the world. My father had already been diagnosed with TB in 1954 and surgeons had removed one of his lungs and half of the other. He ended up spending 18 months in rehabilitation.

I was lucky. They caught it early. I had to spend two months in bed at home and then three months in a rehabilitation centre.

And for several years, I had to take a new drug that had just been discovered called Picamycin. I had to take nine tablets a day and I was still doing so during the early days of my first team career.

I started playing regularly for the Second XI in 1955 when Roy Booth was the first-choice. I was only 19 and I didn't see any real prospect of replacing him at that stage.

Then, totally out of the blue when I was playing for the Seconds against Northumberland at Jesmond, I had a call telling me I'd been chosen for the first team in the Championship game against Nottinghamshire at Trent Bridge the following day, June 25, 1955.

I have to say the whole thing was handled very badly. Yorkshire had been playing at Northampton in their previous game and Roy was still with the side when I arrived in Nottingham on the Friday night.

So he was in the hotel when I appeared as the man who would be replacing him the following day. In fairness to Roy, he didn't show any animosity towards me although he must have been very upset at the way things had been handled.

And at the end of the season, he was released, moved to Worcestershire and never looked back. He played there until 1970, making over 450 first-class appearances and there was never any aggro on his part towards me. And I certainly didn't have an axe to grind. We always got on pretty well.

Roy was a very good wicketkeeper and a useful batsman but that side of the Fifties was not an easy place to be.

They weren't a team, they were a group of individuals and there was a certain amount of acidity among the players if anyone dropped a catch or made a mistake in the field. You found out pretty rapidly that some of your team-mates didn't think you were any good.

The main thing I recall about my debut was that we played on just about the best batting surface I ever saw. It was completely flat.

Ron Giles scored a career-best century for Notts, Len Hutton replied with 194 for Yorkshire and in their second innings, I claimed the first three of my 1071 first-class victims: J D Clay, Giles and C J Poole, all caught behind. I had to wait another two years before I was awarded my county cap.

I could have had absolutely no idea that my debut at Trent Bridge would be the first of 412 successive Championship games for Yorkshire right through to my final game against Middlesex at Harrogate in September, 1969.

Or that I would miss only one of our next 492 first-class matches, against Oxford University at the start of the 1964 season, when I was chosen to play for MCC against Surrey in what was seen in those days as a Test trial.

I suppose it was a pretty incredible record but I never thought so at the time. In fact, I always joke that the main reason I never missed a match was that if we didn't play, we weren't paid!

But that's not quite the whole story, even though it was inevitably a factor. The main thing was that I managed to stay fit enough to keep going, there were no major injuries.

Like a lot of my Yorkshire team-mates, I was prepared to play on with the odd niggling injury here and there, even on one occasion when I had a broken nose. And once when I broke a finger, I just taped it up and carried on.

I didn't have any special fitness routine or any kind of warm-up like they have today. If we practised before the start of a day's play, I was more likely to do a bit of batting.

Nor did I have any particular rituals that I went through before the start of play or during the game. I just padded up and got on with it. I can't even recall my first pair of wicketkeeping gloves.

Before a day's play, the most I would do with the gloves was have someone throw the ball at me, just to get the feel of it. I didn't go in for organised close catching with someone chucking the ball down at a batsman who deliberately edged it behind the wicket.

I thought that was contrived, not how it happened in the real thing. And to be honest, when we were playing Championship cricket six days a week, we didn't need a lot of practice.

But I suppose if I hadn't been a wicketkeeper I wouldn't have got anywhere near playing in so many successive matches. If a batsman had a bad trot or bowler stopped taking wickets, everybody started to notice and eventually he would be left out and sent back to the seconds to regain form.

But I always felt nobody really knew quite enough about wicketkeeping to spot whether I was playing well or not. I was the best judge of that and I certainly wasn't going to tell anybody if I was a bit below par!

Looking back, it must have been tough on up and coming wicketkeepers who were waiting for their chance. But I don't remember giving that much thought at the time. I was a professional and my only interest was making sure I was ready to play.

Strangely, though, there aren't too many of my 491 matches for the county that really stand out, which must seem odd because we won seven Championships and two Lord's finals.

Perhaps our game against Gloucestershire at Bristol in 1959, our first Championship year, has special memories. But for the wrong reasons!

We'd lost the previous game against Somerset at Bath and when we arrived in Bristol, Ronnie Burnet told us to go out and have a drink and forget all about the Somerset match.

We took him at his word, I'm afraid, and it's fair to say we weren't in prime condition as Gloucester racked up 294 for eight declared the following day. They then bowled us out for 35, on the Monday, although by then the effects of our heavy Friday night had worn off.

It was just a disastrous batting performance and when we followed on and lost seven wickets for 136 by close of play on the Monday, we knew we had absolutely no chance of saving the match. So we decided it was time Bob Platt bagged a pair.

Now Bob, as I've no doubt readers will already have heard from the man himself, took his batting very seriously and no one will ever be allowed to forget the 57 he scored against Derbyshire at Chesterfield earlier that season.

Nor was anyone left in any doubt that Bob had never been out for nought twice in the same match. So the night before the final day at Bristol we hatched a plot to change all that.

The following morning the later batsmen did everything in their power to run out Bob...but to no avail. A glance at the scorecard reveals all: R K Platt b Brown 4.

Another match that sticks in the memory more than most is our win over Somerset at Taunton in 1955, only my seventh appearance. Johnny Lawrence, the man who three years earlier had recommended me to J & S Rhodes, was in the Somerset side.

They made 288 in a first innings that occupied 119 overs, slow going in those days. And at the start of our first innings, Norman Yardley said, "Look, we've just got to go out there and hit out or get out. That's the only way we can possibly win the match."

We went for our shots and were bowled out for 157 in 50 overs. But the whole object of the exercise was to get Somerset back in as quickly as possible to give ourselves the best chance of bowling them out cheaply and winning the game. And we did.

We dismissed them for 152 second time around and then Brian Close and Vic Wilson scored centuries as we won by eight wickets. That attitude continued among virtually all our batsmen right through the Sixties.

Look at the averages of specialist batsmen like Bryan Stott, Ken Taylor, Brian Bolus, Doug Padgett, John Hampshire and Philip Sharpe and they may not look too impressive. But bare statistics fail to reveal the number of times those players went out, scored quick runs and were prepared to sacrifice themselves in a winning cause.

Hebden Bridge, January 4. email

A Happy New Year from the frozen wastes of West Yorkshire, Jim. Hope all's well with you. It was snowing when we spoke before Christmas and it's still snowing now!

Would it be OK to give you another call next week to talk about your Test career and the 50 in India in '64 that revealed hitherto hidden batting talents? Please let me know a day and time that would be best for you.

Andrew

Grass Valley, January 4. email

Andrew,

A Happy and Healthy New Year. If you can manage Thursday at 9am that would be fine. We've also had snow recently and couldn't get out for three days. And the frost has killed orange, lemon and avocado trees that we just put in this year. This must be the global warming they keep talking about!

Jim

Hebden Bridge, January 7. Telephone.

My first experience of international cricket wasn't a happy one. I was called up as a replacement for John Murray of Middlesex on the 1962-63 tour of India, Pakistan and Ceylon, as Sri Lanka was known in those days.

But I ended up only playing in two matches out of a possible ten between the start of December and the middle of February. Geoff Millman, the Notts keeper, played in all the rest.

For me the tour seemed to be one endless round of social functions and in the end, I told the management what I thought of it. Predictably, it didn't go down too well but I always had a habit of saying what I thought.

I was given another chance for the tour of India in 1963-64, when I was one of two wicketkeepers along with Jim Parks of Sussex. Mike Smith led a 14-man squad which also included Brian Bolus, John Edrich, Mickey Stewart, Ken Barrington, Phil Sharpe, Fred Titmus, John Mortimore, Don Wilson, Barry Knight, John Price, David Larter and Jeff Jones.

However it wasn't my wicketkeeping that made the headlines but my batting. I wasn't chosen for the first Test at Madras but when the morning of the second Test at Bombay dawned, I was one of only eleven fit players. And two of us were wicketkeepers.

Barrington had broken a finger and Edrich, Sharpe and Mortimore were all in hospital with a serious stomach bug. We'd visited them on the day before the game. Their absence left the batting line-up looking pretty thin, with only Bolus, Stewart, Smith and Parks as recognised batsmen.

Knight, an all-rounder who would normally have expected to bat at seven or eight, was at five, followed by Titmus, another all-rounder, me and the bowlers. Then at tea on the first day, Stewart joined the sick parade.

From the start of the tour, those of us who'd toured the sub-continent before had been telling anyone prepared to listen how tough it could be off the field and how the dreaded stomach bug could strike at any moment.

But Mickey was one of the new boys and as we'd been staying in decent hotels and eating the tinned food we'd taken with us, he didn't believe us. He used to say, "What's the problem? Everything seems fine to me."

Then he was struck down with the same bug that had put three of his team-mates in hospital and joined them within a couple of hours. But unlike Sharpe, Edrich and Mortimore, who returned to action soon afterwards, Mickey had to be sent home and we never saw him again.

He would have been opening with Brian Bolus so his departure created a major problem: how to fill the gap at the top of the order without weakening the batting lower down.

In the first innings, Mike Smith promoted himself. But that exposed the lower order and after India had made 300, we were bowled out for 233.

So after India had declared their second innings on 249 for seven, we were simply looking to save the game and decided to hold back two of the specialist batsmen, Smith and Parks. I was given the nod to open with Brian, my room-mate on the tour.

There were no heroics, it was simply a question of survival and waiting for the odd ball to hit. But we stuck it out, hung in there, reached our half centuries and eventually passed the century mark.

It wasn't pretty and before long the crowd started to boo because we were going so slowly. That didn't worry us at all. I was eventually out for 55, made in three and a half hours, Brian followed two runs later for 57 and we saved the game easily.

Before the third Test, reinforcements arrived in the shape of Colin Cowdrey, who hadn't played since breaking his wrist against West Indies at Lord's seven months earlier, and Peter Parfitt.

They slotted into the middle order but with Edrich and Sharpe still unavailable, I was retained as Brian's partner. We put on 40 in the first innings and 30 in the second and I scored 13 each time.

But by the time we moved on to Delhi for the fourth Test the following week, Edrich was fit again, Parks took over behind the wicket and my Test career was over. Little did I know, however, that my days as an opening batsman were not.

For in 1965, during a spell when Yorkshire were struggling to get a start, Closey asked me to open the innings against Middlesex at Scarborough in July. Batting with Phil Sharpe, I scored 35 in our only innings in that game and then four and 29 in the next match against Essex at Bradford.

But any thoughts I entertained of a new career at the top of the order were shattered when Herbert Sutcliffe, who was on the committee and knew a bit about opening the batting, gave Closey a rollocking on the lines of, "Why do you allow him to open the innings?" The experiment ended there and then.

If my batting had been a plus in India, though, my wicket-keeping was below standard throughout the tour. It's something I've never been able to fathom out.

Whether it was the different light, I don't know, but it wasn't until late in the tour that I really started to see the ball properly and by that time, it was too late. I had no axe to grind about only being chosen for two Tests because I simply didn't do well enough.

I suspected that my chance had gone because in the years between the retirement of Godfrey Evans in 1959 and the emergence of Alan Knott in 1967, there were a lot of good keepers around.

And as the England batting was not always brilliant, the selectors tended to go for a wicketkeeper-batsman, rather than a more specialist keeper like me.

Knott, of course, was an outstanding keeper who also developed into a Test-class batsman. So once he established himself, it was pretty obvious that no one else was really going to get a look-in for some time.

Not that I was a complete duffer with the bat, far from it. I scored just short of 7,000 first-class runs with 18 half-centuries but the Yorkshire batting line-up was so strong that opportunities to really build an innings were few and far between.

I managed to do so a few times and twice, each time at Lord's of all places, I fell tantalisingly close to a century, the first against MCC in the opening game of the 1963 season.

I went in as nightwatchman on the first evening and hung around the next day while another 224 were added for the loss of one wicket. I'd reached 88 when I was caught by wicketkeeper Laurie Johnson off Colin Milburn.

The second occasion was against Middlesex the following year. They made 279 for nine declared and we were in a bit of a hole when I joined Chris Balderstone with the score on 101 for six.

Chris and I put on 126 for the seventh wicket and after I'd added 33 with Don Wilson, I was joined by Fred Trueman with the total of 260 for eight. A hundred was definitely in my sights and I suspect Closey was waiting for me to reach three figures before declaring.

Instead, fate intervened in the form of F S Trueman and a run-out. I was on 95 when Fred played forward to a delivery from Titmus. It hit him on the pad and ran gently in the direction of mid-wicket. An easy single.

I called Fred for the run and set off, only to discover to my horror that when I approached the opposite end of the wicket, he was lost in a world of his own and hadn't moved an inch,

I cut my losses and set off back towards the other end and safety. I nearly made it; I was just a yard short when the wicket was broken.

To say I was brassed off would be the understatement of the decade and even the Middlesex players couldn't believe it. And I let fly at the old son of a gun with both barrels when he returned to the pavilion after scoring a half century of his own.

Hebden Bridge, January 10. email.

Dear Jim,

Thanks again for the other day. And can I give you another call next week to round things off with your thoughts about the Championship years? And while I appreciate you won't want to blow your own trumpet it would be interesting to hear your thoughts about your own role in the side.

Andrew

Grass Valley, January 11. email.

Andrew.

I have no problems about blowing my own trumpet...the only snag is that you said you needed the truth, more or less!

Jim

Hebden Bridge, January 12. Telephone.

After we'd won our first Championship at Hove in '59, a few of us stopped for a meal on the way up to Scarborough for our next match. Ronnie Burnet and three or four of the other guys were there, too.

During the meal, while we were talking in general about the season and what might happen in future, Ronnie asked us, "Should I retire?"

It wasn't an easy question straight after winning our first outright Championship for 13 years. But I replied, "To be honest, I think you should. But please only retire if Brian Close is going to be skipper."

That was no reflection on Vic Wilson, Burnet's eventual successor, who was a great guy and always did his very best for Yorkshire cricket. But I felt that Vic might be a throwback to the Fifties when the philosophy was based more on avoiding defeat than going for a win.

Close, on the other hand, would offer aggression and original thinking and would be looking to win the game all the time. As it happened, Vic was given the job and went on to win two Championships in his three years in charge before Closey took over in 1963 and won four more.

Inevitably people talk about the Wilson era and the Close era and about which side was the stronger. But I view the two eras as one team; I don't see a difference between Vic's side and Brian's.

Apart from one or two changes, there were basically the same players throughout the Sixties and eight of us featured in all seven Championship sides.

And right through the decade, the most significant factor in our success was the absolute team spirit of the players. We were a team and we played for the team and fringe players who came into the side when there were Test calls or injuries took the same stance.

They might easily have adopted a different attitude to press their claims of making the team on a regular basis. But they never did so. The team ethic was everything.

Some of my team-mates have talked about my role within the side, how I was one of four key figures along with Close, Illingworth and Trueman.

And yes, as the wicketkeeper, I felt I always had a role to play. I always seemed to be able to spot a weakness in a batsman and was able to suggest to Vic or Closey how we could exploit that.

Or, on the other hand, how we might combat a batsman's strengths with our field placing, how to make him think about what we were trying to do and plant doubts in his mind.

I was also in the best position to see how our bowlers were performing, if they were not really clicking or if they were tiring.

I could always tell when Fred was not quite firing – nobody can be 100 per cent all the time -- and would suggest to Brian or Vic that they should take him off, give him half an hour.

Having said that, Fred was the best quick bowler I have ever seen and it was a privilege to keep wicket to him.

We all know he was a matchwinner but I will remember also the times when he came on to bowl on an easy-paced surface when nothing much was happening. He would come running in hard and somehow drag some life out of it. On those occasions he was magnificent.

He sometimes needed a gee-up, however, and one of the ways I achieved that was to stand up to the wicket when he was bowling. It was like a red rag to a bull and it always worked, once to my distinct disadvantage.

I don't recall the opposition but Fred was going through the motions a bit so I decided it was time to stand up to the wicket. That would normally have guaranteed that the batsman received one around the ears next ball.

This time, however, Fred bowled a half volley instead, the batsman played forward and missed. I took the ball easily enough but it wasn't until a split second later that I spotted that he had dragged his foot an inch or two out of the crease.

By the time I reacted, his foot was back and the stumping chance had gone. Fred was not a happy man.

After Fred and Illy left the club in 1968 I became senior professional behind Closey and the idea of eventually succeeding Brian did go through my mind as we prepared for the new season.

And in 1969, when he was breaking down a bit more than in his early days, I led the side in nine matches. It went quite well.

By that stage, however, any suggestion that I might be the next captain was purely academic because I had already made up my mind to walk away from Yorkshire cricket, at the age of 33.

It all began at the Roses Match at Old Trafford in May. The match was seriously affected by the weather, with no play after lunch on Saturday and a complete wash-out on the Bank Holiday Monday.

After the game had petered out into a draw on the Tuesday evening, John Hampshire and I were having a drink with the Lancashire chairman Cyril Washbrook and two Yorkshire committee men, Reggie Haigh from Huddersfield and Gerry Shires from Halifax.

It was an informal chat and at one point, Washbrook was telling us about the gulf that had developed between the Lancashire committee and the players and how the committee had been unable to bridge it.

When Reggie claimed there was nothing like that at Headingley, I felt I had to put the record straight. I pointed out that as far as I was concerned, the gulf between players and committee at Yorkshire was a mile wide.

I thought nothing more about it until, about three weeks later, I was getting ready to play one morning at Headingley when I was called into the committee room.

The full cricket committee were sitting around the big table, with Brian Sellers in the chair. And I was dragged over the coals in no uncertain manner for making what I thought had been an informal remark about the gulf between committee and players.

I sat there thinking, "What the hell is going on here?" And I couldn't help also thinking that everything that was happening in that committee room only served to confirm how wide the gulf was.

If I'd had sufficient balls, I would have retired there and then and that was my instinctive reaction. But I had a wife and two daughters to look after.

My mind was made up, however, and on our tour to Bermuda at the end of the season, I told the rest of the lads that I was retiring and explained why. "So that's me out of here," I said.

No one believed me. "Don't be daft," they all said. "You'll be back next year." I wasn't.

When I called it a day in 1969, I was pretty sure I wouldn't play again and that's how it stayed for the next couple of years, while I was working as a marketing manager in Fenner's Hull office.

Lincolnshire was part of my territory, I knew several people who were involved with their Minor Counties team and eventually, I was asked if I might be interested in playing.

I have to admit I was starting to miss the game so I suggested to the people at Fenner's that it might help with my job if I played and they agreed.

I played in six matches in 1972 and two more in '73 and thoroughly enjoyed every minute. There were a few familiar faces on the Minor Counties circuit, like Ken Suttle, the former Sussex batsman, at Suffolk and my old Yorkshire team-mate Ken Taylor at Norfolk.

And we played three matches against Yorkshire Second XI, who were captained by Doug Padgett, by that time the county coach. Don Wilson also played in a couple of games and Phil Sharpe in one.

Then, two years after leaving Lincs, and possibly against my better judgement, I was tempted out of retirement for one last first-class match, for an International XI against Yorkshire at the Scarborough Festival in 1975. It was 20 years after I'd played my first game for Yorkshire.

Our side included current players like Viv Richards, Graham Gooch, Bishen Bedi and Mushtaq Mohammad and a handful of golden oldies like myself and Fred Titmus, the former England off-spinner. Closey was skipper.

All went well until late in the match. Titmus was bowling, the ball popped up, clipped the top of the batsman's pad and took off. It hit me in the mouth, knocking out three teeth. I remember seeing them lying there on the ground.

Closey picked them up, gave them back to me and when the necessary running repairs had been carried out, I put the teeth in a little cardboard box. I still have it today!

But I hadn't learned my lesson and the following year, I played two or three games for Hornsea, where I was living at the time. I kept wicket and it was just a bit of fun...or it was until I broke my nose when a ball popped off a length.

I went so see the doctor straight away and asked him, "What can I do?"

He replied, "To be honest, Jim, if it was my nose, I wouldn't bother." There was no answer to that, really.

1965

We were never alone with a Strand, said the cigarette advert. And Consulate? Cool as a Mountain Stream! Until August, 1965, that is, when cigarette advertising was banned from our television screens.

The year began sadly with the death in January of Sir Winston Churchill. In the same month, Sir Stanley Matthews played his final First Division game at the tender age of 50 years and five days.

Petrol cost five shillings a gallon, the equivalent of 5p a litre today, and a brand new E Type Jaguar set you back £1,867, exactly half the average house price.

In July, Great Train Robber Ronnie Biggs escaped from Wandsworth Jail less than two years after being sentenced to 30 years for his part in the so-called Crime of the Century.

And as Yorkshire opened their season against MCC at Lord's on April 28, the Beatles were on top of the charts once again, this time with Ticket to Ride.

Yorkshire's winning ticket was not in the County Championship, however. After suffering badly with the weather early in the season, they finished fourth, with Worcestershire claiming a second successive title.

Compensation for the White Rose came at Lord's on September 4 in the final of the Gillette Cup when, in what *Wisden* described as "a surprisingly one-sided match," they demolished Surrey by 175 runs.

Even more surprising were the circumstances of Yorkshire's defeat by Hampshire at Middlesbrough in May: they were dismissed for just 23 in their second innings, still the lowest score in the county's history.

Richard Hutton, playing his first full season after graduating from Cambridge University the previous year, has vivid memories of Yorkshire's first Championship defeat at Middlesbrough.

"It was a freak," recalls Hutton. "And apart from the general sense of amazement the main upshot of it all was that Bob England, the poor old Acklam Park groundsman, was sacked by the

Middlesbrough club.

"We thought that was very unfair because the pitch had been the same for both sides and we were level pegging on first innings, when we had high hopes of winning the match. Then it all went horribly wrong.

"In the first innings, I scored 22 out of our total of 121 and was second top scorer behind Fred Trueman. He hit 55, the highest score of the match. In the second innings, I was one of five players dismissed for nought. Don Wilson top-scored with seven.

"The ball swung around from the start, ideal conditions for Derek Shackleton, who took six for 64 in our first innings. He never really strayed at all; he bowled a perfect length and moved the ball just enough either way.

"If you played with a straight bat, the chances were that you would miss it or get an edge. And in fact it was Fred who showed that the horizontal bat was more effective.

"Shackleton's bounce was fairly predictable and Fred simply put his leg down the pitch and smeared him to the deep mid-wicket and long-on area. Our stand enabled Yorkshire to recover from 47 for seven to 113 for eight.

"On the first day, 22 wickets fell for 253 runs but it was close on first innings after we bowled them out for 125.

"Then in our second innings, it was Butch White, Shackleton's opening partner, who did the damage with six for 10 from ten overs. He did bowl exceptionally well because we had to play at virtually every delivery.

"But I can hardly remember anyone playing and missing. Everything caught the edge and every single catch was held – seven of the ten wickets to fall were catches behind the wicket.

"I don't recall the players being unduly fazed by it. Obviously there was a feeling of shame at having registered the lowest score in Yorkshire's history but two days later, we beat Leicestershire in the Gillette Cup and soon afterwards defeated the New Zealanders by an innings."

Richard Hutton.

The Graduate

Richard Anthony Hutton was born in Pudsey on September 6, 1942. The elder son of Sir Leonard Hutton, he made his Yorkshire debut in 1962, the year of his maiden first-class appearance for Cambridge University, and was capped in 1964. Between 1962 and 1974, he played in 208 first-class games for the county, scoring 4,986 runs, including four centuries, at an average of 20.18 and taking 468 wickets at 21.91. He also played in 105 one-day games and his figures of seven for 15 from 7.4 overs in a John Player Sunday League game against Worcestershire in 1969 remain the county's best analysis in the 40-over format. Hutton played in five Championship sides and two Gillette Cup Finals. He also made five appearances for England in 1971. He was editor of The Cricketer magazine from 1991 to 1998 and also served on the MCC Committee.

I played my first formal cricket at Wood Hall School at Linton near Wetherby, a small preparatory school with around 50 pupils. It closed in the 1960s and since then it has been, among other things, a Catholic Retreat and a hotel.

The school was very well appointed and the playing fields were excellent. I was very keen and played a lot of cricket there with a degree of success. For a prep school boy to reach double figures was quite a feat and I was able to do it fairly regularly.

I was awarded my school colours after scoring 17 against Malsis Hall, a prep school near Keighley. Some 25 years later, I returned there with Don Wilson to coach some of the boys.

After a while at Wood Hall, I started to score fifties, which really was pretty unusual. I'm sure the headmaster, who also owned the school, realised that because my name was Hutton, there might be some mileage in it for the school and there was quite a lot of Press interest.

I had my photograph taken once or twice and stories appeared in various newspapers. So from quite an early age, I was aware that there was some attention around me.

Looking back, I suppose that was bound to happen although later, when I was playing at Repton School, there was very little publicity. I have a feeling that the staff there were inclined to control things more tightly.

Obviously my father was away a lot when I was young. He was away on tour with England for six out of nine winters in the years after the Second World War and with a full schedule in the summer, I didn't see a lot of him.

In fact I didn't really get to know him until I was in my mid teens and his travels had finished. But of course I followed everything that he did through the newspapers and on the radio.

I had really started to take an interest in cricket when I was around five. I used to read Wisden in bed and knew the names and initials of all the cricketers.

In 1948, the year of Don Bradman's triumphal last tour, I remember being at the Headingley Test against Australia, although I don't recall which day. I don't think it was the last day when Australia scored 404 in five and three-quarter hours to win by seven wickets. But I certainly remember being there at some point.

I recall vividly England regaining the Ashes under my father in 1953, Coronation Year, and when he retained them in Australia in 1954-55, the photographers again arrived at the school en masse.

There was a picture taken of my younger brother, John, and I hoisted on to the shoulders of two of the bigger boys, surrounded by cheering children. It was a bit like having won the FA Cup.

To follow in my father's footsteps and play for Yorkshire and England was an ambition from an early age, although it would be fair to say that I didn't receive the total support of my parents.

Having been through it all himself, my father knew the pitfalls and I think he thought I was really taking on quite a lot if I was trying to follow him.

He knew there would be disappointments and I feel that to some extent he did try to steer me away from cricket rather than steer me into it. My mother probably took the same view but with a lesser degree of certainty.

Whether my father's unstinting support would have made any difference to my career or not, I don't know.

But with my own son Benjamin, I tried to be as helpful and as positive as possible when he was making his way up the ladder into the first-class game with Middlesex in the late 1990s. I tried not to be negative in any way.

I knew he would have to battle it out for himself, because that's what a young player always has to do.

But I wanted him to feel that I was always there in the background and he could turn to me if he wanted to talk or needed some advice. I didn't really discuss my cricket much with my father.

I went to Repton School in Derbyshire in 1956, when I was 13. I have great affection for the place, although I realise a lot of people don't feel that way about their *alma mater*. I felt very honoured when I was elected president of the Old Reptonian Society in 2009.

The staff there were very cricket-orientated. Several had played some first-class cricket and Eric Marsh, the professional, who had played 66 matches for Derbyshire in the 1940s and coached at the school for 30 years, was a great supporter.

My cricket developed a lot in that environment. It could not have been better and I played in three matches at Lord's, for the Rest against the Southern Schools in 1960 and for the Public Schools against the Combined Services in 1961 and '62.

Then, to have the chance to go up to Cambridge University, where I read economics at Christ's College, and play at Fenner's was also a very important influence.

Fenner's was renowned for its near-perfect pitches. Cyril Coote, the groundsman, had a set of covers that could envelop the entire square so the pitches were always excellent. In fact he was eventually told by the MCC to destroy those covers and instructed not to cover more than one pitch at a time.

Batting at Fenner's was a wonderful experience because you could hit the ball on the rise. And it was also a good discipline for bowlers because you had to be so accurate.

The contrast between that and the pitches on the county circuit, particularly in Yorkshire, required an awful lot of adjustment and it was very difficult for me when I started to play in 1962. In fact, I never fully came to terms with it, although I always felt I could cope well with demanding conditions.

To make matters more difficult, within Yorkshire we played on a vast range of grounds, where the conditions were very variable.

It's all very different now because everything is uniform: the pitches, the materials, pitch preparation. It is ordained that they shall be identical but in the Sixties there was an immense variety of playing conditions.

That made it a more testing game. And the need to cope with vastly differing conditions put far greater emphasis on technique, both in batting and bowling.

If you happened to bowl short on an uncovered pitch the ball would come off slowly and you would be pulled and cut all day. You had to bowl a full length because it was a much tighter game and you couldn't afford to concede runs.

My first experience of Yorkshire cricket came in 1961, when I played a couple of Second XI games after leaving Repton.

My parental home was not in the county by that stage because my mother and father had moved to Surrey. And I think I was only asked to play for Yorkshire because they were afraid I might be snapped up by another county.

In my first game, against Cumberland at the two-match Bridlington Festival in August, I opened the innings with Geoffrey Boycott. It was his seventh game for the Second XI.

We put on 70 for the first wicket and I was first out for 49. He made 156, we declared on 321 for five but didn't have enough time to bowl Cumberland out for a second time. John Hampshire and Don Wilson also played in the match.

Boycott and I opened the innings again against Northumberland in the second game but he was out for one in each innings and our opening partnerships mustered a combined total of 18 runs.

Then, after playing 16 matches for Cambridge the following year, I was called into the Yorkshire side to make my debut in the Roses Match against Lancashire at Old Trafford, starting on August 4, 1962.

I was 19, I'd scored 634 runs and taken 34 wickets for Cambridge and also played in the Varsity Match. But there was certainly a great deal of surprise when I was picked to play against Lancashire.

It was difficult for me and I'm sure it was equally difficult for the other players because they didn't think I should have been playing. I just suddenly appeared in their midst as a University student, the only change from the team that had beaten Kent in the previous game.

Quite honestly, my debut was a petrifying experience and the chap who gave me most encouragement was Fred Trueman. The others were clearly a bit uncertain about it all but Fred took me under his wing. On and off the field.

It was his benefit year and on the Sunday we were due to play in a match at Southport, staying overnight in the resort. Fred said he'd drive me over there after the close of play at Old Trafford. And he did...via Blackpool.

It's all a bit of a blur now – in fact, it was a bit of a blur at the time, too! But I can remember at one point being in the dressing room of a Blackpool theatre and meeting Michael Medwin, one of the stars of the television series, The Army Game.

There are no further details apart from a vague recollection that Blackpool was a hell of a detour and of not arriving in Southport until about two o'clock in the morning.

On the Monday, I repaid Fred for his kindness by dropping a catch off his bowling at deep Third Man. It was the first time in my life that I'd seen a ball spiral off the edge of the bat in that direction and I was so shocked that I dropped it.

At the end of the over, I was, to put it mildly, a bit apprehensive about what Fred's reaction might be. But he just walked over and said, "Don't worry, lad. You'll drop a hell of a lot more before you're finished."

Within the space of a few minutes, another catch went up. This time I was fielding at mid-off and Mel Ryan was the bowler. Brian Statham, one of the last two batsmen, skied one between mid-off and the vacant extra cover position so it was my catch.

But as I moved towards the ball, my foot went into one of the holes containing the attachment for the hosepipe, which was used to water the square. I stumbled and almost fell and how I recovered in time to make the catch I will never know.

However, to my enormous relief, I did, although I sensed there was definitely a hint of, "We thought there was another one going down there," amid the plaudits from my new team-mates as we returned to the dressing room.

The game was badly interfered with by the weather and ended

in a draw. And all in all, my debut had been a pretty nerve-racking experience.

However, in the next game against Sussex at Scarborough I scored some quite important runs in both innings and I think the other players gradually came to realise that I did have a bit of ability. Their suspicions about me dissipated quite soon.

Among supporters, however, expectations were always high. They came with the name, I suppose.

On the whole people were very decent to me, although I would become extremely disappointed with my own failures and frustrated if I didn't live up to expectations. I felt that quite keenly.

On good days, the expectations didn't matter but overall in my early career with Yorkshire there were more disappointing days than good ones. I found that difficult to cope with.

When I look back on my career, I only played the equivalent of seven full seasons with Yorkshire, even though I was in the side from 1962 to 1974.

I was at Cambridge for the first three years and only played a few matches. And then, when I left university, I was articled to Chalmers, Impey, a firm of accountants in London that has gone through several metamorphoses since my day.

I was an audit clerk and while the firm let me off to play in 1965, I hardly played at all in '66 and '67. The odd match but not on a regular basis because I wanted to get my articles out of the way as quickly as possible. So in those two years I really made no progress at all.

Thanks to my employers, however, I had been able to make myself available for a full season in 1965 and played in 20 Championship matches.

But even though I'd been awarded my county cap in 1964, I was very much aware that I was still learning my trade and when I look back at the averages for that 1965 season, I'm amazed to see that I took 58 wickets.

A closer inspection reveals that 30 of them came in the last six matches of the season when I claimed five wickets in an innings three times. The previous 20 matches had been nothing like as productive.

It was an unproductive Championship season for Yorkshire, too, moving up one place in the table to finish fourth, but that relatively modest performance was offset by our first victory in the Gillette Cup.

Thanks to their cavalier batting, Sussex had won the competition, which started in 1963, for the previous two years, although everyone had thought we would be strong because most of our cricketers had been raised on the limited overs game in the local leagues.

But it was not to be. We lost in the second round in each of the first two years, against Sussex in 1963 and Middlesex the following year. And we were a bit nonplussed about why we weren't doing so well.

I suspect that part of the problem might have been that we didn't really regard the competition very seriously. There was a feeling that, with luck, it would all go away after a year or two and we could get back to the proper stuff. How wrong we were!

However we finally got it together in 1965, beating Leicestershire, Somerset and Warwickshire en route to our first final against Surrey at Lord's.

There had been heavy rain in the build-up to the match and when we arrived on the Saturday morning, the place was awash. The pitch was wet and totally alien to anything you would see today.

We took an early lunch and somehow the groundstaff were able to have the pitch ready for a 12.30pm start. But in those days it was a 60-over game and I don't recall there being a plan about what would happen if we didn't finish it that day.

Unsurprisingly, Surrey put us in; then more surprisingly, they proceeded to bowl halfway down the pitch.

Boycott and Ken Taylor made slow going at first and it wasn't until Brian Close went in at the fall of Ken's wicket that we started to make some progress. I don't know the exact words Brian used to Boycott when he reached the crease but the message was simple: we need to bloody well get on with it. And they did.

Boycott flourished on a continuing diet of short-pitched stuff and finished up with a then competition record of 146. Brian scored 79, the innings that really got us going, and we finished up with 317 for four, another record. It seemed a ridiculously high score.

We then bowled them out for 142 in 40.4 overs, with Ray

Illingworth taking five wickets. He combined his usual off-spin with seamers; three of his wickets were clean bowled and two lbw as he did them with his little outswingers.

And before the evening was over the whole team and the trophy were on stage at the Victoria Palace Theatre, home of the Black & White Minstrels.

How that happened I don't know but Philip Sharpe and Don Wilson had close links with the Minstrels and we must have been invited to take the trophy along if we won.

I didn't play regularly again until 1968, the year Yorkshire collected a third successive Championship, the year Fred retired and the year Raymond moved to Leicestershire.

Up to then, the attack had revolved around those two so their departure meant that in 1969, I became one of the front-line bowlers. It was not one of our better years in the Championship. In fact, we finished 13th, Yorkshire's lowest position at the time.

But as in 1965, we provided supporters with the consolation of another trip to Lord's for the Gillette Cup final against Derbyshire. We won by 69 runs, although it did not go down as one of the more memorable finals.

However I do recall being on strike when Harold Rhodes bowled the final over of our innings. I took 12 off the over, all in twos and virtually all mishits that fell between the fielders. In those days we certainly weren't trained to run almost 300 yards in such a short space of time!

That year also marked the start of the John Player Sunday League, a 40-over competition inspired by the success of the televised Sunday afternoon games involving the International Cavaliers XI.

It would be fair to say that, as in the early days of the Gillette Cup, the Yorkshire players were not entirely in favour of the new competition, although it did enable me to make what might well be an indelible mark in the county record books by taking seven for 15 against Worcestershire at Headingley.

I can now reveal, though, that the whole thing was a bit of a fudge and I should not even have played!

I'd been dropped from the side for the game against the New Zealanders at Park Avenue, which started on the Saturday. Peter

Stringer replaced me and was to retain his place for the Sunday League game the following day.

On the Saturday morning, however, Doug Padgett phoned in to say he was ill so I was called in to play against the tourists as an opening batsman. I was not to bowl, Stringer was to do the bowling. I was a straight replacement for Doug. I opened with John Woodford, we put on over 100 and I scored 75.

On the Sunday, I was still filling in for Doug as a batsman and was not supposed to be bowling. I opened the innings and was out for three very early on.

The public address system had been left switched on by mistake after John Nash, the Yorkshire secretary, had given out the pre-match announcements.

And as I made my way back to the pavilion, the voice of John Bussey, Nash's assistant, boomed out over the PA system, "Well, we're off to another good start then, Mr Nash!"

We scored 157 for six and with Tony Nicholson, Chris Old, Peter Stringer, Don Wilson, Close and possibly Woodford available to bowl, I assumed that I had more or less completed my contribution to the day's events.

But after Nick had taken a couple of early wickets, I was brought on as second change.

It was a green top, the ball was going all over the place and I dismissed three batsmen, Tom Graveney, Ted Hemsley and Jim Yardley, very quickly and a fourth, Ron Headley, soon afterwards.

That prompted Brian to call a team meeting in the middle of the pitch as we awaited the arrival of the new batsmen.

It was thought by some of the players that the sponsors would award a cash prize at the end of the season for the best bowling figures in the competition. And with four wickets in the bag for virtually nothing I was clearly emerging as a strong contender.

So Brian came up with an idea. "Look," he said. "I'm going to take you off now and keep you back for nine, ten and jack. Then you can pick up the last three and you'll be in with a real chance of the prize." So I was withdrawn from the firing line.

The arrival of Norman Gifford at the crease at the fall of the seventh wicket, prompted Close to bring me back on and sure enough, I quickly picked up Doug Slade, Brian Brain and Bob

Carter.

Yet when play began, I was not even supposed to be bowling! The whole thing should never have happened.

There was still one final twist to the tale, however: the award for the best bowling figures proved to be a figment of our imagination, no such thing had ever existed! But my weekend performance was at least good enough to enable me to reclaim my place in the side.

At the end of the season there was the expectation that we could motor on in 1970 but we were unable to compensate for the departures of Fred and Ray Illingworth in 1968 and Jimmy Binks the following year.

And towards the end of that season, there were indications that Brian Sellers, the cricket chairman, was becoming increasingly dissatisfied with Close.'

Brian was incredibly loyal to his established players and fought tooth and nail for them in selection committee. But Sellers and his committee perceived this extreme loyalty as a reluctance to introduce younger players from the Second XI.

They operated in the belief that our system for developing young talent would always ensure a plentiful supply of reserves and up and coming players.

They were also very mindful that a lot of former Yorkshire youngsters were playing for other counties and concerned that so many Yorkshire players were leaking out of their regime.

They believed more encouragement should be given to promising younger players; Close preferred to rely on his tried and tested lieutenants.

There was also an incident in the captains' dressing room at Old Trafford in a Sunday League match after Lancashire had clinched the title for the second year in a row.

One of the Red Rose hierarchy gloated about it to Brian, who suddenly lost it and gave him an earful. The Yorkshire and Lancashire committees were as thick as thieves in those days so this was reported back to Sellers. It may have been the last straw.

There was great sadness among the players that Close had been axed and his sacking marked the end of an era. But in my opinion, the beginning of the end was not Close's dismissal. It was Illingworth's departure to Leicestershire in 1968.

For despite the very serious losses of Fred and Binks, the loss of Raymond was crucial. And it all came about in a ridiculous set of circumstances.

Raymond, using the example of his England team-mates at several other counties, wanted the security of a three-year contract, Sellers refused and told him that if he didn't like it, he could bloody well go. He went.

Yet in 1969, the year after Illingworth left, the Yorkshire players were, in fact, offered contracts, even though we hadn't actually pressed for them.

It seemed so absolutely ludicrous that we had lost our key player for that very reason a year earlier and I am convinced Raymond's departure was the catalyst for everything that followed.

The natural thing would have been for him to succeed Brian at some stage and had he stayed, he and Close could have sorted something out about the captaincy as time went by.

Instead, having shot themselves in the foot over Illingworth's departure, the committee chose Boycott as Close's successor in 1971. To my mind, he was totally unsuited to be captain of Yorkshire.

In the early Seventies the atmosphere changed so dramatically. Throughout the Sixties the attitude of a group of highly-talented players was that the team was always bigger than the individual.

Then suddenly that was reversed. It was sad, really sad, although at first, the change of captaincy did not have an adverse effect on my own form. From 1968 my game had been on a rising curve and in 1971, I played five Test Matches for England against Pakistan and India under Ray Illingworth's captaincy. I loved playing for England.

My initial ambition all those years earlier had been to play for Yorkshire. Then, having become established in the Yorkshire side, it was to play for England, in a line of succession from my father, who was at The Oval when I made my fifth and final appearance. He came into the England dressing room at one stage.

To achieve that goal was the pinnacle of my career and I was immensely proud. And to play for my country under Raymond also meant such a lot.

When I first turned up to play at Old Trafford in 1962, he would have been one of the people most surprised. He would have felt that my selection lacked a good deal of justification.

Yet if I look back, Raymond was the one player who probably helped me more than anyone else. He was always ready to offer guidance and talk to me about the game. Over the years, I took a lot of his ideas on board.

In all matches in 1971, I scored 1009 runs and took 80 wickets, statistically my most successful season.

However, the following year I couldn't regain my place in the England side and I think my performance and my commitment probably began to fade from then on. Playing for Yorkshire became increasingly unenjoyable under the new regime.

At the end of the 1974 season, it was time to go. Some of my contemporaries were beginning to move on and I no longer felt the camaraderie that had been such a great team attribute in the 1960s.

For in those days, Yorkshire was like no other county. Before making my debut in 1962, I'd appeared in a couple of matches for Surrey Seconds as well as playing for Cambridge, mainly against county sides.

And the contrast between Yorkshire cricket and cricket elsewhere was so stark, so different.

Yorkshire had a great following with 13,000 members and a large Press corps who came to all our matches. The grounds were more full than empty and the whole thing seemed to have so much more vitality than you would find at another county.

Yorkshire cricket was very conscious of its heritage and the players saw themselves as an extension of the great players and great teams of the past, going way, way back.

Fred had a fund of history and tales about the old timers that he used to keep us amused with and we took a lot of motivation from being an extension of that past, of being part of a long chain of great cricketing tradition.

Wilfred Rhodes was still alive and used to come to some of our matches. So did other illustrious former players and there was also a big involvement of former players in the club.

And compared with other counties there was a great unity of purpose about the Yorkshire team and the way we played. The requirements of the team were far more important than the individual.

We had a wonderful team spirit and everyone tried to be helpful towards one another. And as captain, Brian Close was a very important influence. He was totally involved and put most things before himself.

Whenever he worked himself up into a state or a tizzy, by no means an isolated event, he used to shout, "I'm doing it for Yorkshire! I'm doing it for Yorkshire!" Nothing else mattered.

I remember once when we were stuck trying to take a wicket, I was called upon by Brian and got a couple out. I was absolutely elated and desperate to carry on bowling.

Instead, he took me off immediately to put on Trueman or Illingworth. I was so disgusted that I refused to take my sweater from the umpire. I just ignored him and instead, gave the captain a fearful earful.

As my successor prepared to bowl, I was cursing Close with every swear-word in the book. But it all simply sailed over his head as if nothing had happened. So it eventually registered that I was on a loser and the best thing would be to disappear into the outfield.

There, I was left to conjecture on what I'd said to the captain of Yorkshire and what effect it would have on my long-term prospects. I remember thinking, "God, I'll never play again."

However, my tirade simply hadn't registered with Close and if anyone were to mention the incident to him today, he would have absolutely no recollection of it at all. All he was interested in was the greater good of the side and bugger any individual's aspirations.

And we were all Yorkshiremen, with the common bond that we were representing Yorkshire because we were born within the county boundaries. That made it special.

The unity of purpose manifested itself typically in the search for quick runs. Wickets were thrown away to enable the captain to make a declaration in sufficient time for us to bowl and field out the opposition.

And in Yorkshire the bowling was considered to be the important facet of the game – bowlers were always awarded their benefits before batsmen! They tended to be regarded as the poor relations.

At every pre-season lunch, Sellers would give a resume of the previous season when, more often than not, we'd won the Championship.

He would talk on the lines that the bowling had been very good, supported by superb fielding. And then, he would add, "But the batting, once again, has been woeful..." He was entitled to his opinion, of course.

The Sixties was a wonderful decade for Yorkshire cricket and all supporters will have their own impressions of it.

For me, as a player, it was a very special time, too. And I suppose that if I had to select one moment above all, it would be our victory over the Australians under Fred's captaincy in 1968.

As a bowler, Fred had lost a bit of edge by then but he captained the side in eight matches in mid-summer when Close was out of the side injured.

He enjoyed a wonderful run of success, culminating in that victory, by an innings and 69 runs, over the Australians at Bramall Lane. I think he probably regarded that as the greatest thing that had ever happened to him.

He was never prouder and neither were we. It was a wonderful moment. We hadn't just beaten the Australians, we'd beaten them by an innings!

And Fred's success as a captain prompted Close to call the team together in the dressing room at Park Avenue soon afterwards and inform us in no uncertain terms that he was still the official captain of Yorkshire.

Even so, I think Fred harboured a hope that he might move officially into the captaincy the following season. And I think there were moves behind the scenes, conversations between Fred and Sir William Worsley, the President at the time.

But nothing came of it. And when it became clear to Fred that it wasn't going to happen, he decided there was no point carrying on. It was a wonderful swansong, though, and an uplifting experience for us all.

For there was no other team quite like Yorkshire. Our team.

1966

On July 30, 1966, Bobby Moore raised aloft the Jules Rimet Trophy in front of 100,000 ecstatic fans at Wembley. England had beaten West Germany 4-2 after extra-time to win the World Cup for the first time.

Yet amid the scenes of jubilation that engulfed the nation on that Saturday, few remembered that only the intervention of Pickles, a black and white mongrel, enabled Moore to get his hands on the iconic trophy.

For on March 20, the World Cup was stolen from an exhibition at Westminster Central Hall in London and disappeared off the face of the earth.

Pickles, out for a walk with his owner David Corbett, quite literally struck gold a week later when he unearthed the cup from underneath a hedge in South Norwood, London.

As a reward, Pickles attended England's celebration banquet at the Royal Garden Hotel in Kensington and was invited to lick the plates clean.

Sadly, his hour of glory was short-lived. He collapsed and died the following year while pursuing a cat.

Pickles' *annus mirabilis* was also the year when the Star Trek sci-fi TV series was launched, when moves began for decimalisation of the British currency and when Barclays introduced the UK's first credit card.

And when Brian Close led his Yorkshire side into action in the first match of the season against MCC at Lord's, Dusty Springfield was on top of the charts with You Don't Have To Say You Love Me.

Oh but we did! Because when the dust settled six months later, Yorkshire had won the first of three successive County Championships and we loved them all.

None more so than Don Wilson, the ebullient left-arm spinner who claimed exactly 100 wickets in all first-class matches.

Wilson, nicknamed Mad Jack, was the court jester of the side, the antidote to some pretty hard-nosed cricketers, all of whom became heroes to a generation of Yorkshire supporters. Half a century later, none of them see it that way.

"Heroes?" asks Wilson in disbelief. "We weren't heroes. We were just a group of lads from all sorts of different backgrounds who were lucky enough to play cricket and win trophies for Yorkshire.

"I could just as easily have ended up as a joiner back home in Settle. Instead, I travelled the world playing and coaching cricket and was a member of one of the finest sides the game has seen.

"It was sad that things turned sour for me towards the end but to have played in the Yorkshire side of the late Fifties and right through the Sixties was pure pleasure."

DON WILSON.

MAD JACK

Donald Wilson was born in Settle on August 7, 1937. A left-arm spin bowler, he made his debut in 1957 and was capped in 1960. He played in 392 first-class matches for the county, taking 1,104 wickets at 20.49. He also appeared in 59 limited overs games. Wilson featured in seven Championship sides and two Gillette Cup Finals and won six England caps between 1964 and 1971. An outstanding mid-wicket fielder, Wilson, who also played badminton for Yorkshire, retired in 1974. Three years later he was appointed Head Coach to the MCC, a post he held for 13 years until his appointment as Sports Development Officer at Ampleforth College in North Yorkshire. He also coached in South Africa, where he played a significant role in the establishment of multi-racial cricket.

Settle is just a little market town in the Yorkshire Dales, best known as the starting point for the spectacular Settle to Carlisle railway line. They'd never had any cricketers playing for Yorkshire or anything like that until I came along.

And it was quite amazing how my cricket story began early in 1953. My father worked in the ambulance service and I'd just started as an apprentice joiner. I'd also played a few games for Settle in the Ribblesdale League.

One night my father woke me up and got me out of bed. It was snowing like hell and he'd had some sort of premonition that there was going to be an accident. All of a sudden, there was this great big bang.

The Thames Clyde Express was heading north through Settle and it hit a goods train going the other way. My father and I were first on the scene and it was a dreadful sight, people were killed.

I helped as best I could but it was very upsetting for a 15-year-old. Next day my father wouldn't let me go into work. He said, "You've got to calm down after the shock, just have a day off, a day in bed," which I did.

But when I turned up at work the day after, they'd sacked me because I'd had a day off without telling them.

My father told London Midland & Scottish, the rail company who ran the Thames Clyde Express, what had happened and they said they'd pay me a year's wages as compensation because of my part in the rescue.

It wasn't a lot of money, not much more than a few bob a week, but even so it meant I could spend the summer playing as much cricket as I wanted. So as well as playing for Settle on a Saturday, I played for anyone who'd have me, midweek, Friday nights and Sunday. I even went on a tour to the Isle of Man.

I was as keen as mustard and my dad used to manage to drive me around. Living in a little place like Settle, I could never have managed it without my parents' help.

The following April, Settle started the season with a friendly match against a Yorkshire XI, including the great Len Hutton.

All the townsfolk were talking about it and I didn't think I'd have a chance of playing because I was so young and older players would want the once-in-a-lifetime opportunity to play against Hutton.

Every week the club used to put the following week's teams in the newsagent's window and I'd ride round on my bike after work with my tools over the handlebars – I'd got another apprenticeship by this time – and have a look.

I read down the list for the Yorkshire game and sure enough, right at the bottom was my name, number 11. I was going to play against Yorkshire! At Marshfield, Settle's ground.

I don't know who won the toss but in those games, the amateurs always bowl first, don't they? So we took the field and then in walked the great Len Hutton. I couldn't believe I was on the same cricket pitch as the man who held the world Test record score of 364. He was an idol.

We had a marvellous opening bowler called Jack Buswell. He'd played for Northants and then come up to Settle to manage a paper mill or something like that. A big lad and a quick bowler.

At the other end was the local signal-box man, Harry Robertson. He bowled left arm over and after they'd each bowled a couple of overs, the captain threw the ball to me.

He said, "I want you to bowl at this end." I thought, "You must be joking!" I didn't realise the bowlers just wanted to switch ends.

So I marked out my run-up and ran in to bowl to Len Hutton. First ball, he just pushed it back to me, no run. I thought, "Crikey, you don't have to bowl any more in your life, lad. You've bowled a ball at Len Hutton and he hasn't hit it for four."

In fact he didn't score off me 'til the fifth ball when, being a typical youngster, I thought, "I bet he won't spot my quicker one." It was short, down the leg side and he hit it for four. I thought, "You daft fool, you could have had a maiden over there."

Anyway, sixth ball, I runs up, he plays forward, he must have played for a little bit of turn that wasn't there – I never was a big spinner of the ball -- and it went through between bat and pad and bowled him. I'd bowled the great Len Hutton!

I can't really remember what happened next; I vaguely recall leaping about for a while. But then, as I walked back to my fielding position, all I could see were all these hundreds of people packing their sandwiches in their tin boxes and putting the tops on their flasks.

They'd come to see Len Hutton bat and I'd absolutely ruined their day, hadn't I? Len and Mary Wilson, my father and mother, were the only happy people on the ground.

After the match we went to a pub called The Royal Oak, where we always used to meet after games, and Len came over to me. He said, "You enjoyed that, didn't you?"

I replied, "I'll never, ever forget that as long as I live, sir."

Then he said, "Have you ever been to the Yorkshire nets?"

"No."

"I'm going to see to that then."

I played a full season with Settle and then summer was over and winter came along. Snow on roofs, knocking skin off your thumb wi' t' hammer, a terrible time of year.

But sure enough, in the middle of January, this letter drops on the mat, signed by John Nash, the Yorkshire secretary. A brown envelope.

I was invited to attend the Yorkshire nets in April. They'd pay me £1 and my travel expenses. It added, "You have been recommended by Len Hutton." Well, that was the be all and end all for me.

Settle to Leeds is about 50 miles and when the great day dawned, I caught the very first bus to Skipton for the connection to Leeds. My bus left Settle at half past six, and when I arrived at Headingley at half past nine the gates weren't even open.

Anyway I eventually got into the ground and sat myself down with my little cricket bag. The first people to arrive were the coaches: Maurice Leyland, smart, wonderfully dressed, Bill Bowes, tall, wearing glasses, and Arthur Booth. Maurice coached the batsmen, Bill the fast bowlers and Arthur the spinners.

And there was this other chap, wearing a mac and a black flat cap. He had a silk scarf tied round his neck and he was shouting at some young kids who were there for coaching.

I thought, "My God, who's this fella? Whatever happens I must keep well away from him." Of course it was Arthur Mitchell, one of the great coaches of Yorkshire. But I hadn't a clue at that stage.

Anyway, me and a few other lads who'd been invited went into the dressing room and at around 1 o'clock, all these big cars started to arrive. Driven by people like Len Hutton, Brian Close, Fred Trueman, Willie Watson. My idols.

I'm just sat there wondering what to do next and would you believe Len Hutton comes over and says, "Stay with me, we know you'll be nervous." He was so nice, unbelievable.

Then in walked this Arthur Mitchell chap, still in his flat cap. He looked at Ken Taylor and said, "Put your pads on!" and then the same to Bryan Stott. Then he turned to Hutton. "Len, will you go with them?"

Next he looked straight at me and said, "Pad up!"

I said, "Pad up? I'm a bowler, I can't bat."

He replied, "Anybody who gets here at nine o'clock in the morning for a 2.30pm start deserves to bat first." Well I was completely shell-shocked, I could hardly strap my pads on.

I tried to think, "Don't worry, just make sure you're in that Maurice Leyland's net..." So I walked out to bat with Hutton, Stott and Taylor, they didn't have damn warm-ups in those days, and into my net.

And to my relief, there was Maurice Leyland at the other end. He said, "Eh dear lad, you're as white as a sheet. But you're only going to be here for ten or 15 minutes so you might as well try and enjoy yourself.

"Take a guard and just play as you normally would." That was the problem...I couldn't bloody bat!

I looked up and there was this big tall fellow, wrapping his fingers round the ball. Bob Appleyard. He'd got 200 wickets in 1951 and over 150 in 1954.

Then there was this chap twiddling the ball up in the air with his left hand. Johnny Wardle, another England bowler.

And finally, I spotted a fella marking out his run up further than I'd ever been on my holidays. Fred Trueman. So that wasn't a bad introduction to Yorkshire County Cricket Club, was it? Three of the greatest bowlers of all time.

You can imagine the first five minutes. I kept picking my off stump up and knocking it back in the ground. Then they found the target and I was knocking my middle stump back in.

I was in tears, absolute tears, beside myself. I thought well, that's the end of me. Then I saw Arthur Mitchell walking down the net. I thought I was going to get the biggest bollocking of all time.

He looked at me and said, "Young man, what do you do for a living?"

I said, "I'm an apprentice joiner, sir."

"Really. Well next time you come down to these nets, bring your bag o' tools and board this end up will you?"

All that mattered was that he'd said 'next time'. That was it, that meant everything. There were many 'next times' and Arthur and I became good friends. That's the story, that's how it all started.

In 1957, I played regularly for the Second XI under Ronnie Burnet. We were a marvellous young team and won the Minor

Counties Championship that year and again in 1958 when Ted Lester was skipper.

At that time, the first team had a star-studded side but didn't seem to ever win owt. There were fallings out and all sorts and in the end, in 1958, Ronnie's first season as captain, Johnny Wardle was fired.

I was playing with the second team at Darlington when it happened and I got this phone call telling me to go to Old Trafford to take his place against Lancashire in the Roses Match starting the following day.

The Roses Match? I remembered Len Hutton saying to me that I might play against Australia, West Indies, South Africa and the rest but the hardest game I'd ever play would be for Yorkshire against Lancashire.

I arrived at Old Trafford to be told I was Twelfth Man. But what a crowd! What an atmosphere! I knew then what Len had meant. Just to be there in the dressing room was incredible.

I'd played a few games for the first team before, a couple of them in the Championship, but after Wardle left I started to play regularly. In those days, we used to play home games at seven different grounds: Headingley, Bramall Lane in Sheffield, Bradford Park Avenue, Scarborough, Harrogate, Middlesbrough and Hull.

And they were all different, all a bit special in their own way. Nowadays Yorkshire only play at Headingley and Scarborough but I always thought that we were taking the game to all parts of the county. And we had a terrific following everywhere we went.

Yorkshire's next game after the Roses Match was against Essex at Middlesbrough. And I'll tell you what, you didn't need a damned ice bath after the game there with that wind coming off the North Sea. More like a pint and a pie and a warm.

The Essex opener was a chap called Dickie Dodds, a very religious man. When he batted, if God said, "Whack it all over t'place," that's what he used to do.

But I got him with the fifth ball of my first over, caught by Vic Wilson in the slips. A great way to celebrate my 21st birthday! So I have some happy memories of Middlesbrough.

But like I say, for me all the grounds we used to play at were special in their own way. Take Bramall Lane, for instance. The crowd loved Johnny Wardle and in 1960, we played Surrey there.

I didn't bowl that badly in their first innings and took a couple of wickets. But I couldn't help hearing spectators shouting, "Send for Johnny Wardle!" every time I went for four.

When we batted we lost a few early wickets and when Fred joined me we were 71 for six. We put on 68 for the seventh wicket and I finished up with 83, my highest score for Yorkshire. That was the last time I ever heard anyone say, "Send for Johnny Wardle!"

Harrogate will always be special for all of us because we won three Championships there, against Glamorgan in 1962, Kent in '66 and Gloucestershire in '67.

Against Glamorgan, I took ten wickets in the match, including six for 24 in the first innings, the best figures of my career at that time, and I took a hat-trick against Kent four years later.

And what about The Circle at Hull, where we clinched our final Championship in 1968, beating Surrey with five minutes to spare? One of the umpires was Albert Gaskell, who came from Northallerton. He was a right big fella was Albert and by God, he enjoyed his pints of ale!

Deep into the last session it didn't look like we were going to get them out until Younis Ahmed hit this ball off me and it caught Closey on his leg and split it, right up his shin.

Next ball hit him again only this time it rebounded to Jimmy Binks who dived and caught it. Closey wouldn't leave the field and soon his boots were red with blood.

I trapped Robin Jackman leg before almost straight away and when Arnold Long nicked Tony Nicholson to Jimmy Binks, the whole ground appealed.

And there was Albert Gaskell our 'neutral' umpire from Northallerton, leaping up in the air, putting his finger up and shouting, "That's out...and we've won the Championship!" Well, Surrey went absolutely berserk.

Of course not all the special places were in Yorkshire. What about Hove, where we won our first Championship under Ronnie in 1959? I scored my first Championship 50 in that match and took a few wickets as well.

By that stage my dad had bought me a van; it had three gears and sliding windows. I'd travelled down to Hove from our previous game at Worcester with Dickie Bird, who was Twelth Man, and Jack Birkenshaw but neither of them could drive.

So it was down to me to get us to Scarborough for our next game against MCC. We had a bit of a celebration at Hove and loaded up a few cases of champagne into the van before setting off.

As we were about to leave, Fred said to us, "Now lads, you won't be able to keep up with the rest of us but this is where we'll be stopping on the way up."

Well, Fred seemed to know every damn pub on the A1! When we arrived at our first port of call there were sandwiches all laid out for us. And drinks.

Then we set off again, stopping at Grantham, and it was the middle of the night before we reached our last halt near York. I said to Fred, "I haven't got any petrol."

He replied, "Don't worry, sunshine." It must have been half past one, two o'clock but we drove to a garage and Fred went to this little bungalow and rang the bell.

The garage owner peered through the window, saw who it was and then came out in his 'jamas. He opened the pumps up and filled up our cars -- and he wouldn't take any money.

He just kept saying it was marvellous to see us. "Fancy the Championship side coming here!"

When we got to Scarborough there were people lining the streets waiting for us, we couldn't believe it. It was like winning the FA Cup. And the following morning, when we took the field at North Marine Road, there was hardly a blade of grass in sight. My goodness what wonderful memories!

I got rid of the old van not long after and in the Sixties my regular travelling partner was Phil Sharpe. He used to say, "You do the driving, Wils, I'll do the navigating." He had an MGB, a green one, and we thought it was the bee's knees.

Mind you it had its drawbacks for me because when Sharpey took the roof off, my head stuck up above the windscreen and at the end of the journey my face was absolutely black. By, we had some laughs!

We became big mates. We both loved our music and before long we joined the Settle Operatic Society and did all the shows, Rose Marie, the Vagabond King and so on.

Philip was much more professional than me, though, and went on to join the York Opera. He also got involved with the Open Air Theatre at Scarborough. It used to be beautiful there, although it was bloody cold sometimes.

Scarborough was where I first saw the Black & White Minstrel Show at the Futurist Theatre. I loved it and got to know some of the cast and soon Sharpey and I were friends with quite a few of them.

Eventually we put together a routine based on their shows and the rest of the lads started to join in. We were like one of the old Glee Clubs where groups of men from a factory or whatever got together and formed a choir.

Sharpey was a wonderful pianist and could write music. But he was very finicky. He had this damn tuning fork and he used to go round telling us where we were getting it wrong.

A lot of the grounds we played at used to have marquees around the boundary, like they do at festivals, and after the game someone would invite the boys in for a drink.

And they'd always ask us to sing – marvellous! Most of the lads joined in at one time or another. Fred loved religious songs and if he was with us, it had to be the 23rd Psalm.

And what about Tony Nicholson? A wonderful bowler and what a character! His favourite was Sixteen Tons. He sang it beautifully, too.

Ken Taylor batted for Yorkshire, batted for England, played football for Huddersfield Town, could paint anything. Such talent! But not many people know that he could play the clarinet as well... Stranger on the Shore, the old Acker Bilk number.

We had some escapades! One year we were playing Gloucestershire at Bristol, staying in this marvellous hotel with a spiral staircase. And purely by chance we discovered that the acoustics in the main lounge were bloody wonderful.

So after a night out, Sharpey produced the tuning fork and we launched into our repertoire. Unfortunately, the guests didn't exactly appreciate our efforts and we got thrown out of the hotel.

Inevitably, Brian Sellars, the cricket chairman, heard about it and when we reported for our next home game, he called Fred into the office. He said: "Fred, I hear you've been thrown out of this hotel in Bristol..." and went on to read him the riot act.

But after being rollocked for about 20 minutes, Fred finally got a word in. "By God Brian," he said. "I must have a strong voice – I was playing for England at The Oval!"

I don't know whether the singing and the Glee Club made us a better side but it created a great bond between us all. And one of my lasting memories of that great team was how everybody wanted everybody else to do well.

We were all prepared to go the extra mile for one another and for Yorkshire...like I did against Worcester at New Road in June, 1961.

Early in the game, I broke my left thumb, a compound fracture. I took no further part until the final session when we were trying to save the match. Jimmy Binks was batting with Bob Platt and only me to come.

They hung around and when Binksy was out for 46, we still needed 36 to win with 25 minutes left. I was in plaster right up to my elbow but I said to Vic Wilson, "Right I'm off in to bat."

Vic said, "You're not. If you make that hand any worse, you might never play for Yorkshire again."

I said, "I don't care, I'm going."

Their attack was formidable: pace from Jack Flavell and Len Coldwell and spin from Norman Gifford; good bowling attack. Platty met me on the way out.

"I'll try to take most of the strike," he said. "You just block it out." He fancied his chances as a batter did Platty.

I was holding the bat with my top hand and straight away Norman Gifford dropped two in the perfect spot. I swept them both for four.

By the time Flavell took the new ball with five minutes left we still needed 21. But I'd decided we might win the match, never mind save it. I swung at his first ball and bang, it went for four. I hit two more fours and a two. We ended up taking 18 off the over with the help of four byes.

Platty took a single at the start of Coldwell's final over of the day and when I banged the fourth ball for four, we'd won with two balls to spare. I finished with 29 not out.

Jim Kilburn, the great Yorkshire Post cricket writer, was a very dour man and his reports were pretty straight up and down. But this time his match report stated, "Figures mark the facts but this was fancy beyond the fanciful and it began: Once upon a time...".

And I suppose it was a fairy story. Mind you, I didn't play for Yorkshire again that season.

On the field, people called me Mad Jack. If I got a wicket I used to jump in the air and think it was absolutely marvellous. And I adored fielding. It was made for me.

It's such a vital part of the game. One day you might be out first ball and then bowl absolute crap. So if you don't field well either, you really are a miserable soul.

Yet I was never a fielder until I joined that great side. I'd never thought about fielding, it was all bowling, bowling, bowling. But I soon realised there was so much more to cricket than being able to bat a bit and bowl a bit.

It didn't matter how long we were out there; even if I was feeling tired in the last few overs of the day, I knew the batters were tired, too. They were the times you got people out.

We had Ken Taylor at cover, one of the greatest cover fielders I ever saw, and me at mid-wicket. Very often if Fred was bowling we'd be the only two in front of the bat.

And Ken used to shout across at me, "They shall not pass."

That Yorkshire side used to put pressure on batsmen with our fielding and we became very proud of it. It was very important.

If you look at our scores over that period, we never made massive amounts of runs. But we were always prepared to gamble on the bowlers and fielders finishing the job.

Fielding was just part of my enthusiasm for cricket, for life. I always loved foreign travel and early in my career I was lucky enough to tour New Zealand with the MCC A team in 1960-61 and then in 1963-64, I went to India with the full England side. That's where I scored the only hundred of my entire life.

I'm sure India is entirely different now and the modern players don't go through anything like the kind of experiences we had. Most of the lads were ill at one time or another and, of course, we weren't allowed to drink.

The only way we could get round that was to have our passports stamped: alcoholic. That allowed us one bottle of beer a day and one bottle of whisky a month – Haig Black and White, the one with the picture of the little dogs on the label.

Something like 100 cases of booze were unloaded at the port in Bombay which were then supposed to be shipped on to us at the Brabourne Stadium. The lorry carrying it all had an army escort – but even so by the time it arrived there were only about 20 cases left!

I adored India and I knew all about the possible health problems because I'd had a chat with Hugo Yarnold, the umpire who had been Worcestershire's wicketkeeper just after the War. He'd been to India, too.

He said, "Always remember to clean your teeth in whisky and soda every morning. Every morning without fail. And then drink a tiny spoonful of tap water. After a month, make that a tablespoon."

I did exactly as he said and, do you know, I never missed a match. Everyone else was eating egg and chips all the time but they were still laid low at some stage. Not me.

I followed Hugo's advice and then ate the local food. What's the point of going to India if you're not going to experience how the locals live and see all the wonderful sights like the Taj Mahal and the Golden Temple? How lucky could I be!

My century came at Hyderabad against South Zone, batting with Ken Barrington. Ken was my sort of cricketer and my sort of man. He had a very dry cockney sense of humour.

Before the match started we were told space was a bit cramped in the dressing room so we could only take a few bits of kit. I just took a couple of pairs of flannels, a couple of shirts, socks and so on.

Anyway towards the end of the first day, Mike Smith, our skipper, asked me to go in as night watchman. So I borrowed a bat, pads, gloves, box and stayed until the close, by which time I'd scored 20 or 30. Then I carried on next day, still using borrowed kit.

As I was night watchman I played a few shots and by the time we had a drinks interval, I'd made around 80, not a million miles away from my maiden century.

When the drinks trolley arrived there was a note for Barrington. It was from Gubby Allen, president of MCC, telling Ken to order me to get out because the spectators had come here to watch proper batsmen, not a tailender.

Kenny borrowed a pen from the trolley lad and wrote "Bollocks!" on the bottom of the note. I carried on as if nothing had happened, reached my hundred and at that stage, Kenny asked, "What's Fred Trueman's highest score?"

"104," I replied.

"Well make 105 and then get out. Then for the rest of your life you'll be able to say to Fred, 'What's your highest score then?'"

I was eventually out for 112. And whether Kenny's note had any long-term effect on my England career, I don't know. But I didn't play again until 1970!

Many years later, when I was Head Coach at Lord's, I asked Gubby Allen if he really thought I'd written that note. And he admitted he had.

I didn't tour with England again until I went to Australia with Raymond Illingworth's side that regained the Ashes in 1970-71.

I knew from the outset that I was understudy to Derek Underwood, a phenomenal left-arm spin bowler, and I wasn't going to play in any of the Tests unless he was injured.

Bob Taylor, the reserve wicketkeeper behind Alan Knott was in the same boat and even though I played one Test in New Zealand at the end of the tour, I was little more than a net bowler.

And believe me, it's very difficult to maintain any kind of form and rhythm if you aren't playing much competitive cricket out in the middle.

Early in the tour, I received a message to say that Brian Close had been sacked by Yorkshire, Geoff Boycott was the new captain and I was to be vice-captain. And I knew from that moment that life would never be the same again for me at Yorkshire.

Geoff and I were totally different people. He was a fabulous player and a single-minded perfectionist; I was a bit of a partygoer and a showman. But we were equal in our worth to the Yorkshire side.

When I got back from Australia I couldn't bowl at all. I was in such a state that at one stage, I even forgot how many steps I took in my run-up. Geoff couldn't accept how I was having problems.

From the start there were players who didn't want to play under Boycott and players who were happy to be there. As vice-captain, I was the man in the middle, trying to keep both sides happy.

It all came to a head in 1974, the worst year of my career. I was trying to see both sides of the coin, to listen to both the pro-Boycott and the anti-Boycott players and it was a very traumatic period. It cost me my first marriage.

Eventually I said to Brian Sellers, "You either get rid of Boycott or you get rid of me." The cricket committee met soon afterwards and I left.

Sellers later told me the voting was six-six and he had made the casting vote. A few years later, when the club was in turmoil, I went to see Sellers, who was very ill in hospital. He said, "Don, I buggered Yorkshire cricket up, not you."

By the time I left Yorkshire I was already heavily involved in coaching. In fact, I could write a whole book about my coaching, never mind a chapter!

How I started at Marist Brothers, a Catholic School in Johannesburg, how I became Senior Coach at the Wanderers Club, home of the Transvaal State side, how I helped to set up the Multi Racial Sport programme in South Africa, how I became the MCC Head Coach at Lord's in 1977 and how I ended my career as Sports Development Officer at another Catholic school, Ampleforth, in North Yorkshire. And I'm not even a Catholic!

Helping to get multi racial sport off the ground in South Africa was a bit special, though, it really was.

In 1971, the apartheid system was still in place and as a result, South Africa was banned from international sport.

I had a meeting with Jack Cheetham, a former South Africa captain and president of the Transvaal Cricket Board, and Ali Bacher, also a former national skipper who later became the country's cricket supremo.

Bacher said, "Don, we'll never get back into international cricket if we don't bring the Asians and the Africans into our game." And he asked me to help set up Multi Racial Sport.

It was a big challenge. Next winter, I took a group of players out there, including my old mate Dickie Bird, Peter Stringer, the former Yorkshire fast bowler, and Ashley Harvey-Walker from Derbyshire.

We used to go into the townships – white people didn't go into townships then – and we took along a load of stumps, pads and bats supplied by the Castle Brewery.

On our first visit nobody turned up to start with and Birdie was on edge. He kept saying, "They're not coming, let's go home."

I said, "Hang on, we're in a township now, time doesn't mean a thing." Then I looked up and they were coming from everywhere, hundreds of them. Dickie said: "Wils, I'm off, I think it's another Zulu uprising."

That first time there were about a hundred to a team. We didn't have enough gear and had to play with just one stump. But we created fun for them, got them all wanting to play.

Over the years we went to Port Elizabeth, Cape Town and Pretoria as well as Jo'burg and in 1975, I was asked to take a multi-racial side to Uganda. Phil Carrick, who later skippered Yorkshire, was with me that year.

But with Idi Amin's brutal regime running the country it would have been far too dangerous. So instead we headed for Bulawayo in Rhodesia, or Zimbabwe as it is today.

When we arrived in Bulawayo, we were ushered towards the bus that had been hired to ferry us around. Problem: there was no driver. And who was the only person with an international driving licence? Me. Jack of all trades, never mind Mad Jack!

On the first evening, I called them all together and said, "Remember you are representing the coloured people of Africa, not the white people. You are the trailblazers.

"And we're here as a team so we'll all sit down and have dinner together so we get to know each other properly."

We sat at this great long table and I remember Phil asking some of the lads if they'd ever had a prawn cocktail. They'd never even heard of it but when it arrived, they tucked in. Then we had steak and chips.

They went off to bed soon afterwards, leaving me and Carrick to have a couple more drinks.

Next morning we set off down the corridor for breakfast, nursing a bit of a hangover, and as we walked along, all the bedroom doors opened behind us and the lads followed in our footsteps.

And when we sat down to eat, we were faced by 28 prawn cocktails that the boys had ordered. For breakfast! We screamed with laughter. What a way to start!

We had a pretty useful quick bowler, Samuel Nontshinga, and

after his first five or six overs in our opening match, I said, "Well bowled lad, great. Have a rest."

Phil took over and after looking round the field before his first over, he shouted, "Wils, we've only got 10 players on the field." Our fast bowler was missing.

We found him fast asleep on a bench across the boundary. I said, "What the hell's going on? When I said have a rest ...I didn't mean a sleep!"

My last trip to South Africa was in 1976, for the second season of a two-year stint as manager of Eastern Province in the national competitions.

Just before Christmas, I received a letter from Jack Bailey, the secretary of MCC, asking me if I'd be interested in becoming Head Coach of the new indoor school at Lord's.

I had an interview when I returned to England the following spring and started my new job when the school opened in November. Another phase of my life had begun.

I've never been back to South Africa. And people say I'm a fool, that I should go out there one more time and meet all my old pals, see how the work I helped to start has come to fruition.

Maybe. But the real satisfaction for me is to switch on the telly, see coloured cricketers in the South Africa side and know that I've played my part. Another wonderful memory.

And I still live on those memories. I look around at the pictures on the walls of my living room and I see the players, the friendships, the way of life, the people I met through playing and coaching.

What could have been better? Yes, I've been a very, very lucky man.

Fred Trueman.
February 1931 – July 2006

Frederick Sewards Trueman was born in Stainton, South Yorkshire, on February 6, 1931. One of the finest fast bowlers the game has seen, he made his Yorkshire debut in 1949 and was capped in 1951. He played in 459 first-class matches for the county, taking 1,745 wickets at 17.12. In all first-class cricket, he took 2,304 wickets at 18.29. He played in seven outright Championship sides and was a member of the team who shared the title with Middlesex in 1949. He also played in two Gillette Cup finals. Trueman made 67 appearances for England between 1952 and 1965 and in 1964, he became the first player to take 300 Test wickets. In all he claimed 307 wickets at 21.57. Following his retirement in 1968, Trueman became a sports journalist and was a member of the Test Match Special team for 25 years. He served on the Yorkshire committee and in 2009 was inducted into the ICC Cricket Hall of Fame. He died on July 1, 2006.

Don Wilson remembers: Fred was a genius, simple as that. In my book, the finest fast bowler the game has seen. People have no real idea of how good he was and he was as strong as a lion.

Yet the true wonder of Fred wasn't his bowling, it was his character. He was quite the funniest man I ever met in my life. Everybody who played with or against Fred could tell a few stories about him.

We once played against Worcester when they had people like Tom Graveney and Don Kenyon at the top of the order. Fred didn't reckon much to Kenyon -- I think he thought he'd nicked it once and hadn't walked. We always walked in my day.

The match was pretty even late on the second day and the new ball had been due for 15 or 20 overs. But we'd kept whittling them out with the spinners and Closey wouldn't let Fred have it.

He was absolutely livid but Closey stuck to his guns and by the close of play we'd got seven of them out. Fred hadn't bowled since just before lunch and at the close, he was not a happy chap. He sat in the dressing room – I can see him now – with his head in his hands.

Eventually Closey said, "Fred, I know tha's been sulking all afternoon and evening but I want you down here in t'morning early and loosened up 'cos I'm going to take t'new ball first thing.

"Worcester have got the three of the worst batters in the country at nine, ten, jack and I want you to bowl 'em out."

And Fred took his head from his hands and said, "Down here early? I'm going to sleep here all night with t'new ball in my hand!"

And sure enough, he bowled 'em out next morning.

Off the field, he had this tough image but deep down, he was an old softie. If you were in trouble, he'd be the first to offer a helping hand.

His last Championship match was against Surrey at The Circle in 1968, when we won our seventh and last title.

It went right down to the wire and when the new ball was due with a handful of overs to go, Closey threw the ball to Fred.

I remember this wag in the crowd shouting out, "Come on Fred, Yorkshire expects!" But for once, he just couldn't do it. He tried everything but he was jiggered.

A week or so later we played our last match of the season against MCC at the Scarborough Festival.

By that time, most people knew he was going to retire and when he walked back to the pavilion after his last innings, the brass band played "Wish me luck as you wave me goodbye," the old Josef Locke song.

And believe me, when Fred walked into the dressing room the tears were rolling down his cheeks.

1967

They don't make 'em like Donald Campbell any more: the archetypal British hero who broke eight world water and land speed records and was, at one stage, the only man to hold both records in the same calendar year.

Barely had we returned to business as usual after the Christmas and New Year festivities, however, than Campbell was gone, killed when Bluebird K7, travelling at over 300mph, cartwheeled out of control during a record attempt on Lake Coniston. It remains one of the decade's more chilling pieces of footage.

For better or worse, January also saw the foundation of Milton Keynes New Town – could anybody have dreamed then that one day it would inherit a Football League team from Wimbledon, of all places?

And in September, Queen Mary, the three-funnelled icon of Cunard Line and the golden age of transatlantic crossings, sailed to New York for the last time.

Yorkshire's season opened against MCC at Lord's on April 29, three weeks after Sandie Shaw had won the Eurovision Song Contest with Puppet on a String, by now number one in the charts.

Their 157-run victory provided a curtain-raiser to a campaign in which Yorkshire would win their second successive Championship. And during a season when Brian Close would be away leading England in six Tests against India and Pakistan, with Raymond Illingworth by his side, a new name burst on to the White Rose scene: Geoff Cope.

In Illingworth's absence, the bespectacled Leeds-born off-spinner seized his opportunity and in nine appearances, claimed 32 wickets at 12.78 to head Yorkshire's bowling averages. A glittering future beckoned.

Then it all started to turn sour. His action came under official scrutiny in 1968 and suspension followed four years later. "The worst part was never knowing exactly what I was doing wrong," recalls Cope.

"I was never no-balled throughout my career. All it needed was for a captain and/or an umpire to report doubts about my action and a TCCB 'committee' would hire a film crew to come and have a look.

"They'd record me bowling from several angles and report back to the 'committee'. I never really had any idea who was on the 'committee' who sat in judgement.

"There was never any discussion; I was never given an opportunity to ask exactly what they thought I was doing wrong. The 'committee' made its decision and walked away."

Cope, his action re-built by Yorkshire's legendary left-arm spinner Johnny Wardle, returned in 1973 and was selected for England's tour of Pakistan in 1977-78. And if England skipper Mike Brearley, unsure about whether or not he'd taken a clean catch at slip, had not recalled Pakistan batsman Iqbal Qasim, Cope would have become only the eighth Englishman to take a Test Match hat-trick.

At the age of 37, he was diagnosed with Retinitis Pigmentosa, a hereditary eye disease. He was registered blind in 2002, although he is still able watch his cricket and remains a familiar figure at Headingley.

Kemp, his Labrador-Retriever, is never far from his side and it is testimony to Cope's enduring determination that in three years he has raised around £100,000 for the charity, Guide Dogs For The Blind.

Geoff Cope.

Living the Dream

Geoffrey Alan Cope was born in Burmantofts, Leeds, on February 23, 1947. An off-spin bowler, he was capped in 1970. Cope played in 230 first-class matches and 36 limited overs games between 1966 and 1980, taking 630 first-class wickets at an average of 24.80. He also featured in 28 limited overs games. Cope played in two Championship sides and made three appearances for England on the 1977-78 tour of Pakistan, claiming eight wickets at 34.62. He later served on the Yorkshire committee and in 2002 became a member of the new four-man Board of Directors. He was closely involved in the formation of the Yorkshire Players' Association in 2005.

I learned my cricket at Manston Junior School in Cross Gates, an east Leeds suburb. The head teacher was Ernest Smelt. He was an old-school head, the sort who, within a fortnight of the school year starting, would know every pupil by his or her Christian name.

There were 500 of us at Manston. I was always Geoffrey. He insisted that my Mum had christened me Geoffrey, therefore I would be called Geoffrey. People had no business cutting names short.

It was a happy school with a lot of teachers who'd been there for a number of years, including Mr Smelt and Ken Fletcher, who looked after the sports teams. Four times a week, we'd meet at the school gate and in the winter we'd run to the park, half a mile away down a ginnel and up a footpath, and play football until it was dark.

Afterwards Mr Fletcher took us all home individually. We were never left to walk home in the dark. In the summer we'd go on to the park and play cricket until six o'clock. From the start, he and Mr Smelt encouraged me to bowl my off-spinners.

When I was ten and playing for the Under-11s, we had a bit of a special weekend. All the Leeds schools played one another for the Sheldon Trophy, which was an absolutely huge pot; so big we put our wicketkeeper in it for a bath!

We'd reached the semi-final and were due to play against Headingley Junior School the week before school finished for the summer. But it was rained off so we ended up having to play the semi-final the following Friday, the day before we finished school, at the Leeds Police ground at Gledhow.

We bowled them out for 74 and knocked them off for five. I managed to score 36 not out, batting at three, and took five wickets. For the final against Upper Wortley the following day, we were without four players, including our two opening bowlers and an opening bat. They'd all gone off on holiday.

Mr Fletcher came up to me before the game and said, "You'll be opening the bowling."

"Does that mean I'll have to bowl quick?"

"No, I just want you to bowl your off-spinners as usual. You'll be all right." So I opened the bowling and finished up with figures of 16.1-4-26-10. They made 54, we replied with 55 for five and I scored an unbeaten 36. They didn't have a Man of the Match in those days but I think I might have been in with a chance!

My mum, Marjorie, was at the match, sitting in a deck chair, doing her knitting. She always turned me out immaculately with creases in the trousers and so on. Both my dad, Tim, and Mr Smelt had tears running down their cheeks afterwards and we all dashed over to Mum. My dad said, "Do you realise what t'lad's done?"

Clearly, she didn't. "No, what's he done?"

"He's taken all ten wickets!"

And Mum simply replied, "Well, what about number eleven?" The Yorkshire Evening Post headline read Cope (10) takes all 10 to see Manston to victory. And the report added that "perhaps Yorkshire may be interested in this young man in a few years' time."

Even then, that was the dream...in fact it had been since the age of seven when I used to dash back to the park in the summer after tea. I was always Fred Trueman. I lost count of the number of sandals I wore out because of Fred.

When we went back to school in September, Mr Smelt brought me out at assembly. He presented me with the ball, which had been mounted on a little plinth. I still have it today.

Once, when I was off sick from school, my godmother came round to look after me. She brought me a copy of Happy Go Johnny, the autobiography of Johnny Wardle. She arrived just before lunch and I gave it back to her at teatime, finished. Fred Trueman in the park, Johnny Wardle in my sickbed. Little did I know the part those two would one day play in my life.

Ernest Smelt gave me my first taste of senior cricket when I was 11. He'd once played for Durham in the Minor Counties but by the time I went to school he was playing for Leeds Zingari, a club he'd formed with Jack Walkington, the old Hunslet and Great Britain Rugby League full-back, and a chap called Norman England.

They didn't have a ground and just played friendly cricket. But when the Dales Council lost a club five weeks into a season, they agreed to fulfil the fixtures. Over 50 years later they still had a team in the Dales Council and still didn't have a ground!

During the summer holiday between leaving Manston and going to Temple Moor Grammar School, I saw Mr Smelt walking up the drive at home. When Mum opened the door, he said, "Mrs Cope I wonder if you'd allow Geoffrey to come and play cricket with us."

"But I thought the school had finished with cricket now."

"Oh, it has. But this is with my men's team."

"But he's only a lad."

"Mrs Cope, I've looked after him since he was four and will continue to do so." And in fairness to him, he did. It wasn't until three years later that I discovered players used to go for a drink after the match. He talked me through all aspects of the game and even though I was only 11, he put me on to bowl.

Norman England was the wicketkeeper and before each over, he'd take off his glove and produce a packet of Polo mints. He'd say, "Come on, Geoff, if you really make it spin you can have one of these."

I used to rip my fingers off trying to make it turn enough for a Polo! It was his way of making a boy part and parcel of a men's team and that's where I started to learn what the game was all about.

Their first team played in the Yorkshire Council so I had a few seasons with them before, at around 14 or 15, I started playing boys' cricket for Leeds CC, who played in the Yorkshire League. Thanks to an intervention by a chap by the name of Herbert Sutcliffe, who I was told could bat a bit.

Dad and I went into his shop off Briggate in Leeds to buy a bat and he asked where I played my cricket. I told him and he replied, "Do you play any junior cricket?" I said no.

So he went on, "Well you go up to Headingley next Wednesday. Mr McConniff will be waiting for you." Gerry McConniff was there as promised and I started playing for the juniors, then the Seconds and finally the first team.

I always stayed in touch with Mr Smelt and Ken Fletcher and sometimes I'd pop and see Ken in September and ask who he'd got for the football season.

He'd say, "You see that tall lad. He can catch the ball so he can be my goalkeeper. That big lad can be centre-half and that one over there can run a bit so he'll be centre-forward. I don't know what else I've got." But he always used to turn out a good side.

In the late Seventies, the Yorkshire Evening Post and Rothmans ran an award scheme called Service to Youth and I nominated Mr Fletcher. In 25 years, Manston had won the cup and league double for football and cricket 17 times. There was only one year when they didn't win anything.

We held a presentation evening for him in the Manston Hotel near the school and traced as many of his old pupils as possible. They came from all over the country.

I went to see Mr Smelt just a week before he died. He looked up as I walked into the room and said, "Come and sit down, Geoffrey." I sat on his bed. He said, "We've had some good times, haven't we?"

I replied, "I've probably had better times because of what you gave to me so early."

And he said, "Well, we're only there to try and help. And I hope I've been able to." They were wonderful words and yes, he had helped tremendously.

Soon after Mr Fletcher's 90th birthday, we took him to Headingley for a day. He was in his wheelchair and he absolutely loved every minute.

He was with his son and daughter and I told them that because of all the hours their dad had put in with me in Manston Park, Headingley had become my park. He died soon afterwards.

But if Manston Junior School had provided a perfect grounding for my sporting ambitions – I fancied my chances at centre-half in those days, too, and played for Leeds City Boys – it was a different story when I moved to Temple Moor Grammar School, three miles away in Halton.

At first, we played football and rugby union in the winter and combined cricket with athletics in the summer. Then, when I was 14, the headmaster, David Breese, announced that Temple Moor would become a 'rugger only' school. I played fly-half but my heart was never in it.

And when I had to do athletics as well as cricket, it was a complete disaster for me. I was on my way by that stage, I'd already played for the City Boys and age group cricket for Yorkshire, the North and England. I had my goals and I felt that if I couldn't concentrate on cricket, it might never happen for me.

Even so, two of us from Temple Moor, David Bradbury and myself, were chosen for the England Schools cricket trials down at Hastings.

Two from the same school was almost unheard of and on the last day of term, we turned up wearing our England Schools' Cricket Association blazers. We ended up in front of the head for not wearing school uniform.

Every county bar one had a representative looking at the young talent on show at Hastings; Yorkshire were the odd ones out. Perhaps the expenses were too high.

And after going back the following year, I came home knowing that nine counties were interested in signing me. I could have joined the Lord's groundstaff as well.

My only disappointment was that Yorkshire had not been there and, it seemed to me, weren't interested. It hurt. I was ready to take one of the opportunities on offer but Mum put her foot down.

She insisted that I got a job before I even thought about playing cricket for a living. She said, "If your cricket is successful, fine. If not, you'll have something to fall back on."

I wasn't happy about it and we argued. At 15 years of age, I just saw it as Mum trying to stop me doing something I'd always wanted to do. But looking back, it was the best advice I was ever given.

I went into the paper trade, gained my qualifications and in the end, I worked in that line for the next 38 years; first in the winters while I was playing cricket and then full-time after I retired.

The penny finally dropped with Yorkshire when several counties wrote asking for clearance for me to join them. Instead of agreeing to let me go, they decided they'd better have a look and I was invited to the winter nets at the old indoor school at Headingley. My first encounter with Arthur 'Ticker' Mitchell, the Yorkshire coach.

It was always freezing in the winter shed and when we arrived, Ticker would be wearing two Yorkshire sweaters under his county blazer. He'd have a white cravat round his neck and his Yorkshire cap on his head. He used a walking stick.

The young players had to hang around at the back of the net for ages before we had a chance and we'd stuff our hands into our pockets to try and stop them going numb before we had to bowl.

Every now and then Arthur would walk along in front of us, spot a lad with his hands in his pockets and give him a crack across the knuckles with his walking stick. "Lad," he'd say, "Tha's had long enough to find thi 'ankie." We got the message.

I'd been going there for a while when dad took me to one side and said, "Now then, how are you doing?"

"I don't think I'm going to make it, Dad."

"Why?"

"Well every time I go, Ticker Mitchell is on my back straight away, even if I'm not in his net. He shouts all the time. I can't be doing it right if he keeps on at me like that."

Soon afterwards we went to a function where Tony Nicholson, the Yorkshire fast bowler, was speaking. Dad happened to mention that I was going to the winter nets and that Ticker had been giving me a hard time. Nick replied, "Good."

My dad said, "What do you mean?"

"Just tell Geoff to have a look round and see how many players Ticker shouts at. Make a note of the ones he doesn't speak to and see if they're around the following week.

"If he makes his mind up that there's something there, he won't let you go. If he doesn't think you're at the right level, he keeps quiet." That eased it a bit for me...except I started to panic if Ticker wasn't shouting at me! I was growing up in a hard school.

I started playing for the Second XI in 1965. I played four games and took 15 wickets. Only Ken Taylor finished above me in the averages and he only bowled 4.4 overs! Chris Old, Barrie Leadbeater and Peter Stringer were just starting out as well, although there were a lot of people who just played the odd game and moved on.

I played regularly at the start of 1966 and then on June 13, I received a telegram from the Yorkshire secretary, John Nash. It simply said: "Report Bradford tomorrow. Nash." So two days later, I turned up at Park Avenue to make my Yorkshire debut against Hampshire.

I arrived at half past nine, much earlier than anyone else, and picked a corner of the dressing room where I thought I'd be out of the way. I got changed, went out on to the ground and saw straight away that the pitch was totally different from anything I'd ever seen there.

For a league game, there was always a bit of green but this was a white, concrete strip. Over the years I discovered that it was never as hard as Headingley but it was the whiteness of it that struck me.

There were one or two people around like Ron Healey, the groundsman, and on my way back to the pavilion I met Phil Brown, the sports journalist from the Evening Post for the first time.

He was known to some people as the man with white eyeballs... he also covered Leeds United and in his view, they never, ever did anything wrong. If they lost 7-0 they'd still been magnificent.

He asked where I was from and where I was employed. I told him I was in the paper trade and worked for Wiggins Teape, a Leeds firm of paper manufacturers and merchants. "Oh yes, I know them very well," he replied.

That night's EP reported that Geoff Cope worked for a well-known Leeds tea firm! That went down exceptionally well with my employers.

After chatting to Phil I climbed the steps up from the pitch to the pavilion and then up towards the dressing rooms. I started to panic as I approached the last five yards between the top of the stairs and the dressing room.

This time I could hear voices on the other side of the door and I remember thinking that perhaps I should have been going in there with an autograph book. I went in with my head down and a few voices chimed up straight away.

"Hey up, he's here..."

"Come on in, lad..."

"Well done, son..."

Then I looked under the big table in the centre of the room and saw my suit, the one my dad had pressed that morning, and the shirt he'd ironed – sadly my mum died before I made my Yorkshire debut – that I'd hung on the peg in the corner.

From that same corner, a voice boomed, "Are them thine, lad?"

"Yes, they are, Mr Trueman."

"Well, tha' sees that peg in t'corner. It's been my peg for t'last ten year and if tha' thinks I'm changing it for thee, tha's another think coming. Tha can borrow Illy's...for this match."

I was horrified. I started to pick my things up from the floor and Phil Sharpe said, "Come on, Geoff, put your stuff over there." I turned round and there was Fred.

He put his arms round me. "Lad," he said. "I hope this is t'start of a long journey. There's nowt better. And don't worry, thi Uncle Fred'll look after thee." I sort of buckled at the knees because Fred, above all, was the person I wanted to say that to me. And to Fred's credit, he was a massive player for me throughout my career.

I was still recovering from my initial encounter with the Great Man when Brian Close took me to one side. "I know you can bowl, I know you can bat a bit but can you field?"

I muttered that I could. I was despatched to fine leg and fairly early on, a ball was turned round the corner towards me off one of the quicks. My arms felt like lead, my legs were even worse and here was this ball bouncing towards me.

I just thought, "Whatever you do, don't miss it, don't miss it!" I gave it the long barrier, collected the ball and the throw landed right back in Jimmy Binks' gloves at the top of the bails. I just thought, "Thank goodness."

At the end of the over, Closey came storming over. "Did you enjoy that?"

"I'm glad I got it back all right."

"Well, if you'd picked it up and thrown it in straight away, you'd have saved one." And he stormed off again. Like I said, a hard school.

In those days, the captain was often called off the field late in the day to discuss selection for the next few games with the committee.

During Hampshire's second innings, Closey left the field and while he was off, Fred said, "Right lad, come and have a bowl." I'd completed my first five overs in Championship cricket, nought for 19 with two maidens, when Closey returned.

"Who put you on?" he asked. Then, pointing in the direction of fine leg, he said, "Get back down there." And that was it, thank you very much. My first and only game of 1966.

But just being in the dressing room had been an eye opening experience because virtually all the players were past, present or future international cricketers. And there were specialists in all areas.

Could any side have fielded a better opening attack than Fred and Tony Nicholson? Was there a better spinning combination than Ray Illingworth and Don Wilson? Was there a better slip fielder in the world than Sharpey? Where would you find better cover and mid-wicket fielders than Ken Taylor and Wilson?

And I haven't said anything yet about the man behind the stumps, Jimmy Binks. He was so good that we never really knew he was there. We rarely saw him diving around because his anticipation was uncanny.

His nickname was Byes -- because he hardly ever gave one away – and quite simply, he was the best I ever saw by a long way. And that includes people like Alan Knott and Bob Taylor; great keepers but not as good as Binksy.

Binks, Illingworth, Trueman and Close were four players from the very top tier of professional cricket and giants in the Yorkshire dressing room. By 1970, they had all left the club and the backbone of the side went with them. It was like breaking the spine of a rhino.

In 1967, when Illy played six games for England, I made nine appearances for Yorkshire and finished second in the first-class averages with 40 wickets at 13.8.

Between June 7 and June 27, I played in four Championship matches, against Somerset, Glamorgan, Northants and Surrey, and took 23 wickets for 229 runs, including my first Championship wicket against Somerset at Bath. Appropriately enough, it was their opener, Roy Virgin, stumped Binksy.

Bill Alley was my second victim, thanks to a remarkable catch by Ken Taylor. Alley swept and Taylor, stationed at deep square leg, raced round the boundary and caught the ball low down at deep mid wicket. Alley said, "Against any other fielder in English cricket that would have been four runs. And I had to pick him out!"

That night I was having a wander round Bath and was passing a hotel when a window opened and an Australian voice boomed, "Come on in, lad. Come and sit with Uncle Bill!" It was Alley.

I left the hotel two hours later and a lot wiser. It was a special era when senior players like Bill were great company and just happy to talk to young cricketers about the game.

From Bath, we moved on to Swansea and my first encounter with Glamorgan and their great off-spinner, Don Shepherd. He was a true artist with the ball and a lovely man. With people like Shep,

A watchful eye. Binks and Close in the Headingley nets. (YP)

Benefit Year. The fixture list for Binks' 1967 Benefit matches. (Ron Deaton)

Back home. Binks and Don Wilson at a Yorkshire Players' Association meeting, 2009. (YPA)

The 1965 side pictured at Bradford Park Avenue.

The Cup that cheers. Close holds aloft the Gillette Cup for the first time after victory over Surrey at Lord's in 1965. Joining in the celebrations are (from left) Don Wilson, Padgett, Hampshire, Taylor, Illingworth, Trueman, Hutton, Binks, Sharpe and Boycott.

Runs in the family. Richard Hutton takes the field with his father, Sir Leonard, for a charity match. (YP)

Three wise men. Hutton with Sir William Worsley (centre), the Yorkshire president, and cricket chairman Brian Sellers. (YP)

Master class. Hutton and Don Wilson during a coaching session for pupils at Malsis Hall School, Keighley.

Yorkshire at The Oval, 1966. Back row (from left) Fast bowler John Waring, Sharpe, Binks, Don Wilson, Hutton, Hampshire, Padgett, Boycott. Front Illingworth, Close, Trueman, Taylor.

Treading the boards. Don Wilson (centre) and Sharpe (seated right) during rehearsals for the Settle Amateur Operatic Society's production of the Vagabond King in 1963. (Daily Mail)

The Wilson Years. A telegram from team-mate Dickie Bird marks the first of Don Wilson's three hat-tricks for Yorkshire in 1959...

...and after a coaching career in South Africa and as Head Coach to the MCC at Lord's, Don returned home as Sports Development Officer at Ampleforth College in North Yorkshire in 1990. (YP)

Hat trick. A night out at the Pigeon Pie, Sherburn, near Scarborough. Trueman hams it up with Don Wilson and his first wife Jill.

Back row: Left to right: G. A. Cope. P. G. Sharpe. A. C. Nicholson P. Stringer. J. Waring. J. H. Hampshire. G. Boycott.
Front row: Left to right: D. E. V. Padgett. J. G. Binks. F. S. Trueman. D. B. Close. R. Illingworth. K. Taylor. D. Wilson.

The Yorkshire squad pictured during pre-season training at Headingley, 1967.

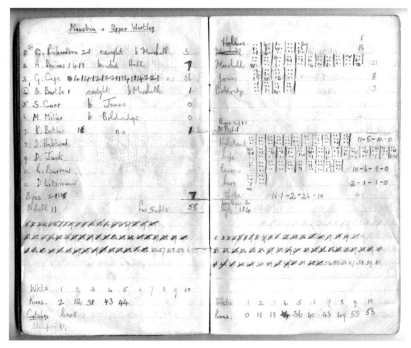

Ten out of ten! The scorebook showing ten-year-old Cope's all-ten for Manston Junior School against Upper Wortley.

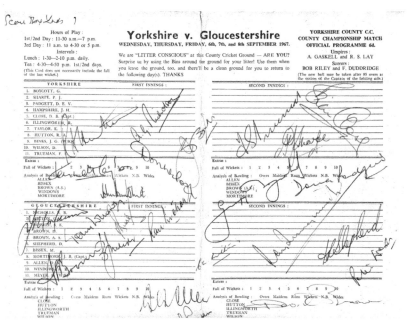

Thanks! A signed scorecard, donated to the scoreboard staff, from Yorkshire's Championship clincher against Gloucestershire at Harrogate in 1967. (Ron Deaton)

A safe pair of hands. Pre-season catching practice for a youthful Cope at Headingley. (YP)

Guest stars. The retired Johnny Wardle and Trueman going out to bat during Yorkshire's tour of Bermuda in 1969.

The end of an era. Yorkshire's 1968 Championship side. Back row (from left) Hampshire, Nicholson, Hutton, Wilson, Padgett, Sharpe. Front Binks, Trueman, Close, Illingworth, Taylor.

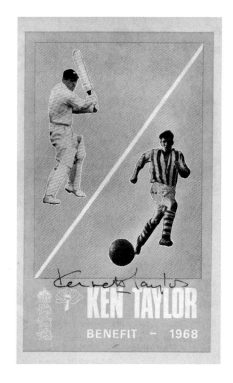

Double life. Taylor's 1968 Benefit brochure displays his all-round sporting prowess.

Winter's tale. Taylor (front row centre) and his football team-mates
from Stile Common School, Huddersfield. (Huddersfield Examiner)

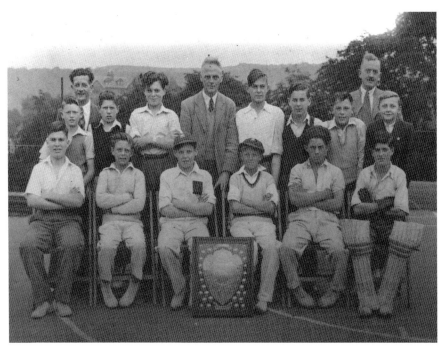

Summer game. Taylor (front row, third from left) and the Stile
Common cricket team. Wally Heap, an inspirational head, is extreme
right back row and Colin Garthwaite, an early cricket mentor,
extreme left. (Huddersfield Examiner)

Taylor-made. The artist's eye view of (clockwise from top left)
Trueman, Bird, Illingworth and Close.

Yorkshire, now without Illingworth, Trueman and Taylor, in 1969. Back row (from left) Balderstone, Hampshire, Nicholson, Hutton, Chris Old, Boycott, Cope. Front Sharpe, Binks, Close, Padgett, Don Wilson.

Wedding bells. Sharpe and his wife Susan on their wedding day in 1970. The guests include (from left) Nicholson, Boycott, Hampshire, Close and Padgett. (YP)

Eye on the ball.
Slip catching
must be a doddle
after this! (YP)

Eyes front. Sharpe on his
way to the middle. (YP)

In a good cause! Adverts from
former colleagues Ryan and
Platt in Sharpe's 1971 Benefit
brochure. (Ron Deaton)

Final fling. The match programme for Yorkshire's Gillette Cup victory over Derbyshire in 1969. (Brian Sanderson)

White Rose giants. Close and Trueman take a breather in the nets. (YP)

Front runners. Close and Illingworth with Derek Ibbotson (right), the Huddersfield athlete who broke the world mile record in 1957. (YP)

Next in line. Close with Geoffrey Boycott, who succeeded him as captain in 1971. (YP)

David Evans, Tony Lewis, Majid Khan and Jim Pressdee around, I always enjoyed playing against the Welshmen.

Fred was captain when we played Northants at Bramall Lane. That year Closey was captain of England and played in all six Tests against India and Pakistan. He missed 15 of our 28 matches.

With Illy also playing regularly it was down to Fred to lead a side that included several younger players like myself. We won a second successive Championship and I don't think Fred was ever really given the credit he deserved.

Against Northants, we fielded first and I didn't bowl a ball in the morning session. When we came off for lunch I put my nosebag on and was zooming off for lunch when Fred shouted, "Get yourself back 'ere and sit down."

"What's up?"

"You're going to bowl this lot out this afternoon."

"But it's seaming."

"That's Bramall Lane early doors but there's a bit in it for you if you bowl right in your 'ead. You'll be all right this afternoon. You'll bowl 'em out."

The omens weren't promising. Colin Milburn was 60-odd not out at lunch and Roger Prideaux 24 and they were 101 for none. Fred said, "Now then, tell me how you're going to bowl at Ollie Milburn."

I thought, I just want my lunch! Instead, I recalled Ernest Smelt's advice and said, "Off stump, off and middle."

"Rubbish."

"Middle."

"Tha's not even thinking abaht it."

I thought of Mr Smelt's philosophy of 'If they miss, you'll hit,' and couldn't work out what Fred was getting at. After five minutes' getting nowhere I said, "Fred, I'm going to be honest with you." And I told him what Mr Smelt had said.

"Well," he replied. "That's good advice, lad. But this time we're dealing with an individual. Ollie's a one-off."

"Right, Fred. Can I say to you that I just don't know."

"You can, lad, 'cos tha's being honest wi' me. Nah then, listen. Tha's gonna bowl in at his legs."

"If I do that and he misses it, I'll miss leg stump."

"Aye."

"So...why?"

"Because he can't bring t'bat round his belly to bray thee. If I just let you bowl at him like you want, we haven't enough balls on t'ground to let t'game continue past tea.

"So you've got to stop 'im playing 'is shots. All you have to do is concentrate and bowl the line I've tell'd thee. All the time. I'll sort t'field. Tha'll be reight."

The rest of the lads were digging into their steak and kidney pie by this stage; I was sat looking at a sandwich. Fred said, "You're not sure are you?"

"I'm not, Fred."

"Don't worry, your Uncle Fred's wi' thee."

We went out after lunch and I remember looking at Milburn's massive frame and wondering... But Fred never left me and said, "Right, come on. You can start at t'Pavilion End."

He set his field with a man out at cowshot corner and said, "Right, you're OK. There's nobody 'ere, just you and me. Nobody else, just you and me." And he wandered off to short leg with that familiar bow-legged walk.

So I bowled three deliveries as per his plan and each time, he called back, "Well bowled, Sunshine, well bowled." Then after the third, he called, "Just a minute, hold on, Sunshine."

And he moved cowshot corner half a yard, no more. "We're reight now, carry on." I got away with a maiden.

After the second ball of the next over, he was at it again. "Just a minute, Sunshine." Then he shouted to the fielder at cowshot corner, "Tha's moved. Go back half a yard."

It was all done to unsettle Milburn, to let him know we were thinking hard about how to combat him. I bowled two maidens. Then, after the second ball of the third over, he called, "Go round t'wicket, Sunshine." I stopped.

"Fred, can I have a word?"

"Certainly." He walked down the wicket and put his arm round my shoulders. "What's up Sunshine?"

"I can't bowl round the wicket at him."

"Don't worry, I'm going to move the field a bit so if he picks you up, he'll hole out. You'll be reight." So the next two balls, I tucked it in as he asked.

Then I made a mistake and pitched it on middle. Milburn aimed to drive, got an outside edge. Binksy was stumper so we don't need to say any more.

Ollie gave me a long stare and started to walk down the pitch. Then he stopped. I thought, "Christ, even at this level, they don't walk." But he just looked at me and said, "If you keep listening to that old bugger round the corner, you'll get a few more wickets by the time you've finished!" And he walked off.

The old bugger in question simply said, "Bit of a mistake there, lad. Got to concentrate all the time." There was no well bowled or anything like that. But we'd done Milburn and I finished with 27 overs, 20 maidens, three for 15. Second innings. 7-5-2-3.

I took eight wickets in a rain-affected match against Surrey at Headingley and I look back at those four games as my initiation into a very tight-knit unit.

At the end of the day, we always had a drink in the dressing room and that was a time when any cricket issue could be raised. I was very young and just sat quietly and listened to what was an education in itself.

But one night I went out with Fred for a meal and started talking about my cricket. He said, "We don't talk cricket after seven. You had your chance earlier." I told him I was a bit nervous about that so in the end, we talked cricket.

Next day at 6.30, Closey said, "Right, has anyone got anything to say?"

"Aye, t'young 'un," said Fred.

I started to say, "No, no, it's all right..."

But Fred wasn't having it. "No, come on, what were you saying to me last night?" And he made me say what I'd been talking about and in the process made me feel I really was part and parcel of that gang.

Often on away trips, a few of us would be hanging around in the evening, wondering where to go, and sometimes we'd call over to Binks. "Where are we going tonight then, Bink? Can you afford a drink?"

And Jimmy would bring out this little leather purse he used to have, shaped like a horse shoe. He'd shuffle a few coins around and say, "All right, I can afford a Guinness." And off we went.

At one of our annual reunions a few years back, I was recounting the tale of Binksy's purse to David Ryder, a long-serving Headingley official, when the man himself walked by our table. I said, "Binksy, come and tell David about your old purse."

"You mean this one?" he replied, and produced the self same purse!

In 1968, after Closey had been sacked by England, he and Illy were available far more regularly and I only played in four Championship matches. I bowled 92.5 overs, taking 20 wickets at ten apiece.

The first of those games, against Glamorgan down at Cardiff in July, marked the beginning of my Cruel Time.

There had been a few whispers about my action on the circuit the previous year, although I had not been no-balled, and questions were still being asked in 1968. So when I learned before the game at Cardiff that one of the umpires had been changed and Syd Buller would be in charge, I was a worried man.

I realised things could go very wrong for me. Buller was the man who'd called several players for throwing, including the South African fast bowler Geoff Griffin at Lord's in an exhibition match after the 1960 Test had finished a day early. I didn't have to be a brain surgeon to realise why he'd been sent to Cardiff.

First Buller stood at square leg, then he stood at point and he couldn't have made it more obvious that he was scrutinising my action every time I bowled. But the call never came.

And as he left the ground, he shook my hand and said, "Well bowled, young man. It can't have been easy for you. But I've no problems." My figures were 19-4-42-7 in the first innings and 34-12-74-5 in the second.

To record those figures under that pressure made it probably the most magic game I ever played. And more important, we won the match by ten wickets on the way to our third successive Championship.

But the whispers wouldn't go away and midway through the 1972 season, Yorkshire received a letter from the 'committee' saying I had been suspended. Just a couple of months before I was due to get married.

Jim Laker rang and said he would help me when he could. So

did Fred Titmus and a few more. Then Fred rang. "Now then, this is ridiculous. But there's only one fella to sort thee out and it's Johnny Wardle. Do you know 'im?"

I'd met Wardle once, at the end of the 1969 season when Yorkshire went on tour to Bermuda. Because Don Wilson was tied up with his coaching commitments in South Africa, Johnny came with us as a replacement left-arm spinner.

He was 45 but I had a glimpse on that tour of what a fine bowler he must have been. And what a great entertainer, too.

In one match, he and I were sharing the attack when one of the batsmen cut loose and took us for 50 in about six or seven overs. Johnny was fielding at deep mid-wicket for me and when the batter fired another missile in his direction, he set off running for the catch.

He launched himself at the ball, landed, rolled over several times and stood up with his arms aloft. Everybody stood there aghast, not least the batsman. "Go on, get off!" Johnny barked. And off he went.

The new batter came in, took guard and then one of the lads said, "Where's t'ball?"

Cue Wardle from the mid wicket boundary. "Aye, that's a good idea. Umpire, do you mind if I leave the field?"

"No, not at all, Mr Wardle. Have you been caught short?"

"No I'm just off into that field to fetch t'ball back!" He'd fooled everybody: the players, the umpires, the spectators. We all thought he'd caught it but it had sailed past him for six. The bemused batsman was recalled and missed a straight one next ball.

A few overs later, Johnny was bowling and the batsman hit a straight drive that looked to be flying low and just wide of his left hand. Fred was fielding at mid-off and Johnny shouted, "Go on, Fred, get after it."

Fred turned and set off and the batsman started to run. When he reached the bowler's end, Johnny said, "Has tha run enough?"

The batsman couldn't understand what he was talking about and just said, "Why?"

"Well tha might as well stop now cos I caught thee. And he produced the ball out of his pocket." Again, nobody had seen what had happened.

He showed the other side of his nature, too. When he'd bowled about six overs, he shouted down the wicket to Binks, "Look, Binky. Tha couldn't spot me when you were a young 'un and tha can't spot me now.

"When I take my hankie out of my pocket it's the Chinaman, when I scratch my head it's the top spinner." It wasn't a joke. Even though he was nearly 50, playing a friendly game on tour, he expected perfection from everyone.

So I didn't know quite what to expect as, in the summer of 1972, I drove down to the Ponderosa, Wardle's home at Thorne, near Goole, about 60 miles away. It was a smallholding and he later developed it as a night club.

For over a year, five days a week until the closing stages of the 1973 season, I would report for duty at nine o'clock in the morning. Johnny's wife, Edna, would always have a bacon buttie and a pot of coffee waiting for me and then we'd go into Johnny's shed, which had two nets, each with a green indoor wicket.

We'd spend the first half hour or so talking and then the bowling would start. We'd go through until one o'clock. I'd have a sandwich for lunch and set off home. Some days, I'd go back after tea for an evening session.

The Press were invited on the third day. Johnny told them, "Right, you can have as long as you want, ask whatever you want and take all the pictures you need. Then that's it. From the moment you leave, I don't want to see any of you here again."

When they'd left, he turned to me. "Right, they've gone, lad. And I'm going to tell you something. When I've finished with you, you'll play for England. If you don't, it's my fault; if you do, it will be all down to you."

From that moment, I listened to every word he said. For around 15 months, I was virtually living with Johnny and when you spend as long as that with someone, you get to know them deep down. I got to know Johnny Wardle so well that before long, I came to call him Dad.

He changed my action totally, adapting the action he'd used as a left-arm spinner to my own off-spin. I became a right-arm Johnny Wardle. It was like learning to ride a bike again, completely changing everything.

I started by walking to the crease instead of running. Johnny would guide me through the new action every inch of the way, holding my arms from behind. And for the first few weeks, there was no gentler man. It was 100 per cent encouragement, 100 per cent knowledge and I had 100 per cent faith in my mentor.

At first, I went weeks without even hitting the green mat. I hit the top, both sides, everywhere except the mat. Then, when I started to hit the mat with any kind of regularity, Johnny began to change.

He put a newspaper down as a target and if I failed to hit the target, he started to get a bit upset; shouting and demanding. The wonderfully warm man became a tiger on the prowl. Now we were going for the kill. "We're nearly there," he'd say. "Come on, we're gonna do it."

He was magnificent. There's no other word to describe him. His patience was amazing. I'd heard all the stories about Johnny being difficult, awkward. When I was alone with him in that shed, those stories were utterly unbelievable. And it was this gentle man that I came to know.

Eventually I was hitting the newspaper regularly and finally, Johnny said, "Right you're going to play some cricket this weekend." I started playing for Bradford in the Yorkshire League.

Playing? Not strictly. I was just thinking, "Right foot here, left foot here, left arm here...am I going to make an arse of this?" Johnny would come along with his cine camera.

In a game against Sheffield Collegiate at Abbeydale Park, I'd bowled five overs and was really starting to feel that it was all going to come right after all when, as I went back to my place in the field, Johnny's voice boomed out from the boundary, "Come 'ere!"

The umpire said, "I think he wants you."

"I think you're not wrong," I replied.

Johnny was not a happy man. "Haven't you worked 'im out yet? He can't play off his legs. Bowl leg and middle at him, put a short leg and a silly mid-on in and you'll tie 'im up." Fifth ball of my next over, he drove me straight to silly mid-on.

"Come 'ere!"

"You see, if you think about this game..."

"Johnny, I've enough to think about with my action..." I didn't get any further.

"Never mind your action, that's natural. Start thinking."

Once when I was at the Ponderosa, he had a call from the secretary at Rishton, the Lancashire League club where he played for six years from 1963. "T'pro's out for a fortnight, Johnny, will you come back and play?"

"What do you mean? I'm 50. I haven't played for years."

"It doesn't matter. If we just say you're coming we'll fill t'ground."

"I don't know, I'll see..."

I could see the look in his eyes and as he put the phone down, I said, "You want to play, don't you, Dad?"

"I'd love to play, lad. But I daren't"

"Why not? We'll get some more Radox in. You'll be all right."

So in the end, he rang them back. "OK, I'll come."

Monday morning I walked into the kitchen, the bacon buttie and coffee were waiting. He was just finishing the sports pages. He spoke first. "How've you gone on this weekend, then?"

"Never mind me, I've been all right. But how are you? Are you a bit stiff?"

"I've never played with such a fielding side. I gave some right bollockings out, I can tell you. I got six for 42 and it should have been six for 24. The fielding was dire. I've given 'em a right do."

"And did you get a bat?"

"Aye and I got run out for 40. What a muck-up! I could have had a collection."

The following week, he went back and took seven-fer. But again, the fielding had been a disaster and the bollockings fearsome. I began to get some idea of how some of the younger players in the Yorkshire side of the fifties must have felt.

In 1976, after taking five for 27 from 14 overs in a Test Trial at Bristol, I was chosen for the England tour to India. The following year, I went to Pakistan where I won the first of my three caps. The night before the match, I rang Johnny. "Hello, Dad," I said. "It's me."

"Now lad, how are you?"

"They've picked me...thank you." And then I had to put the phone down. I couldn't say any more.

He rang me back at the end of the match. I said, "I'm sorry about last week, I hope you didn't think I was rude."

"No lad, I know what state you were in. I bowled every ball with you. I bet it was a right low, slow pitch 'cos you bowled 39 eight-ball overs, which is about 52 of our overs, and you've given 'em two an over. That's not bad bowling, you've kept your concentration." And he was spot on...at a distance of 6,000 miles.

Of course Johnny had been something of an outcast at Yorkshire since his sacking in 1958 but the club eventually healed the wounds and I like to think I had some part to play in his return.

First he was made a life member; he was delighted about that and there were a few tears. And then, because of all he'd done for me, he was offered a role as a bowling consultant. It is one of the biggest disappointments of my life that illness prevented him from taking up the offer.

Soon after returning from Pakistan, however, the rumbles about my action resumed and the film crews re-appeared. I soldiered on. Then at the end of the 1980 season, I was called to Headingley to discuss a new contract.

The committee said they were 100 per cent behind me because I'd never been no-balled for throwing. But they said they could ill afford to give me a one-year contract when there was a risk that the phone call might come after six games and I'd be suspended. So they were only prepared to offer me a match-by-match deal.

My work in the paper trade was going well, my son Andrew was going on three and my daughter Nicola was one. There was no way I could accept. I felt I had a lot to offer as a senior player but I couldn't afford the uncertainty of not having a contract through to September.

If only I could have gone back to those early days when playing cricket was all about fun, enthusiasm and enjoyment, instead of worrying about my action, wondering if the cameras would be there. But no. It was time to go.

I received the message saying Johnny had died on August 23, 1985. I was about 40 miles outside Swansea on my way to play in a three-day match for MCC against Wales. I rang his home straight away. I spoke to Gerald, the younger of his two sons and told him I was turning round and heading back north.

"Wait, while I talk to Mum," he replied.

He called back a few minutes later. "Mum says he would have wanted you to play and that's what you must do."

Roger Knight was the MCC skipper. He knew how close we'd been and said it would be OK for me to leave at any time in the match if I wanted to. I was still in two minds until Gerald rang next day.

"I'm just ringing to make sure you're still there and don't you think about coming home." Then he said, "I just wanted to tell you it's family flowers only. But you're part of the family."

I sent a bouquet of white roses with the inscription: "Dad, without you, your patience and perseverance, I would never have achieved the greatest day for any cricketer: to represent his country. You said I'd do it...and we did it. Bowl well up there."

1968

The abolition of theatre censorship threatened to open a veritable Pandora's Box of licentious behaviour on the West End stage with Hair, a musical that featured full frontal nudity, launching the Age of Aquarius at the Shaftsbury Theatre in September.

Rather more sedate fare was on offer on the small screen with the launch of a new series about life on the home front in the fictional town of Walmington on Sea. Yes, Dad's Army really has been going that long.

The Government's I'm Backing Britain campaign urged us to work an extra half hour a day for no pay to make the country more competitive while yachtsman Alec Rose flew the flag on the high seas by completing a 354-day solo circumnavigation of the world.

In the Unites States, Civil Rights leader Martin Luther King and Robert Kennedy, younger brother of the late President John Kennedy, were assassinated and on both sides of the Atlantic concerns were growing over the number of imported Japanese cars.

Meanwhile Yorkshire began a successful defence of the County Championship in time-honoured manner by playing MCC at Lord's.

And sitting on top of the charts as they strode down the pavilion steps for the start of the only day's play in a rain-affected match was What a Wonderful World by Louis Armstrong. For Yorkshire supporters it was.

As ever, the man patrolling the covers as Fred Trueman bowled the first delivery of the new campaign was Ken Taylor, starting what proved to be his final season in first-class cricket.

A gifted all-round sportsman, Taylor lived a double life for over a decade: summers playing cricket for Yorkshire, winters on the football field with Huddersfield Town.

He was by no means the first to combine the two and in 1968, the roll call included Arthur Milton, Stuart Leary, Graham Cross, Jim Cumbes and Ted Hemsley. Not to mention Taylor's Yorkshire team-mate Chris Balderstone.

A decade later, however, cricketer-footballers were on the verge of extinction, with Arnie Sidebottom, a Yorkshire and England fast bowler who played football for Manchester United, Huddersfield Town and Halifax Town, one of the last of a dying breed.

Taylor has fond memories of the dual challenge. "I always looked forward to the change-over at either end of the season," he recalls.

"I was actually short-listed for three or four winter cricket tours but I really don't know whether I would eventually have said 'yes' because I did enjoy going back to football. I don't think I would have liked to play 18 months' continuous cricket.

"But my involvement with cricket explains why I played in every position for Town apart from left-wing and goalkeeper. When I returned from cricket, the side had played a few games and until things settled down, I tended to slot in wherever and whenever Huddersfield needed me.

"In fact I remember one game at Plymouth when I still didn't know whether I'd be playing at left-back or outside-right 15 minutes before the kick-off!"

Ken Taylor.

The Man for all Seasons

Kenneth Taylor was born in Huddersfield on August 21, 1935. An opening batsman and medium pace bowler, he was capped in 1957. He made his Yorkshire debut in 1953 and went on to make 303 first-class appearances for the county, scoring 12,864 runs, with 16 centuries, at an average of 27.37 and taking 129 wickets at 28.52. He also appeared in ten limited overs games. He played in seven Championship sides, two Gillette Cup Finals and won three England caps. Taylor played football for Huddersfield Town between 1954 and 1965, making 250 first team appearances before moving to Bradford Park Avenue. An art teacher, he now lives in Norfolk, for whom he played Minor Counties cricket in 1970 and '71. His son Nick, a fast bowler, spent two seasons with Yorkshire in the early eighties.

When I was young, it never crossed my mind that people might think I was a bit special because I could play cricket and football so well. I just enjoyed my sport and took everything in my stride.

And I was very fortunate that I went to Stile Common School, close to our home in Primrose Hill, Huddersfield, because sport was such a big thing there. We had a great headmaster, a chap called Wally Heap, a real enthusiast.

No matter what you were good at, he encouraged you, whether it was academic subjects, sport, art or anything else. He helped me all along and took me and other boys to various trials for schoolboys at both football and cricket.

I used to bat and bowl for the school cricket team and played on the wing for the football team. We were always pretty successful at both sports.

I'm slightly dyslexic, which meant that academic lessons were a bit of a problem. I could do the work OK but it took me a long time. And in those days, if you wanted to go to Grammar School, you had to pass the old 11-plus. That was all about speed and I didn't pass.

So instead of following Jeff, my elder brother, to Almondbury Grammar School and probably on to university like him, I stayed at Stile Common until I was 15. I remember Wally Heap being very disappointed that I hadn't passed the 11-plus but looking back, it was probably a good job because it meant I could stay where I was and concentrate on sport.

And it really was an excellent environment to grow up in. In the winter we used to play the staff at football every couple of weeks on the old recreation ground on Newsome Road. We used to mark out the pitch with sawdust from a sawmill down by the river.

The staff were all young men who had just come out of the Forces. They were fit and wanted to expend some energy. One or two of the boys made up their team but the majority were members of staff and they took it seriously. There was never any suggestion of easing off and letting us win

We used to play against the staff at cricket, too, at the top of the playground. We used a dustbin for the wicket and we didn't have pads or gloves. We played with an old cork ball, which bounced and turned a lot.

We didn't play proper matches, more a knock-about. But I remember that if the sun was shining at lunchtime and everyone was enjoying themselves we didn't have to go back to lessons in the afternoon.

We started in the morning break, carried on at lunchtime and in the afternoon break. Then we'd start again after school. The batsman stayed at the crease until he was out; no time limits or restrictions on the number of balls he could face.

And if he was not out at any of the intervals he carried on when play resumed. Sometimes I even carried my bat in the evening and started again as the not out batsman next morning.

One of the teachers was a chap called Colin Garthwaite, who was a big influence on my cricket. He was the pro at Cleckheaton in the Bradford League for donkey's years and bowled leg breaks and googlies.

He was very successful and he'd also played for the Navy against the Army at Lord's. He was, to say the least, a pretty useful bowler with a corkie ball on a concrete wicket.

He taught me to use my feet and I suppose playing against him for so long explains why I was always able to handle leg-spin better than off-spin. And learning how to play a turning ball on that concrete surface was a pretty important part of my development.

Cricket had a more structured system than football, starting with the schoolboy sides. I made it into the Huddersfield, Yorkshire and North of England teams and eventually played for England against Wales, by which time I was also playing for Primrose Hill in the Huddersfield League. I started there when I was 13.

I made my first appearance for Yorkshire Schoolboys when I was about 11 and carried on for the next four seasons. Keith Kettleborough, who went on to play football for Rotherham and Sheffield United among others, was in the side.

So was Terry Allcock, who later played football for Bolton and Norwich City, where he spent ten seasons. Terry tried his hand at various jobs after leaving football until one of his sons started an undertaking business.

It really took off and in the end, Terry, his five sons and their wives were all involved. He still goes into the office part-time as well as doing some corporate hospitality at Norwich.

And Yorkshire Schoolboys was where I first met Bryan Stott and Doug Padgett. We soon became good friends. They were a little bit older than me but we played together in all the Yorkshire sides on our way up into the first team.

A bond developed between us as we progressed through the system and if you look at the team picture taken at the start of the 1959 season, we're there on the front row, sitting on the ground. The Three Musketeers!

They haven't changed. Doug never had a lot to say but when he did have a point to make it was always sensible. Stotty was more outspoken and outgoing, a great motivator. He and I are still in contact regularly and visit one another two or three times a year.

When I was 13, I played for the North of England Schoolboys against the South at Denton, near Manchester. Stotty and Padge were both playing, too.

England were playing New Zealand in a Test at Old Trafford at the same time and the night before our game, Denis Compton and Walter Hadlee, who was the New Zealand manager, came and gave us a talk. It was quite an event.

All the time I was moving up the ladder at cricket, I was also playing football. But even though I played football for school, I made my way into the professional game mainly with the help of Jeff, my brother.

He was five years older than me and when he was 13 he was spotted by Huddersfield Town playing for Priestroyd Ironworks junior side in the Huddersfield Red Triangle League.

He was a centre-forward and made his first team debut for Town in 1949. He scored 29 goals in 71 games before moving to Fulham and then Brentford while he was at University College, London, and later at the Royal Academy of Music, where he trained to be an opera singer.

While he was at Leeds Road, my father took me down for trials and I signed on as a junior, starting in the third team, who played at Beck Lane in Heckmondwike. I was playing on the wing for school in the morning and then for Town's third team in the afternoon.

They mainly played against colliery sides so it was a pretty tough school. Let's say we learned how to jump! I played in the forward line most of the time although even at that stage, I could slot in more or less anywhere.

I didn't play too many games for the reserves in the Central League because on March 6, 1954, I was pushed into the first team for my league debut against Liverpool at Anfield. I was 18.

Don McEvoy, the first choice centre-half, was injured. The previous year he'd been a regular member of the side who were promoted into the old First Division. The goalkeeper and all five defenders played in every game.

It was a tremendous experience, running out of the tunnel with the Kop at one end, making an incredible noise. I was marking a chap called Louis Bimpson, who put himself about a bit. But we won 3-1.

The following week we played Newcastle United at home – I marked Jackie Milburn and we won again, 3-2. Then we went to Old Trafford to play Manchester United. This time I was marking Tommy Taylor and we lost 3-1. I played another four games before Don was fit again.

Soon afterwards he was transferred to Sheffield Wednesday and I took over on a regular basis in the 1954-55 season. So the football developed quicker than the cricket and for the next couple of years, it was my main priority as I tried to balance the two.

The start of the cricket season wasn't really a problem because in those days there wasn't much cricket in April and the County Championship didn't really get under way until early May, by which time the football season had ended.

But it was different at the start of the football season. Not only did the players have to report for pre-season training in July but when the season began, usually around my birthday on August 21, the cricket season still had another two or three weeks to go.

So when Bill Shankly took over as Town manager in 1956, we came to an arrangement. If Yorkshire were in with a chance of winning the Championship, I would stay with them until the end of the cricket season.

If not, I would return to Huddersfield for the start of the football season. That continued after Eddie Boot took over when Shankly moved to Liverpool in 1959.

And as Yorkshire won the title four times between 1959 and 1965, the year I left Town, I didn't see a lot of my football team-mates at the start of their season. But I was naturally quite fit and the cricket kept me ticking over.

Even so, Shankly and later Boot were pretty strict about me reporting as soon as Yorkshire's Championship season was over... which explains why I always seemed to miss out on the celebrations.

I never featured in the annual match between the Champion County and the Rest at The Oval, which was played for the last time in 1961. There was always a team photo and I was never on it. And I hardly ever appeared at the Scarborough Festival.

I really don't know how my two sets of team-mates viewed my double life, I just got on with the job at both clubs. As long as we were performing on the field, it didn't really matter.

There was no aggro, no jealousy. I can't think of any awkward person, someone you would dislike, in either dressing room. Everybody was pleased for everybody else to do well.

Certainly that was the thinking at Yorkshire from the time Ronnie Burnet took over as captain in 1958. I'd made my debut against Northants in 1953 and played three more games that year before making a total of seven appearances over the next two seasons.

I played more regularly in 1956 and '57, when I was capped, but it wasn't until 1958 that I held down a more or less permanent place in the side.

Ronnie had inherited a group of very talented individuals who never really played together as a team. He changed all that, because above all, Ronnie was a team man and insisted that everyone played for the team.

He drilled that into the young players when we played for him in the Second XI and when we progressed into the first team we had that same attitude. Vic Wilson kept the ball rolling when he succeeded Ronnie in 1960 and the spirit was the same when Brian Close took over in 1963.

It stayed with the team right through to the late Sixties when things began to change and one or two players were thinking about themselves and not the team. You simply can't do that and expect to win a Championship.

But the team ethic that was so strong for so long was basically down to Ronnie. He was an amateur and not a particularly good player but he was a great motivator and an absolutely super chap.

He used to drive a big Jaguar and some of us travelled with him to away matches. He had a special petrol tank fitted so that he wouldn't have to stop at a filling station.

So we'd fly down to Lord's, The Oval, Taunton or wherever and then fly back home. All on the old roads. I remember once doing 139mph on the old A1. Quite an experience!

I scored just short of 1,000 runs in 1958 and the following year won the first of my three England caps in the first Test against India at Trent Bridge. It was a good ground for me as I also scored my maiden first-class century there in 1956.

I opened the innings with Arthur Milton, the Gloucestershire opener who had also played football for England in 1951. We lost a couple of early wickets but Peter May and I took the score past 50 before I was given out lbw by Eddie Phillipson.

Phillipson always used to talk about how he gave more people out in a season than any other umpire – he was very proud about it. And I was definitely unlucky this time.

I was on 24 and played a long way forward to their leg-spinner, Subhash Gupte. The ball hit the outside of my front leg and went down for a leg bye.

When I reached the other end, Gupte turned to Phillipson and in a half-hearted way, said "How's that?" He gave me out. It was a very dodgy decision and May was a bit upset about it.

He went on to score a century, we won by an innings and I didn't bat again. So that was a bit of a disaster. I played in the second Test at Lords but didn't do anything and was left out for the third game at Headingley.

To be honest, I wasn't too disappointed because it meant I probably wasn't going to be selected to go on an overseas tour that winter and wouldn't have to make the difficult decision about football.

I only played one more Test, against Australia at Headingley in 1964, when I was called up as a late replacement for Colin Cowdrey. I had to bat at number six and made nine and 15 and rejoined the county set and played under Brian Close for the rest of my career.

As a captain, Brian led from the front and we knew that if he asked us to do something, he could do it just as well – perhaps twice as well in some cases. But for some reason he seemed to under-rate my bowling talents.

I always fancied my chances as a bowler in my early days. In fact, I took four wickets for 40 from 22 overs on the first day of our 1959 Championship decider against Sussex at Hove.

And while I always say I only came on because everybody else was knackered after a hard season, dismissing four of their first five batsmen in the first innings was pretty important.

I did a fair bit of bowling under Ronnie Burnet and Vic Wilson and always felt that if I failed with the bat I might chip in with a wicket or two. But I hardly bowled under Brian, even though I dismissed Garfield Sobers twice in our game against the West Indies at Middlesbrough in 1963.

In the first innings, he was caught by Fred in the leg trap. Then I clean bowled him in the second innings. To this day I can picture him throwing his head back in the air as he walked away, obviously thinking, "How have I let this doolally bowl me out?"

In March, 1964, I was chosen for E W Swanton's Commonwealth tour to Singapore, Kuala Lumpur, Hong Kong, Bangkok and Calcutta. Garry was also in the party and in Kuala Lumpur he took five wickets in five balls – followed two days later by a century after playing 18 holes of golf in the morning!

He was undoubtedly the greatest all-rounder we have ever seen and I'm sure he would have been exceptional at any sport he tried to play. And such a nice chap. So dismissing him twice at Acklam Park was special.

And I also like to look back at the win over Glamorgan at Harrogate that clinched our third Championship in 1962.

We'd retained the title by beating Worcestershire there two years earlier but this time it was the last game of the season and Worcester, who had finished their matches, were ten points in front. So we had to win.

There was a lot of rain around in the build-up to the game and we knew that when the Harrogate wicket was wet, it was always going to do a bit. We put them in, Don Wilson took six for 24 and we bowled them out for 65.

We lost wickets steadily in reply but I managed to survive and make 67 out of our total of 101. It was one of those wickets where if you were going to stick around, things had to be working in your favour. And they were. Even so, I was proud of that knock.

Glamorgan were 13 without loss at the close when rain washed out the second day. When we arrived on the final day, the field was under water and everybody had to work hard to get the pitch fit to play on.

While the work was going on, Peter West, the BBC commentator and cricket presenter, arrived at the ground. At that time, he was also presenting the old Come Dancing programme on the television.

We spotted him walking through the entrance at the far side of the ground from the pavilion and as he walked round in front of the stand, the crowd starting singing, "One, two, three, one, two, three" in waltz time. We all thought it was a huge joke but I don't think Peter was too amused.

Anyway, when play finally got under way we again bowled them out cheaply and needed 66 to win. This time I was out first ball, giving Jeff Jones, who had taken the last two wickets of our first innings with successive deliveries, his first hat-trick. But, with apologies to Peter West, we waltzed home in the end by seven wickets.

By the time we arrived at Hull for the final game of the 1968 season against Surrey, I had made up my mind to retire.

Perhaps, on reflection, I should have carried on for a bit longer. But I wasn't as interested as I had been, my results were going down and it was no longer quite so much fun to play.

So it meant a lot to walk off the field at the end of my final match knowing that I had helped Yorkshire win another Championship, our last for 33 years.

I suppose it really started to wane for me after Stotty left in 1963. I couldn't understand why he was allowed to leave because he was still doing well with the bat and he was no slouch in the field.

But Brian Sellers, the cricket chairman, had this bee in his bonnet that we couldn't have more than 12 capped players and at the end of the 1963 season, Geoff Boycott, John Hampshire and Tony Nicholson were all capped. So, according to Sellers, somebody had to go.

Stotty had the family plumbing business to go into and he softened the blow by convincing himself that the business was more important than cricket at that stage. But deep down, I think he would have liked to stay on.

Bryan was enthusiastic, he made you want to play. And we had this understanding as an opening pair all the way through schoolboy cricket, the Yorkshire Federation, the Second XI and the first team.

We once ran five singles in the first over of a Roses match – nobody had ever done that before – and even now, people talk about Stott and Taylor as one of Yorkshire's best opening pairs. That means a lot.

Something went out of the game for me when Stotty disappeared and by the end of the 1968 season, I knew it was time for something new, something I'd prepared for since going to Huddersfield Technical College as an art student when I was 15.

I was there for five years, studying for the National Diploma in Design. And then, in the autumn of 1956, I won a place at the Slade School of Fine Art in London.

Throughout my student days, I was combining three different component parts of my life: cricket, football and art and while I was at technical college, I rarely trained with my Huddersfield team-mates. I just turned up on a Saturday and played. If we were away from home, I was allowed to take Friday off.

And during my year at the Slade, my brother Jeff was playing for Brentford and I was allowed to train with them two mornings a week before catching the train on a Friday afternoon to join up with Town again.

It was a really good time to play football. It was back in the days of the maximum wage so we were all paid more or less the same and it was a happy dressing room.

I suppose when the maximum wage was abolished in 1961 and some people started being paid more than others, a bit of niggling and grumbling crept into the game. But it wasn't like that in my early years at Town.

Even though we were relegated in 1956, we had a good side and it was a nice team to play with. And of course from the start of the 1956 season, we had the one and only Bill Shankly as manager.

Bill had arrived the previous December as reserve team coach but took over when Andy Beattie left after we'd gone down. I think

Bill liked me. As a player I was reasonable in the air, I was fast on the ground and I could tackle hard.

There was usually a place in the side for me somewhere and while wing-half was my most regular position, I was pretty versatile. But Bill didn't like it when I was off playing cricket. He called it a lassies' game.

Denis Law arrived for a trial in 1955. He was a frail, skinny 15-year-old from Aberdeen and had these horn-rimmed glasses and a squint. He didn't really look as if he was going to be any kind of a player.

But as soon as you saw him on the field, you realised he was special. He was playing in the first team at 17 and for Scotland the following year.

Ray Wilson signed for Town at the same time as me in the summer of 1952. He was an inside-forward then and never really looked as if he would make the grade. I think that towards the end of the 1954-55 season they were ready to let him go.

Then one day we were short of a full-back in a practice match and Bill McGarry, who was the skipper, said they should give Ray a chance there. He went from strength to strength. Five years later he was playing for England and he won a World Cup winners' medal in 1966.

They were good times with people like Denis and Ray, Les Massie, John Coddington, Kevin McHale, Bob Parker and Gordon Low. A few years ago, Les came up with the idea of a get-together at the Golden Cock in Farnley Tyas on the outskirts of Huddersfield.

We meet up every winter now. Some of us have changed a bit, some haven't. But it's always a good day.

And even though we weren't in the top flight we had some pretty memorable matches. Like Charlton at The Valley on December 21, 1957. We were leading 5-1 against ten men with 28 minutes left and ended up losing 7-6. We became the only team to score six goals and lose a match.

Their centre-half Derek Ufton, who also played cricket for Kent, dislocated his shoulder and was taken off after 15 minutes. We weren't in any real trouble but then all of a sudden this chap Johnny Summers, who played on the left wing, popped up and scored five goals. With his right foot.

Sandy Kennon was our goalkeeper and he was always a bit of a showman, who liked to make every save look a bit more difficult than it was. The only problem was that on this occasion, he kept missing the ball!

It was a pretty silent ride back to Huddersfield. In fact I don't recall Bill Shankly saying a single word on the entire journey.

Another big game was against West Ham in a third round FA Cup replay at Upton Park in 1960. We won that one 5-1. They were doing well in the First Division at the time and after we'd drawn one-all at Leeds Road, nobody gave us much of a chance.

There was a hard frost overnight in London before the replay and when we arrived at the ground, half the pitch was still as hard as iron while the other half, which had been bathed in sunshine, had thawed.

So the players had to decide whether to wear leather boots with proper studs or training boots with rubber studs. We decided to wear rubbers first while they wore ordinary boots. And they couldn't stand up.

The following year, after Denis had moved to Manchester City for a then record fee of £55,000, we were giant-killing again, this time against Wolves, a really strong side.

We somehow contrived to hold on for a draw at their place and the replay was fixed for the following Wednesday. It was the night when the Leeds Road floodlights, paid for with some of Denis's transfer fee, were switched on for the first time.

I'd never seen a crowd like it. I couldn't get near Leeds Road in the car and had to park in the middle of Huddersfield by the viaduct and walk down to the ground – all the car parks were for the directors and visitors. Imagine a player doing that before a big Cup-tie today! We won 2-0

I left Town in 1965 and over the next four summers, I played for Yorkshire in three Championship sides and won two Gillette Cup finals. But by the end of the 1968 season, I was 33 and I knew it was time to start a new career in teaching. And the sooner the better.

So when the opportunity arose to move to South Africa and take up a part-time post at Rondebosch High School in Cape Town, working in the art department and coaching cricket, my wife Avril and I decided to give it a go.

I did that for 18 months and then worked as a football coach in a scheme run by the Rembrandt Tobacco Company. But the political situation out there was not very comfortable and we always feared something drastic was going to happen.

So we decided to come back, although we had no firm plans at that stage about where we might go or what we might do.

However before we left, a friend in South Africa mentioned that East Anglia was a nice part of the world to live and said there were good schools like Gresham's, Framlingham and Felsted. I wrote to them all.

Logie Bruce-Lockhart, who'd played rugby union for Scotland, was headmaster at Gresham's and he invited me to see him when we returned to England. He couldn't offer me a job in the art department that year but there would be something the following year.

Then he asked if I did pottery. I said, "No. But I know someone who does. My wife."

So Avril was given a job at Gresham's and I went to work part-time at Beeston Hall preparatory school nearby. The following year, I started at Gresham's and Avril went to Beeston Hall.

She's been there ever since as head of the art department. And I pop in part-time on four days a week for a couple of hours. I work with the kids who are hoping to get a scholarship to a senior school.

I didn't have much contact with Yorkshire when I got back from South Africa but in 1982, I became involved again when my son Nicholas joined the county staff. He'd learned his cricket at Gresham's and he was a good fast bowler.

I was unsure about whether to take him to Yorkshire because of my own links. But I thought that as I'd been a batsman and he was a bowler, there wouldn't be a problem.

He spent two years there but he had a terrible time. The other players didn't like public schoolboys and he was really given a hard ride. Illy was manager in 1982 and captain the following year and Doug Padgett was the coach.

They were both men for whom I had a lot of time but I don't think they really made any effort to make Nicholas feel wanted and confident or to sort out the people who were causing problems.

He performed quite well on the field but during his second season, he was ringing every week saying he wanted to get away. My instinct was to leave a decision until the end of the season but he insisted.

So I phoned and asked for his release. I was told he could not be released mid-season and instead he was made Twelfth Man in six consecutive first team matches. It was awful.

I had hoped he might go to Nottinghamshire the following year because Richard Hadlee and Clive Rice were there at the time and he would have learned a lot. Instead he went to Surrey and played on a pitch that was as flat as a pancake before spending the 1986 season at Somerset.

That was my last contact with the county game, really. I watch a bit every now and then but it has changed. Sadly it's a bit of a nonentity nowadays.

The counties exist because of the money they get from the ECB so the ECB has the say in what the system is. But they've done nothing for county cricket; I don't think it's changed for the better.

Switching from a three-day to a four-day match was ridiculous. We always looked to win the toss and go in to bat aiming to declare before the end of that day's play.

We'd want to get the other side in for three-quarters of an hour and have a go at them in the evening...and then another again next morning.

Now the idea seems to be for the first innings to go on till lunchtime on the second day and if that happens, the spectators on the first day only see one team bat. It's a bore and as a spectator I'd be very disappointed.

Chris Balderstone.
November, 1940 – March, 2000

James Christopher Balderstone was born in Huddersfield on November 16, 1940. A middle order batsman and left-arm spinner, he made his Yorkshire debut in 1961 and played in 68 first-class matches and 13 one-day games before joining Leicestershire in 1969. Balderstone scored 1,332 runs and took 37 wickets in first-class games for the county and 17,627 runs and 271 wickets in 319 first-class matches for Leicestershire, for whom he also played 225 one-day games. He played in four Championship sides for Yorkshire and one for Leicestershire and made two appearances for England. After retiring in 1986, he joined the panel of first-class umpires. Between 1960 and 1976, Balderstone also played in 524 Football League games for Huddersfield Town, Carlisle United and Doncaster Rovers. He became a first-class umpire in 1988 and stood in two one-day internationals. He died on March 6, 2000.

Ken Taylor remembers: I knew Chris from when he was a little lad. He lived close by and went to Paddock School. Then he played for Paddock in the Huddersfield League before moving into the first-class game.

I even used to keep an eye on him when he was courting because Madeleine Carson, who later became his wife, lived opposite me in Primrose Hill. She was the daughter of the manager of the Theatre Royal in Huddersfield.

Chris was always outstanding at both sports, one of three people born in Huddersfield who went on to play cricket for Yorkshire and England and football for Huddersfield Town. Willie Watson and I were the others.

I actually took him down to Town for trials in the late fifties when I was a first team player. I always tried to help him during his time there.

He was an old-fashioned inside-forward, great on the ball and a superb passer. He reminded me of Johnny Haynes, the Fulham and England captain of the Fifties and early Sixties.

They didn't look to be using a lot of energy and dashing about here, there and everywhere. But they had this ability to control the ball quicker than other players and didn't need three touches to kill it stone dead.

He was a great distributor but the Town crowd tended to like hustle, bustle players. It didn't help that he came into the side on a regular basis after Denis Law had been transferred to Manchester City for a record fee of £55,000 in 1960.

In 1965, Chris decided to leave. In those days there was no money, not officially anyway, for the player in a transfer but I said, "Wherever you go, ask for a couple of thousand quid."

Soon afterwards, Town accepted an offer from Carlisle and when Chris had talks with the Carlisle officials, he asked for the money... and got it! He was very successful up there and went on to play in the old First Division when they were promoted in 1974.

The following year he joined Doncaster Rovers and on one occasion played cricket for Leicestershire and football for Doncaster on the same day!

In any sport, you need to be in the right place at the right time and at Yorkshire, I was lucky. I just happened to be around when several senior players were leaving and they were looking for young players to come in.

Whereas between 1959 and 1968, we had an established side and opportunities were very limited for people like Chris, Barry Wood and Jackie Birkenshaw, all very talented players, who couldn't get into the side on anything like a regular basis.

In the end, Barry moved to Lancashire and Chris and Jack to Leicestershire and they all went on to play for England.

Chris was very unlucky not to have a longer career with Yorkshire. He was a lovely chap and a fine cricketer and his death at the age of just 59 really was a terrible shock.

1969

On July 20, 1969, time stood still across the world as Neil Armstrong, the US astronaut, took one small step for man, one giant leap for mankind and became the first man to set foot on the Moon.

It was the year Colonel Gaddafi seized control in Libya, Richard Nixon succeeded Lyndon Johnson as President of the United States, Concorde underwent her first trials in Toulouse and the QE2 embarked on her maiden voyage from Southampton to Las Palmas.

The halfpenny ceased to be legal tender and at London's Victoria Palace theatre, the Black and White Minstrel Show was still packing them in during its ten-year run of over 6,000 performances.

On the face of it, any connection between Yorkshire cricket in the Sixties and the Black and Whites may seem a little tenuous. However Philip Sharpe and Don Wilson, both of whom played in seven Championship sides, would beg to differ.

Over the years, the two players enjoyed their fair share of time in the Minstrels' company and whenever Yorkshire played in London, they called in at the Victoria Palace.

And it was on their first trip to the capital in 1969 that Sharpe scored the first century of the new season in the traditional curtain raiser against MCC at Lord's.

It proved to be a propitious day for Sharpe, who went on to score more than 1,400 first-class runs, play six times for England and record his only Test century, against New Zealand at Trent Bridge.

He also featured in the final showpiece of the season at headquarters, the Gillette Cup Final on September 6, in which Yorkshire defeated Derbyshire by 69 runs to win their last trophy of the golden age.

It would be another 14 years before they won more silverware, in the shape of the John Player League, and the Championship pennant would not fly at Headingley again until 2001.

"Seven Championships in ten seasons was an unbelievable achievement," says Sharpe, who now runs a travel business, based at his Wetherby home, organising cricket tours for England supporters during the winter.

"But somehow we always felt the supporters didn't quite appreciate what was involved. They *expected* us to win the Championship and people seemed to get more worked up if we failed to do so.

"That's when the inquests started and it was always the batters who came in for most of the stick. People conveniently overlooked the fact that we had to bat on the same wickets on which our bowlers were running through the opposition."

PHILIP SHARPE.

TAKING CENTRE STAGE

Philip John Sharpe was born in Shipley on December 27, 1936. A middle order batsman who was equally at home as an opener, he made his Yorkshire debut in 1958 and was capped two years later. He made 411 first-class appearances, scoring 17,685 runs, with 23 centuries, at an average of 29.72. He also played in 89 limited overs games. Sharpe featured in seven Championship sides and two Gillette Cup finals. He won 12 England caps between 1963 and 1969, scoring 786 runs at an average of 46.23, and was one of the finest slip fielders in Yorkshire's history, taking 525 catches for the county and 635 in his career. He left Yorkshire in 1974 and spent two years with Derbyshire before enjoying six seasons of Minor Counties cricket with Norfolk. Sharpe served on the Yorkshire committee, was a Test selector from 1983 to 1988 and later joined the panel of ECB Pitch Inspectors.

There can't be too many Test cricketers around who also worked backstage with the Black and White Minstrels. Tell us about it.

How long have you got? I could give you a chapter or two on the

Black and Whites alone...but then I'd have to leave the country!

It all started at the Futurist Theatre in Scarborough. Before setting up a permanent base at the Victoria Palace in London in 1962, the Black and Whites spent their time touring theatres all round the country and in 1961, they spent a week at the Futurist.

Don Wilson wasn't in the Yorkshire side at the time – he'd been injured early on and Keith Gillhouley did well as his replacement. So when the Minstrels arrived for their week at the Futurist, Don was playing for the Second XI at North Marine Road.

One evening, he went along to their show and, in true Stage Door Johnny style, introduced himself afterwards to Dai Francis, Tony Mercer and John Boulter, the principal singers. Tony and Dai were keen cricket fans and when Yorkshire played at Scarborough the following year, Wils was back in the side and gave them a couple of tickets for the match. In return, he and I were invited to the show. That's how it started.

It was what you might call a reciprocal arrangement and it continued right through the Sixties. They loved their cricket so we fixed them up with tickets. And, of course, we loved the girls, the dancers! Occasionally one or two of the Minstrels would play in a charity game or a benefit match and some of them weren't bad performers.

When the Minstrels were in London, they played at the Victoria Palace and if we were in the capital, too, we'd head for the theatre in the evening. Where else? If we'd been the superbly honed athletes of the modern era, I don't think we'd have got away with it somehow. But it was a different world in those days. There were no warm-downs after the close of play; in fact, there wasn't much of a warm-up before the start, come to think of it.

And at the end of the day, the old tray of drinks would come in... so many pints of beer, so many lagers, a whisky for Closey and so on. How Brian managed to drink a whisky after a day's play, I'll never know. But I digress...

Then after we'd got changed, we'd wander off to the pub for another drink, have a bite to eat and then around ten o'clock take a taxi to the Victoria Palace, arriving as the show was winding up. We knew Tony, Dai and John well by this time so we'd go into the theatre via the stage door and into their dressing room. And at the end of the show we'd all head off into the night and party.

We only had a maximum of three games in London, against MCC, Middlesex and Surrey, and it wasn't a case of going to the Victoria Palace every night we were there. But I suppose you could say it was more often than not! And after we won the Gillette Cup for the first time in 1965, Leslie Crowther, who was the resident comedian at the time, invited us up on stage with the trophy.

Then one winter, Don and I found ourselves as part of the ensemble when they were doing a week at the Alhambra Theatre in Bradford. We were waiting backstage when they arrived on the Monday and the first person we saw was Keith Leggatt, who was the head minstrel behind Tony, Dai and John. He was usually our first point of contact and as soon as he saw us, he came straight to the point. "Look, boys, wardrobe are struggling for a dresser, how are you fixed?"

One look at all the girls, one whiff of the greasepaint and one nod between us was enough. I replied, "Well, sounds all right to me." So Wils and I were signed up as dressers for the week. Sadly the job didn't turn out to be quite as exotic as we'd hoped; in fact, we turned out to be more like odd job men.

For instance, if the Minstrels were strutting their stuff with a soft shoe shuffle, complete with top hats and canes, Wils and I would be waiting in the wings, one at either side of the stage. At the end of the routine, the Minstrels would sashay towards the wings, hand us the hats and canes and we'd take them back to the wardrobe. Ah, the glamour of showbiz!

But it was great fun for a week and after the show we'd all repair to the tap room bar at the Alex, the pub round the corner from the Alhambra, and have a few beers, pre-breathalyser days of course.

Looking through your 1971 Benefit brochure, there are tributes from actors Ian Carmichael, Brian Rix and Ray Barrett, Leslie Crowther and Liverpool comedian Jimmy Tarbuck. So clearly you were no stranger to the entertainment world.

The Benefit brochure! Yes, in its time, it wasn't a bad product. Now, of course, it would pale into insignificance with all the elaborate material they come up with on the Internet and so on.

I met Ian Carmichael, who died early in 2010 and was originally from Hull, when I was playing in my first Test against the West Indies at Edgbaston in 1963.

Ian and two of his friends from the acting fraternity, Michael Craig and Donald Sinden, were all big cricket men and they happened to be in the same pub as me and one or two other players after a day's play. We got chatting and when it came to the Benefit brochure, I asked Ian if he'd mind jotting down a couple of hundred words, which he duly did. That was nice.

I first met Ray Barrett, who was a big name for his role in the TV series The Troubleshooters, in another charity game in Kew Gardens. John Hampshire, Don Wilson and I all played in that one along with David Frost, now Sir David, who wasn't a bad wicketkeeper. It was organised by Tom Sloan, who I recall was Head of Light Entertainment at the BBC. He must have had access to a lot of entertainers who were keen on cricket.

Brian Rix, star of the Whitehall farces, I encountered in a charity game in Morecambe in 1966 and he also played in a benefit match for Ken Taylor at Hull two years later. I met Jimmy Tarbuck at a health farm, of all places, and, of course, Leslie Crowther was involved with the Black and Whites for a while. But generally, a lot of actors were keen on cricket and enjoyed playing in benefit and charity matches and there was a real camaraderie.

But cricket always took centre stage for you.

Yes, from an early age. My father -- he was called Frederick Gilbert but everyone knew him as Bert -- was very keen. He was a good sportsman, too, but he always said he gave it up for women and motorbikes at the age of 19. He used to race bikes; he was the sidecar man, hanging over the side on bends, no helmet!

He saw that I could play a bit, even as a youngster, and he was instrumental in my development as a fielder. He used to tell me that if there were two guys of the same ability going for one place, the better fielder would always be chosen. So we'd practice catching for hours: half a dozen catches to my left hand, half a dozen to my right. From the age of eight, first with a soft ball, then a hard ball.

From quite early on, I saw myself as a slip fielder. And do you know why? It was a glory thing. If I brought off a spectacular catch, I could think, "Aren't I good!" But when I told my father, he wasn't happy. "No," he said. "You want to be in the outfield!" But I didn't. I wanted to be at slip

He came to accept the idea eventually but there was one thing he was very strict about. "Never, ever throw the ball up when you take a catch," he said. "That's swanking."

To a certain extent it was and I learned what could happen when I went to Park Avenue with my father to watch a Yorkshire game. Don Brennan was behind the stumps for Yorkshire and he was a great thrower-up of the ball. Don was also a very fine keeper but on this occasion, as he took the catch, he started to throw the ball up and spilled it. "There you are," said my father. Point taken.

I never forgot that day and throughout my career, I hardly ever threw the ball up to celebrate a catch. Perhaps half a dozen times, later on, when I was playing Test cricket. I remember doing so when I caught Joey Carew, the West Indies opener, off Basil D'Oliveira in the first Test at Manchester in 1969. But since *Wisden* described it as a 'memorable catch,' I suppose I was entitled to celebrate a bit.

And I seem to remember throwing the ball aloft twice more in the same series after catching Garry Sobers. Those were also a bit special because they were the result of a plan I'd hatched with Barry Knight, the Essex all-rounder and a very useful seam bowler indeed.

Like just about every seam bowler in those days, and unlike most of the current generation, Knighty was very accurate, so accurate that he was confident he could tuck up even Sobers. So the idea was for Knighty to keep Garry tied down for a couple of overs then slip him the old wide half volley. He'd chase it, get a nick and thank you very much! And it worked. We did him twice and it might easily have been three or four times.

So all the hard work with your father paid off?

Indeed! And it had moved up a rung when I went to Worksop College in Nottinghamshire at the age of 12 and discovered the slip cradle. I spent more time practising my catching than my batting. ⟋

Cradles are a bit more sophisticated these days but still operate on the the same basic principal: bouncing the ball off strips of wood attached to a bow-shaped metal frame. The only problem was that they were a bit predictable and you could more or less guess the angle of the ball as it bounced off the cradle...unless it caught a corner or something like that.

Much later, when I was a county player, we used to cover the cradle with a white cloth so we couldn't see exactly which fret the ball had hit. I think it was Bill Alley of Somerset who gave me that tip. That was back in the days when players from both sides would meet in the pub in the evening and senior pros were always happy to talk to junior pros from other counties.

Worksop has always had a reputation as a strong cricket school but when I there I was very small. My father was 5ft 4in and I came up to his second waistcoat button. There's an early team picture from Worksop of the junior colts in my first year. The team photos were always taken at the bottom of a row of four steps in the main quadrangle. Half the players would sit on chairs at the front with a second row standing behind.

The steps were not part of the set-up...until I came on to the scene. I was so tidgy that I had to stand two steps up and I was still smaller than the two guys who were standing next to me. At face value, I'm taking my place in the row of standing players...but if you look carefully at the picture, you can see the top half of my body, but no legs!

I played in the first team from the age of 14, batting at six, seven or eight. But because I was so small, I didn't have enough strength to hit the ball off the square. I could defend OK and nudge the ball into the gaps but I couldn't really hit it properly. That was enough to prompt the then headmaster, Canon B C Maloney, to say, "This boy will never play cricket, he's too small." How ludicrous a statement was that about a 14-year-old?

I was lucky to have a good coach in John Hall, who'd played for Notts in the Thirties. A medium pacer. I was even more lucky to be able to bat on some fantastic wickets, prepared by Jack Wigmore, who was groundsman there for many years. One year, he had an offer to take over at Bramall Lane but fortunately for us, he decided to stay put. The wickets were great for the batters, heartbreaking for the bowlers and that's where I learned to play.

In 1955, my last year at Worksop, I scored 1,252 runs, including two double centuries, and played twice at Lord's, for The Rest against Southern Schools and for Public Schools against the Combined Services.

Yorkshire had already been along to Worksop to have a look and after the school year ended, I played a couple of games for the Second XI, against Northants and Durham; straight from school into a county dressing room, which was quite an experience. Ronnie Burnet was the skipper.

At Northampton, Jackie van Geloven, the all-rounder who moved on to Leicestershire the following year, was claiming to anyone who would listen that he'd been having trouble with his eyes. He insisted to Ronnie, "I can't bloody see, I can't bloody see." So Ronnie suggested he should go to a specialist and find out if there was anything wrong.

When we arrived at Bishop Auckland for the Durham game, van Geloven was not happy. "That specialist has charged me five guineas just for telling me there's nothing bloody wrong!" He then proceeded to take seven for 69 and four for 39 so the old eyesight can't have been too bad after all.

Those two second team outings were as far as it went with Yorkshire for a couple of years because I joined the Army in '56. First up was a stint of officer training. I failed. So I stayed in the ranks and was moved on to Honiton in Devon, where I started to play some cricket.

If you were any good, it wasn't long before the call came and soon I was playing two-day games for my regiment, the Royal Electrical and Mechanical Engineers, then for the Army and eventually three-day matches for the Combined Services. So I fought most of my 'war' on the greenswards, which was very, very lucky.

Then back to Yorkshire in 1958. Given your Public School background was there any chance that you might play as an amateur and pursue another career?

Never. I'd always wanted to be a professional cricketer so I just turned pro at the first opportunity. I made my first team debut against Sussex at Worthing in July, 1958, and finished the season with 12 appearances and 461 runs to my name.

At the start of 1959, there were four capped batsmen at the top of the order: Bryan Stott, Ken Taylor, Vic Wilson and Brian Close. Ray Illingworth was going to bat at six so that left three of us, Brian Bolus, Dickie Bird and myself, vying for the same spot unless one of the senior players had a poor run and was left out. That's what happened to Vic eventually...and, unfortunately, to me as well.

I played in 18 games early on then lost my place for the Southern Tour at the end of the season after a dreadful run in which I scored 73 runs in 11 innings. As it happened, my father had already arranged to go down to Worcester for the first game of the tour so I said, "Look, Dad, I've been dropped so why don't I come down with you?"

"Good idea." And off we went.

When we arrived at the ground on the first morning, we discovered that Cyril Turner, the Yorkshire scorer, had been taken ill and they needed someone to fill the gap. "Why doesn't Sharpey do it?" asked Doug Padgett. And Sharpey did...first for the game at Worcester and then on to Hove for the Championship clincher against Sussex.

Which explains how, as Yorkshire chased 215 in 105 minutes to clinch their first outright title since 1946, I was scoring away alongside the Sussex chalker, George Washer. In that amazing second innings, Bryan Stott, Ken Taylor and Closey had scored 50 in the first four overs before I'd even got the names of the batsmen and bowlers written down in the book!

But George was a great bloke and he was telling me what to do all the time. Thank goodness it was just a straightforward, old fashioned scorebook and not all this technical mullarkey they have to handle today. I couldn't have managed that.

In 1960, you scored 1,000 runs for the first time and were capped along with Brian Bolus, Don Wilson and Mike Cowan. You scored 1,000 runs again in '61 and then everything really started to happen for you in 1962.

Yes, and not just on the field, where I scored over 2,000 runs.

The Trueman Episode also occurred at Taunton in 1962 and I happened to play a significant supporting role.

Fred and I had been playing in what proved to be the last Gentlemen v Players match at Lord's; Fred was skippering the Players. After the game, he was doing a television stint as a guest on the Marion Ryan Show and we'd arranged to meet afterwards at our hotel, the Clarendon Court in the Edgware Road, and set off for Taunton from there. No M4 in 1962 so it was going to be a long haul. To cut a long story short, we arrived in Taunton at three o'clock in the morning.

After checking in with the night porter, I arranged for an 8.30 call. To my certain knowledge, Fred did the same: 8.30 and a bacon sandwich. Then, after arranging to meet in the foyer at ten o'clock next morning, we went off to our rooms. At five to eleven, there was still no sign of Fred and as it was the first day of the match, we were supposed to report at 10.30, an hour before the scheduled start.

I was pacing around in the foyer of the County Hotel, which was only five minutes' walk from the ground, when I spotted Don Mosey, a member of the Press corps who followed us around in those days. He was with the Daily Mail at the time.

I said, "Look, Don, I can't wait any longer for Fred, I've got to get to the ground, even though all my kit's in Fred's boot. Vic will be playing bloody hell." I was dead right there. I got a fearful bollocking.

Fred eventually arrived at 11.20 and was informed by Vic that he'd been left out. He was actually sent home as well but as our next game was against Gloucestershire at Bristol, he didn't leave Taunton and hung around for the next three days. Fred was just about the biggest name in the game at the time so needless to say it was a huge story in the national Press.

Even though I'd been late, too, I escaped the axe and scored 138 on the first day...not bad after an overnight trip from London. On another occasion I would probably have got nought. But that was 1962, my year.

The main beneficiary from Fred's absence, however, was Peter Wight, Somerset's West Indian batsman. Peter was a very good player but he was scared to death of Fred. He must have thought it was his birthday when Fred was dropped and he cashed in with

215. And I didn't help by shelling him at slip off Mike Cowan. It was pretty much straight in but it went down. Mind you he'd already scored 100-plus by that stage.

One way or another, quite a year. Another Championship, Young Cricketer of the Year, 71 catches and so nearly a place on the 1962-63 Ashes tour to Australia. Disappointing to miss out?

Very disappointing indeed. But I had an inkling, in fact considerably more than an inkling, courtesy of Brian Sellers, the Yorkshire cricket chairman. We were playing at Bramall Lane and he asked me to go into the dining room for a word. He came straight to the point. "Although you're scoring all these runs and being talked about, I've told the selectors you're not ready."

I thought, "That's bloody brilliant, that is. My own chairman!"

Even so, I think I might have gone if David Sheppard, who later became the Bishop of Liverpool, hadn't made himself available to tour. Sheppard had first played for England in 1950, while he was still a student at Cambridge. Then he opted for a career in the Church and only played cricket as and when the day job permitted.

He played two Tests against Australia in 1956, two more against the West Indies the following year and a couple against Pakistan in 1962. So when he announced that he would be available to tour Australia in 1962-63, there was little doubt that he would be selected. He was even touted as a possible captain but Ted Dexter was given the nod instead and Sheppard was named as one of seven specialist batsmen.

Colin Cowdrey and Geoff Pullar were expected to open, with Dexter, Ken Barrington, Sheppard, Tom Graveney and Peter Parfitt contesting four places in the middle order. In the event, Cowdrey had a wretched start, dropped down the order and Sheppard ended up opening the innings in all five Tests.

So instead of Australia, I was invited to tour South Africa in March, 1963, with the International Cavaliers, managed by Ron Roberts, a cricket writer who worked for the Daily Telegraph. We had 13 players, nine Aussies and four of us from the UK. Richie Benaud was skipper and after a one-off in Bombay against an

Indian XI, we played seven matches in South Africa

John Edrich, Mickey Stewart, Roy Swetman, myself and, later in the tour, Ted Dexter represented the Mother Country while the Aussie contingent consisted of Benaud, former Test opener Arthur Morris, Bill Alley, Norman O'Neill, Barry Shepherd, Johnny Martin, Graham McKenzie, David Sincock and Des Hoare.

Exchanging the frozen wastes of an English winter for a South African summer was inevitably quite a culture shock but I started to score a few runs towards the end of the tour. That was when Shepherd, who went on to play nine times for Australia, told me, "You'll play for England next season."

"What? No chance, I replied." But he was deadly serious and I ended up betting him a pound that I wouldn't.

The West Indies were touring England under Frank Worrell that year. But even though David Sheppard was no longer available and I played for the MCC against the tourists at Lord's in what was always seen as an unofficial Test trial, I wasn't included in the side for the first Test. Stewart and Brian Close were chosen ahead of me and at that stage, I had no reason to suppose that the situation was going to change over the next few months.

I assumed my bet with Barry Shepherd would be safe but even so, when Yorkshire played Notts at Trent Bridge, I decided to lay off the pound. We were having a drink in the Trent Bridge Inn one evening, accompanied by one or two Yorkshire supporters, one of whom was a landlord from a hostelry I knew back home. So I struck the bet with him that I'd be playing for England before the season was over.

And sure enough, I was. Cowdrey was wounded in the second Test at Lord's when he was hit by a short one from Wesley Hall, breaking a bone in his arm. He was clearly going to take no further part in the series and England were going to need someone who could bat and field at slip. So they sent for me and all of a sudden, I owed Barry Shepherd a pound!

But how to repay the debt? By chance, Graham McKenzie was in England later in the summer so I said, "Look, Garth, I don't know when I'll be seeing Shep again so will you give him his quid when you go back home." He did...but I never got my pound back from the landlord! Still, I should worry. I was paid £100 for playing for

England.

A lot of money in those days, as they say. But surely your selection as a specialist slip fielder cranked up the pressure a bit? Dropping a catch in the first over wouldn't have been a good idea.

Pressure? No, not at all. Because I knew it was something I could do. I thrived on the fact that zillions of people were watching me. It got the adrenaline going. The point is that in those days, a player was selected for two matches at most. If you didn't do well, it was a case of, "On your bike...next, please!"

Now in my view, that was good. It made you concentrate doubly to make sure you did well. These days, if you're a centrally contracted player, you can normally reckon on being in the squad week in, week out. Now for me, if you know you're going to be in the side – be it England or Yorkshire -- for the next yonk, you can coast.

That certainly happened occasionally with me at county level. I was confident that I would always get into the Yorkshire side because of my catching so there were times when I tended to coast a bit with the batting. That's a terrible admission, isn't it? But I did.

Then there would come a time when I'd think, "Mmmm, I haven't been getting too many runs, I'd better knuckle down a bit." It didn't always work, of course, but usually if I wasn't scoring runs, I'd bring off one or two catches and people would say, "Yes, that's why he's there."

But nowadays, we've reached the stage where Test cricket has almost become like the county game for centrally contracted players. The squad situation creates an environment for lazy players. It's much better to put people under stress – I prefer that word to pressure. That brings the best out of them. If they can't play under that premise, then they shouldn't be there in the first place.

In three Tests in 1963, you topped the averages with 267 runs at 53.40...and took four catches. And you were playing against a pretty potent attack.

Very much so. Wes Hall and Charlie Griffith to open the attack with Sobers and Lance Gibbs following on behind as light relief. With Hall and Griffith we never knew when the next bouncer would be coming.

In the modern game, just about every ball seems to be a bouncer so batsmen have needed to develop a technique to get out of the way. Whereas then we were used to the ball being pitched fairly well up to give it time to swing. We were expecting a fuller length so when the bouncer came, either from Wes's extreme pace or Charlie's suspect action, it could be very nasty indeed.

Charlie was a particularly dangerous proposition at Headingley and The Oval, the two grounds where there was no proper sightscreen, and picked up nine wickets in each of the Tests played there. They won the series 3-1 after winning the final Test by eight wickets when Fred was unable to bowl in their second innings because of an ankle injury. It must have been the only time he was injured in the eleven years I played with him.

After touring India in 1963-64, you played a couple of Tests against the Aussies in '64 but didn't play for another five years. You returned in 1969 and scored your only Test hundred against New Zealand at Trent Bridge. But they made you wait for it.

I was on 98 for half an hour, waiting, waiting, waiting. I was facing Hedley Howarth, the left-arm spinner, for most of the time and he was a tidy bowler. But there was no way I was going to give it away, not like they do today. Having a slog in the nineties? Excuse me! Finally, he bowled me a full toss, I turned it through the mid-wicket area for four and I'd made it. I enjoyed that one.

I was eventually out for 111, caught and bowled by Howarth, who also happened to bat at number 11. So the old electronic scoreboard read, ct 11, b 11, 111. No chance of getting past Nelson that day. But that was only the start. I was courting my missus, Susan, at the time; she was an air stewardess and had arranged to come up to Trent Bridge to see me.

And on the same day that I scored 111 and was caught and

bowled by their number 11, Susan's bank balance was 111 pounds, eleven shillings and eleven pence. Amazing! So we simply had to get married.

I finished that summer with a Test average approaching 50 from 11 matches but I only played one more game for England, the first match against the Rest of the World the following year. I made four and two. It was one of those matches at Lord's when the ball was swinging all over the place and people like Sobers, McKenzie and Mike Procter weren't bad bowlers in those conditions. If I'd scored runs there, I might have carried on and made it to Australia for the 1970-71 tour under Illy.

You had been appointed vice-captain to Brian Close at the start of the 1970 season. He was 39 at the time so did you see yourself as the heir apparent?

I thought I had a chance, yes. But it wasn't to be. Let's leave it at that. Thereafter it all went a bit sour. Did I see it coming? No, not at the time. But if you look at it with the great gift of hindsight, it was inevitable. We'd lost four great players in Closey, Fred, Illy and Jimmy Binks and they hadn't been replaced. Bowlers win matches, as well as catchers, and the attack was useful but a bit thin.

They weren't particularly pleasant times in the early Seventies but in 1973, when Geoff Boycott missed several Championship matches because of Test calls, I took over as captain. Yorkshire only won three games all season and tied another against Middlesex at Park Avenue. I was skipper in all four matches. The following year I was sacked and moved on to Derbyshire.

I had two good years there...and then I was sacked again! But somebody up there must have been working on my behalf because that meant I was able to get fixed up with Norfolk in the Minor Counties and start one of the happiest phases of my career. It was a delight after the years I'd had in the early Seventies.

I joined them as skipper in 1977 and stayed for six years. I like to think I brought out the professionalism in a gang of amateurs. They were very good cricketers but they just went out and played at it. I told them no. I said, "We can't do this, lads. We've got to play it properly, think about what we're doing, bowl straight."

I made them think about the game as a professional would and it was a great pleasure for me. I was passing on Closey and Illy's thinking to some talented amateurs and they appreciated it.

We still had a lot fun, of course, like the Magic Hat for Idiot of the Day. It was a grey sombrero, about three feet wide with a black band, and was awarded to a player who'd done something silly during the day. Somebody nicked it in the end.

One of the fast bowlers was Teddy Wright, a great mate now. He was the production director at Bernard Matthews, the poultry producers, and his main claim to fame is that on his Gillette Cup debut against Leicestershire in 1982, he bowled a maiden over to David Gower.

Mind you they were absolutely walking the game and Gower won the Man of the Match Award for his 65 not out. But even so... We still have a reunion every two years, first a dinner, now it's a lunch.

And after Norfolk, an unexpected career swerve.

One morning in 1983, I had a call from D B Carr, the secretary of the TCCB. He said, "For some reason, I have your name on a pad in front of me."

"Oh, yes?" says I.

"We'd like you to be a Test selector."

"Oh, right." It came totally out of the blue. Apparently he'd sounded out Ray Illingworth, who'd recommended me. Illy must have thought that after all those years standing at slip alongside Binks, Closey and Raymond, of course, something must have rubbed off on me. We weren't paid but received expenses.

Alec Bedser was in his final year as chairman with myself, Peter May and A C Smith as selectors. Peter took over as chairman the following year, with Alec joining AC and myself, and when Smith was appointed chief executive of the TCCB in 1987, Fred Titmus joined the panel of selectors.

Contrary to the old cartoon image of selectors spending more time at the bar than watching cricket, it was a very serious job. During a Test Match, we hardly missed a ball unless we were delayed after lunch because we'd had to wait to be served. Apart from perhaps a glass of something at lunchtime, drink was off limits during the day's play.

We would all meet up before the start of the season when we'd discuss the players who'd been touring the previous winter and who might be in the pipeline for the coming season. Everyone had their say and we would eventually reach a consensus.

For most of my six years in the job, the side was pretty settled but of course there were gaps here and there and the selectors would be despatched around the country to watch potential candidates. We were on the road a lot.

There was never any suggestion of trying to watch a player incognito. In fact, we would always let a club know that we would be on the ground and, in the hope that we would select one of their players, we'd be given a decent lunch.

I never said who I was actually watching, although in most cases it was pretty obvious. And over the years, I lost count of the number of times a club chairman would say, "Oh, you should have been here last week...he did this, he did that! You've got to pick him, you know."

And the standard riposte was, "OK, if we pick him, who would you leave out?" That set them thinking.

Ian Botham gave us our biggest headache...but only when he was unfit. There weren't that many all-rounders about and obviously no one of Botham's calibre. Derek Pringle was probably the nearest thing to Ian, a good bowler but his batting was not quite up to it. Not in the same street as Botham, who could easily have moved up to number five if necessary.

Ian really was a good batsman, he played the straightest of the lot. So if he wasn't around, we usually had to decide whether to replace him with a specialist batsman and lose a bowler. Or vice versa.

The eighties marked the end of an era when cricket at all levels had a big social side, too. People like Botham, Mike Gatting, David Gower, Allan Lamb, John Emburey and Phil Edmonds played it the same way as we did in the Sixties. They played hard on the field and enjoyed themselves afterwards. So even though I was from the Sixties and they were the Eighties, we all had the same approach.

However they had the misfortune to be around at the time when the Press were just starting to come in and nail 'em about being out late and all that sort of thing. And it all stopped anyway when Graham Gooch took over as captain in 1988. He was a fitness fanatic, trained with West Ham United and was supremely fit. So the regime changed at England level and from there it went down the ladder into the first-class game.

Cricket wasn't the only sport; hockey and rugby union were the same. I used to play hockey for Yorkshire, although I finished in '71. It was my benefit year and I simply couldn't combine the two. But I played the whole of my hockey career with the county, the North of England and a couple of England trials without any serious training. I just went out and played.

The preparation and training they do today means that hockey and rugby players are far better. No question. But I'm not sure the same applies to cricket. They are better at the limited overs game, although we would have learned to manufacture shots and so on. And they are more athletic. We were fit enough to do the job – I was fit enough to stand at first slip all day -- but everything was at a much slower pace.

We never really netted, not even at the start of the season. In April, if the weather wasn't so good, we'd have half an hour indoors or maybe work for a while on the slip cradle. Then we'd wander off to the Original Oak in Headingley for a pint. Or halves for me in the fifties. Even when we were outside, it was a case of 20 minutes each for the batters and then a bit of fielding practice. And that was it.

And I suppose today's game is more fun to watch for the general public because the ball is whizzing to all parts all the time. But that's because they can't bowl straight. It's the same game but not the game I played, which was a competition between high-class bowler and high-class batter, each trying to outwit the other. Playing and missing was a cardinal sin...or it was if you were a Roman Catholic. If not, it was just a bloody awful shot!

Six of Yorkshire's seven Championships were shared by Brian Close and Vic Wilson. Who was the better captain?

Closey. A captain is only as good as his players but Brian was very much the man in charge, the leader of men. The idea of Closey working alongside a coach or team manager as they do today is unthinkable. He used to do everything himself.

And when we were having a bad run, as we did from time to time even during the Sixties, he would come up with some amazing ways of turning things round. Like banning our nights out at Chinese restaurants.

It may not be very politically correct these days but there used to be an old saying on the lines of, "If you kill a Chinaman, it's bad luck for the next 30 years." I've absolutely no idea where it came from. But once, Closey was convinced that our bad run had been caused by eating Chinese food too often. So trips to the Chinese were off limits until we started winning again.

Of course, Brian was lucky to have Illy as a sidekick. Raymond was methodical and straight down the middle whereas Closey would do something ludicrous and it would work. It was the ideal combination.

And do you single out one of the seven Championships?

Not really. The 1959 win at Hove seemed to set the tone for tense finishes and three more of our seven Championships went right down to the wire, two of which were decided at Harrogate.

In 1962, the second day of the game against Glamorgan was completely washed out – there were still 5,000 people in the ground, though! But Don Wilson took ten wickets in the match and we got home by seven wickets.

It went to the last game at Harrogate in 1967 as well, with Illy taking 14 wickets in the match against Gloucestershire. And in 1968, we beat Surrey at Hull with just five minutes to spare. So we were never really like the golfer who's about 200 under par in the Open with three holes to play and can afford to relax and savour the moment.

Perhaps that was a feeling we might have enjoyed in winning our last trophy, the 1969 Gillette Cup. We beat Derbyshire by 69 runs in the final and were never really in any trouble. But quite honestly, apart from Barrie Leadbeater winning the Man of the Match award, I can't really remember anything about the match. I was out for three, chopping a ball from Alan Ward on to my wicket and I didn't take a catch.

Even though it was a Lord's final, the day was all a bit low key somehow. It certainly didn't feel like the end of an era.

But it was.

When the final season of Yorkshire's golden age began, the Beatles were on top of the charts with Get Back. And as the 1969 campaign ended, the number one slot was occupied by Zager and Evans, singing In The Year 2525. Hopefully Yorkshire supporters will not have to wait quite so long before the White Rose gets back to where it once belonged.

AFTERWORD.

BY BRIAN CLOSE

They were a magnificent group of lads, they really were. On and off the field. A team in the true sense of the word. Totally committed, working 100 per cent for one another.

Above all, we were all Yorkshiremen, which meant such a lot to everyone. We weren't the best-paid players in the land and none of us had a proper contract...we were just told in August whether we were going to be retained the following year.

But from April to September we were eleven Yorkshiremen playing for Yorkshire and we knew all about the cricketing traditions of our county.

We were a great side and we became a great side because we had so many options in the field. You are never, ever going to win a Championship unless you are good in the field.

Your batsmen, and make no mistake we had some bloody good players, can put you in a winning position. But to go on and win the match, you have to bowl the other side out twice. And we were equipped to do that week in and week out.

On the fast bowling front we had Fred Trueman, supported early on by Mike Cowan, Melville Ryan and Bob Platt and later by Tony Nicholson and Richard Hutton.

And if the ball was swinging, Ray Illingworth and I could chip in as well. We both started as youngsters bowling swing – in fact, in 1948 and '49 I was as fast as Fred.

I had a long delivery stride, though, and used to land heavily on my heel. I jarred it badly and eventually had to stop bowling fast. But I could still bowl a bit of swing if I had to and if the quicker bowlers were tiring, Ray and I could come on.

We had two off-spinners, me and Ray, and Don Wilson with his left-arm spin. And then there was Ken Taylor bowling medium pace. He could always chip in with a wicket and provide another alternative.

And with all those options we could continually change the questions we were asking the batsmen, changing the scene, never letting them settle down. That's the way to play cricket.

On top of that we had a bloody good fielding side. Philip Sharpe at slip, Illy in the gully, Fred at backward short leg, Don Wilson at mid-wicket and Ken Taylor at cover were all top-class. Jimmy Binks was as good a wicketkeeper as I've seen and I just fitted in any bloody where.

I used to have the odd chat with Jimmy, who could tell me how the bowlers were performing. It was no good having bowlers who were bowling people in, we needed them to bowl batsmen out! If Jimmy didn't feel they were likely to beat the bat they were taken off and replaced by another bowler.

It was magnificent. We were always on our toes and we won matches that we had no right to win because of the way we played.

We loved the game and we played it honourably. If you cheated in those days your own players would play hell, never mind the opposition. And four times in my career as a captain I called a batsman back who'd been given out.

One of them was Tom Graveney when we were playing Worcestershire at Scarborough. Tom was injured and needed a runner, just a young lad who was there as Twelfth Man.

I was bowling, Tom played and missed, Jimmy took it down the leg side and had the bails off in a fraction. Tom was in his crease all right...but his runner wasn't! So the umpire gave him out.

Tom was looking really crestfallen so I said to the umpire, "Look, the young lad didn't understand. I'd like to call Tom back." So we gave him another knock – fortunately he didn't score too many more!

They do all kinds of things now that we would never have done. We considered ourselves a good side with good players and we didn't need to cheat. But because of all the money involved now the morals of the game have declined. That's a great pity.

We enjoyed our cricket. And a lot of people used to say how much they enjoyed playing against us because if they did well it was a real feather in their cap. Bomber Wells, the off-spinner who moved from Gloucester to Notts in 1960, always said how much he liked playing against Yorkshire.

Why? Because at the end of the day's play, the opposition's young players could go into the bar, spend half an hour with Fred, another half hour with me and learn more in that hour than they would in a whole week.

We talked openly about the day's cricket, who'd played well, who'd made mistakes, what they could do to put things right. We were never reluctant to talk to lads from other teams because it helped to improve the game overall.

We had our arguments because no two people think alike. Not even Ray and me and I'd known him since we'd first played together when we were 16. Same with Fred. I knew them inside out.

In some respects Ray was slightly negative; he'd be happy to bowl 20 overs for 30 runs and take two wickets whereas I'd rather have him take four wickets for 50. But when push came to shove, all that mattered for both of us was Yorkshire.

In the early post-War period, there were two great teams: Surrey, who won seven Championships in the Fifties, and Yorkshire, who won seven Championships between 1959 and 1968.

And while Surrey had arguably the finest bowling attack of them all – pace from Alec Bedser and Peter Loader, spin from Jim Laker and Tony Lock – I believe we were better.

Our batting was stronger and we were a better all-round fielding side, although Locky was an incredible fielder both in the leg trap and to his own bowling. He was responsible for the best two bits of fielding I ever saw...although obviously I never saw myself!

I never sampled Surrey's off-the-field antics either but I'd be prepared to bet they couldn't match us in that department. We knew how to play hard on and off the field.

We used to have a load of members following us round because we played the right sort of cricket. Many of them stayed in the same hotels and we used to entertain them in the evenings.

I'll always remember the sing-alongs we had with Sharpey and Don Wilson and I had a few party tricks up my sleeve, too.

I could balance a pint of ale on top of my head, go into the press-up position and pick up a box of matches in my teeth – without spilling a drop!

Or what about balancing a pint on the back of each hand and then slowly turning my hands over so that the pints were in the palms of each hand? And I've even been known to drink a pint of ale off the top of my head with my hands in my pockets!

I took over as captain in 1963, although I'd more or less been doing the job for four years anyway.

In 1959, Vic Wilson was Ronnie Burnet's senior professional, vice-captain in other words, but was left out in the middle of June because he couldn't score a run. He only played two more Championship games that year.

So Ronnie came to me and said, "Brian, you're the senior professional now." Now Ronnie was a lovely fella but he was no great shakes as a captain. Sometimes he didn't seem to know what time of day it was.

So I replied, "Right, well look here Ronnie. If I suggest something and you don't do it, you can find someone else."

We won our next three matches. I was telling Ronnie who to bowl and how to move the field around and it was working fine. But once we were up with the leaders Ronnie started to ignore my suggestions.

We had a bit of a row and I repeated that he could find somebody else if he wasn't going to listen to me.

He more or less did as he was told after that and after beating Worcester at New Road, we went to Hove for the last game against Sussex with a chance of the Championship.

Throughout the match we were reasonably in command but at lunch on the last day, they had seven down and were nearly 200 in front with just one session to play...the game was scheduled to end at 4.30pm.

Robin Marlar, their captain, was never going to declare and let us win the Championship and as we were walking out for the afternoon session, I said, "Ronnie, what are you going to do now? We've got to get 'em out straight away or we aren't going to win."

He replied, "Well all we can do is let Fred bowl down the hill towards the sea."

"Forget Fred," I said. "He's had a hard season and he hasn't bowled well here. Let Raymond have that end and Don Wilson the other end and if they can't do it, we've had it." Ray got the last three wickets and we got the runs with a few minutes to spare.

After a few days of frolicking at Scarborough, enjoying our Championship success, we went down to The Oval for the Champions v The Rest.

They fielded a hell of a side. Mike Smith had scored over 3,000 runs and Geoff Pullar and Ken Barrington had both topped 2,000. Trevor Bailey, Godfrey Evans and Tony Lock were also in their line-up.

Ken Taylor was back playing football for Huddersfield Town so Vic Wilson was brought into the Twelve. The night before the match, I asked Ronnie who he was going to play. "I'm going to leave Vic out and play Jackie Birkenshaw," he replied.

I said, "Don't. Vic hasn't scored a bloody run since God knows when; he's bound to come good sometime."

"Yes but we might need Jackie as an extra spinner because Ray's finger's not so good."

That was news to me. I asked Ray if he was OK and he said, "Yes, I'll be all right as long as I don't have to bowl on the first day."

"Right. Tell Ronnie you'll be OK and I'll see to it." So he left out Jackie Birkenshaw.

The Rest batted, made a big score and Ray only bowled seam. Vic made 41, the top score, but we ended up following on. This time Vic made a hundred and then Ray and I bowled them out.

That winter Brian Sellers, the cricket chairman, took Ronnie out for lunch and, according to Ronnie, this was the gist of his words: "Well, you've won the Championship and you're entitled to do it again.

"But if you stay for another year, we'll have to get rid of Vic and then we'll have no option but to give the job to Brian Close when you retire. And we mustn't do that." Sellers was never a pal of mine.

And he went on, "But if you retire now, you'll leave as a Championship-winning captain and Vic can take over." And that's what happened.

Vic was a hell of a nice fella but he wasn't quick in making decisions. Something to do with being a farmer, I suppose; they take three months to decide whether the grass needs cutting.

And unbeknown to Vic, the lads used to watch me in the field instead of him. Anyway, we won the Championship again in 1960 and again in '62, Vic's third and final season.

By the time I was appointed for the following year, I knew the ins and outs of the job. I'd played for so many different kinds of captains.

At Yorkshire there was Norman Yardley, Billy Sutcliffe, Ronnie and Vic, not to mention Len Hutton, who was captain of England from 1953 to 1955. I used to sit alongside him and listen to every word he said. It was always sound common sense.

And I'd played for England teams under Freddie Brown, Donald Carr and Peter May as well as Ted Dexter when I was recalled in 1963 for the series against West Indies.

I wasn't stupid, I observed everything that was going on in the game of cricket. I always looked at other captains and learned something, asked myself why they did this or that. I'd seen the good and the bad and it was up to me to pick out the good bits.

Captaincy is about being in command of your players and knowing their strengths and weaknesses. And obviously it helps to know the strengths and weaknesses of the opposition as well.

A captain also has to lead from the front and that's something I was always prepared to do. I was never going to ask other people to take risks I wasn't prepared to take myself.

I used to field at what some people thought was suicidally close to the bat at short leg and I was hit all over the bloody place.

I used to get down with my legs half bent with my upper body always horizontal and my head stuck out in front. The only places they could hit me point blank were my legs, my shoulders and my head.

Getting hit was all part of the job but a few incidents stand out. Once we were playing Kent at Gravesend and it nearly was my grave's end!

There were about ten minutes left and we were struggling to bowl them out after I'd declared and set them 50-odd an hour to keep them interested.

Wils was bowling with about ten minutes left and Alan Brown, their big, tall fast bowler, had a real crack. It hit me on the forehead, flew sky high and landed on the pavilion steps.

I'd already shouted, "Catch it" because I knew Dougie Padgett was fielding in front of the pavilion.

Next ball I moved half a yard nearer. Up comes Wils again, Brown tried the same thing, missed and Jimmy stumped him. We won by 22 runs.

There was another time when Gloucester opener Martin Young

swept Illy, the ball hit me flush on the forehead and rebounded to Sharpey at slip.

Quite a few people were caught from rebounds off my head over the years and I reckon I must have caught half a dozen catches or more where the ball never went more than two feet off the bat. Standing so close made batsmen a little bit nervous.

The players I inherited in 1963 were already a bloody good side and were reinforced by the emergence of three younger players, John Hampshire, Tony Nicholson and Geoff Boycott.

I played a part in the development of all three, especially Boycott. Before Vic retired he had apparently told the committee that they should release Boycs, who had only played five first team games at that time.

He had been involved in a couple of run-out incidents with Ken Taylor and Philip Sharpe and as I understand it, Vic felt that as long as Boycs was around there would be problems.

But when I was made captain, I said, "No, don't release him. Let me look after him and see where we go from there."

Geoff scored his maiden century, batting at five, in the Roses Match at Bramall Lane at the beginning of June. Seven weeks later, I made him into an opening batsman, even though he wanted to stay in the middle order.

In one of his early games as an opener, we were playing Surrey at Bramall Lane and in the first innings, Peter Loader bowled him for a duck. Boycs came into the dressing room and was in tears. I wasn't having that.

I said, "Stop feeling sorry for yourself and grow up. I've chosen you to open because you've got the right technique to be an opening batsman. I'd do the job myself but it's better if I stay in the dressing room and see how I can help the other batsmen later.

"If it's not working out, I have the experience to pull it round. I'll help you all I can." And I did. I also spent hours talking about how to read different bowlers.

And no messing, a couple of weeks later, he scored his first hundred as an opener against Lancashire at Old Trafford. The following June he was opening for England against Australia.

In 1963, we won the Championship with a bit to spare and the only cloud on the horizon was the introduction that year of the first one-day competition, the Gillette Cup or whatever it was called in those days.

At Yorkshire we were in the business of winning championships and the one-day stuff was the total opposite of everything we believed in and were trained to do.

In first-class cricket, it's the bowling and fielding side who ask the questions and the batting side who have to find the answers. In limited overs cricket it works the other way and that's why bowling standards have declined so much in recent years.

I must admit that as captain, I believed my job was to win championships and we didn't put as much effort into the one-day competition as we might have done. The first time we really did so was in 1965 and we won it, beating Surrey in the final by the record margin of 175 runs.

Early in that season we had loads of rain in the north of England and hardly finished a home match by the end of June. Halfway through the season we basically had no chance of winning the Championship and set ourselves a target of the Gillette Cup.

We did the job properly and by then I'd realised the time had come to ask my bowlers to bowl negatively to a negative field. It hurt and it was totally against the grain. But we had to do it and we won the cup.

Then it was back to the serious business of winning championships again and we lifted three in a row from 1966, the year I was appointed captain of England for the final Test against the West Indies.

We won that game by an innings and in 1967 I led England in six more Tests against India and Pakistan, winning five and drawing one. It wasn't good enough to keep me in the job.

The Establishment wanted me out and after the second Test against Pakistan in early August, Crawford White, who wrote for the Daily Express, warned me something might happen

He said, "For heaven's sake, Brian, watch your step. If they have any possible chance, the MCC are going to get rid of you and put their own man in."

A few days later, they were given the chance they were looking for when I was accused of time wasting in Yorkshire's drawn game against Warwickshire at Edgbaston.

We did absolutely nothing wrong. We were accused of delaying the game to avoid defeat in the final session but in fact we had to play in drizzle and our lads actually broke a rule to try and get through their overs quicker.

That season there was a new rule, designed to counter ball tampering by certain counties, stating that if the ball was wet, any bowler wanting to dry it had to do so in front of the umpire.

Instead, Fred, Tony and Richard, took the cloth from the umpires and wiped the ball on the way back to their mark after each delivery. If they'd followed the letter of the law, far more time would have been taken up.

Because the ball was wet, I couldn't bowl my spinners, Illy and Wils, so I had to rely exclusively on the three seamers. And with four or five minutes to go, I took off Nick and replaced him with Richard. He went and had a practice run!

I didn't know he was going to do it and to put it mildly, it didn't go down too well with the Warwickshire supporters. But he explained afterwards that he hadn't bowled at that end before all match and needed a warm-up. Fair enough.

They still required nine to win when he started his over and as Richard could be as dozy as hell sometimes, I shouted across to him from extra cover, "Richard, for heaven's sake bowl straight. If you get a wicket this will be our last over."

He bowled a straight one, clean bowled Alan Smith and the game was drawn. As I came off the field, a Warwickshire supporter said something rather rude. I walked along the row where I thought the comment had come from, put my hands on a fella's shoulder and asked him, "Did you say that?"

He replied, "No, I didn't." So I said I was sorry and went into the dressing room. It was subsequently reported that I'd picked him up by the scruff of the neck and tried to throttle him.

Next day the so-called quality press, the Times, Telegraph and Guardian, representing the amateur side of the game, went for me in a big way. As well as my so-called assault on a member, they accused the Yorkshire team of wasting time.

We hadn't. It was a wet ball, we couldn't use the spinners, we had to rely on the quickies and I wasn't going to tell Fred to bowl off a short run, was I?

At the subsequent hearing at Lord's, I was asked to apologise. I refused. I had done nothing wrong. But that was their way of getting rid of me as captain and Colin Cowdrey took over for the winter tour of the West Indies.

I covered the tour from the Press Box, writing for a national newspaper here and also for a paper in the Caribbean. Colin must have read my articles because by the end of the tour he was ringing me up to ask what he should do!

The 1968 Championship race went right down to the wire when we beat Surrey at Hull with five minutes of the final day left. But unfortunately I missed out on the celebrations because I was in hospital receiving running repairs after being hit twice by Younis Ahmed.

The first time the ball rebounded off me and hit John Hampshire at backward short leg. He was hopping about all over the place so I shouted, "Never mind that, get the ball back to Wils!"

Next ball, Younis hit me in the groin and this time it rebounded to Jimmy Binks, who caught it.

Wils soon trapped Robin Jackman leg before with his arm ball and then Nick had Arnold Long caught at the wicket and we'd won another Championship.

In 1969, Fred had retired, Illy had gone to Leicestershire and we had three players involved with England on a regular basis – Geoff Boycott, Philip Sharpe and John Hampshire.

We didn't make much of an impact in the Championship so once again we turned our attention to the Gillette Cup...and won it again, beating Derbyshire by 69 runs.

I missed four games early in the 1970 season with a shoulder injury and at first we struggled a bit. Even though my right arm was more or less useless, I came back after missing four games.

We recovered well and at one stage we were in with a chance of another Championship. But then Chris Old and Don Wilson were called up to play for England against the Rest of the World and we were short of bowlers. In the end, we finished fourth.

Little did I know as we went our separate ways for the winter, that my days were already numbered.

It had all come to a head at Old Trafford after a Sunday League match. Lancashire won to clinch a second title in a row. They were lucky to win, we were annoyed and weren't going to shrug off a defeat like that in a few minutes.

At Old Trafford, there was a separate dressing room for the captains and I was back in there when a bloke I'd never seen before in my life burst into the room.

He was full of himself, bubbling over about how well Lancashire had played. I said, "Don't talk so bloody daft. You were lucky." He turned round and walked out of the room.

I packed up my gear and walked out of the pavilion to jump in my car and go straight home. I was halfway to the car when this voice boomed out, "Close! Close!" It was Brian Sellers, chasing after me, demanding an explanation.

I told him my side of the story and then it emerged that the man I'd been talking to was Lionel Lister, the Lancashire president. When I got home, I wrote him a letter of apology.

The following week, I was hauled over the coals by Sellers and John Nash, the Yorkshire secretary. I showed them a copy of my letter and thought that would be the end of it. It wasn't.

In November, the day after the monthly committee meeting, I received a phone call from John Nash, the Yorkshire secretary, telling me Sellers would like to see me. We fixed a time, 11.30 next morning.

Sellers came straight to the point. "Well, you've had a good innings, Brian. We have two letters here, one saying you've resigned the captaincy, the other saying you've been sacked. We'll give one of those out to the Press at two o'clock."

I didn't have a clue it might happen. And neither had the committee when they'd gathered for the fateful meeting the night before. The agenda, on which the first item was my future, had not been circulated in advance.

I'd assumed Sellers wanted to talk about the 1971 season. Instead, I was given five minutes to decide whether to resign or be sacked. Five minutes! After 22 years with Yorkshire, that's all I was given to decide how I would leave!

I'd won eight Championships – I played in 1949 when we shared the title with Middlesex – and two Gillette Cups. And I'd given my life to Yorkshire cricket for bugger all in terms of financial reward.

I said, "Oh well, if that's the case, I'll resign." I thought there would be less bother that way and I'd had enough trouble in my life. I walked out. I felt terrible. On the way home, I had to stop at Kirkstall Abbey and I was as sick as a dog over the wall.

When my wife Vivienne came in, she took one look at me and said, "What's the matter?"

"I've resigned."

"Resigned?" I explained what had happened. She told me to call Roy Parsons, a great friend who was an influential figure in Yorkshire cricket, and Jack Mewis, my solicitor.

They both said I shouldn't have resigned; that by doing so I was taking away Yorkshire's responsibility for getting rid of me.

So between 12.30 and one o'clock I tried to ring Nash to say I'd changed my mind. But the line was permanently engaged. When I finally got through, I told Nash, "I've decided you can sack me." I left it at that.

I was too late. The statement that I'd resigned had already been released. As soon as I put the phone down, I had a call from Reg Hayter, a journalist who ran a sports agency in London. He was a good pal.

"Brian, for heaven's sake, find a suitcase, pack your toothbrush and your pyjamas and get yourself out of the house. It will be flooded with Pressmen any time now. Get yourself down to London.

"England are playing East Germany at Wembley tonight. I'll have a ticket for you and I'll try and get you on Sportsnight." That was the BBC's weekly sports programme introduced by David Coleman.

I told David that I accepted that the Yorkshire committee ran the club and were entitled to make what they thought were the right decisions. But after 22 years' service I thought I was entitled to better treatment.

So in 1971, they gave the captaincy to Boycs and I went to Somerset. They made me captain the following year. I had seven good seasons at Taunton, bringing on people like Viv Richards, Ian Botham and Brian Rose, to name just a few, and we made real progress.

And if Tom Cartwright hadn't struggled with injuries from 1974 onwards, there's nothing we could not have won. Tom was a superb medium-pace bowler. I could give him the ball on a good wicket and still have five or six men around the bat.

I even ended up playing for England again, leading the side in the one-day series against Australia in 1972 – we won 2-1 – and three matches against the West Indies in 1976, at the age of 45.

Meanwhile Yorkshire had been having problems and in 1975, my fourth year as Somerset skipper, we played them at Harrogate. At one point, I was walking round the ground towards the pavilion. And who was coming the other way? Brian Sellers.

He couldn't dodge me…and I certainly wasn't going to avoid him. We met face to face and he looked me straight in the eye.

He said, "You've done a great job at Somerset, Brian, and I've got an apology to make. I can honestly say that sacking you was the biggest mistake of my life." I retired a couple of years later.

None of the men who played for Yorkshire between 1959 and 1969 will ever forget that time. We never made much money but it was a great life and a wonderful way to make a living. We enjoyed being together and working for one another. We played the game hard but above all, we played it with honour.

Dennis Brian Close was born in Rawdon on February 24, 1931. A middle order batsman and off-spin or medium pace bowler, he made his Yorkshire debut in 1949. In 536 first-class appearances for the county, he scored 22,650 runs, including 33 centuries, at an average of 31.94, claimed 967 wickets at 24.29 and took 564 catches. He also featured in 32 one-day games. Close played in seven outright Championship sides and was a member of the team who shared the title with Middlesex in 1949. He captained Yorkshire between 1963 and 1970, winning four Championships and two Gillette Cups. Between 1949, when he became England's youngest Test cricketer, and 1976, Close played 22 times for England, including seven unbeaten matches as captain. Close joined Somerset in 1971 and went on to play for another seven seasons, scoring 7,567 runs and taking 74 wickets in 142 first-class matches. He also played in 126 one-day games. Close later served on the Yorkshire committee and was president of the club from 2008 to 2010.

ACKNOWLEDGEMENTS

Magnificent Seven would not have been possible without the 15 former Yorkshire players who, so willingly, have given up their time to take part in the preparation of the book. Without exception, they have been unfailingly friendly, helpful and hospitable. A warm and sincere thank you to them all.

Special thanks also to Ron Deaton for allowing access to his compendious collection of photographs and other memorabilia. And for his unstinting work in collating archive material, team pictures and portraits.

Thanks, too, to the former players who loaned illustrations and memorabilia. And to *Yorkshire Post Newspapers*, for access to their picture archive, and Colin Abba, H & J Jelley, Brian Sanderson, the Yorkshire Players' Association, *Huddersfield Examiner*, *Scarborough Evening News* and the *Daily Mail* for permission to use photographs and other illustrations.

Thank you also to the team at Great Northern Books, to my Press Box colleague David Warner, for his expert advice and meticulous eye, and to Bill Hudson, for his professional assistance.

And finally, thanks to my son Tom, for his support and encouragement, and my wife Lynne, for her ideas, expertise and endless enthusiasm.

Fire and Ashes
How Yorkshire's finest took on the Australians
Introduction by Geoffrey Boycott

Includes interviews with Yorkshire and England cricketing legends, including Michael Vaughan, Matthew Hoggard, and Darren Gough

There are eighteen Yorkshiremen still alive who, whilst playing for Yorkshire, also participated in the Ashes Tests. In this book they recall favourite memories and stirring moments in their own words. Collectively they reveal how Yorkshire's finest took on the Australians in one of international cricket's most famous rivalries. The memories go back to the early 1950s with Brian Close and Bob Appleyard, and range over the next half century up to the 2005 Ashes that included Michael Vaughan and Matthew Hoggard.

The Yorkshire County Cricket Club Yearbook

Relive every moment of Yorkshire County Cricket Club's season, meet all the players and get the lowdown on what it's like to be a professional cricketer for one of the most famous sporting clubs in history. Featuring articles on players past and present, records from the history of Yorkshire Cricket and Internationals played at Headingley Carnegie, this book is essential reading for fans of Yorkshire cricket.

Sweet Summers
The Classic Cricket Writing of JM Kilburn
Winner of Wisden Book of the Year

Capturing a time when the true spirit of cricket existed. Some of the game's legends are brought to life including Donald Bradman, Fred Trueman, Jack Hobbs, Keith Miller, Garfield Sobers, Hedley Verity and Len Hutton. Kilburn is worth reading not only because he was a knowledgeable and respected interpreter of cricket, but also for the historical and social perspective.

www.greatnorthernbooks.co.uk

Frith On Cricket
Half a Century of Writing by David Frith

Multi-award winning and bestselling author, David Frith, is arguably one of the greatest living cricket writers. Cricket is his passion and for the past 50 years he has written extensively about the game. In Frith on Cricket, he has selected the very best of his writings on the game's colourful history, personalities and of course, its controversies over the last 50 years.

Frith on Cricket is wide-ranging with book reviews, magazine articles, major obituaries, fun cricket and even a little verse. It takes in cricketing events right from 1952 up to England's victory over Australia in the 2009 Ashes Test. It is a wonderful anthology of the best cricket writing and is sure to appeal to all fans of the game.

Play Cricket The Right Way
by Geoff Boycott

Geoffrey Boycott is a real legend of cricket both as player and respected commentator. He's one of England's finest cricket players, making over 48,000 runs and scoring 151 hundreds during his career and has never been afraid to speak his mind about his beloved game.

And now, in this richly illustrated, updated edition of his original, highly successful coaching book, Boycott shares his techniques with the next generation of cricket players. In Play Cricket the Right Way, he takes the reader through every step of the game from batting and bowling to fielding and captaincy. It also been updated to include new techniques such as the switch hit and the controversial Doosra.

The easy-to-follow instructions from the master himself are all clearly illustrated, making the book an ideal guide for both for the young, aspiring cricketer and experienced players alike. The perfect gift book.